# PERSPECTIVES ON URBAN AMERICA

MELVIN I. UROFSKY teaches history in the Allen Center at State University of New York at Albany. He received his doctorate from Columbia University and has taught at Ohio State University. He is the co-editor of THE BRANDEIS LETTERS and the author of BIG STEEL AND THE WILSON ADMINISTRATION and WHY TEACHERS STRIKE.

# PERSPECTIVES ON
# URBAN AMERICA

*Edited by*

MELVIN I. UROFSKY

ANCHOR BOOKS

*Anchor Press/Doubleday*
*Garden City, New York*
*1973*

*The Anchor Books edition is the first edition of*
PERSPECTIVES ON URBAN AMERICA
*Anchor Books edition: 1973*
*ISBN: 0-385-04446-1*
*Library of Congress Catalog Card Number 71–186056*
*Copyright © 1973 by Melvin I. Urofsky*
*All Rights Reserved*
*Printed in the United States of America*
*First Edition*

*For*
D.W.L. *and* L.H.L.
*urban refugees*

# CONTENTS

# PREFACE

ONE of the truisms in American life today is that our cities are in deep trouble, a trouble bordering on disaster. In the last decade, there have been hundreds of news stories on racial riots, crime in the streets, impending financial insolvency, and strikes or breakdowns of essential services. Nor are these woes limited to the big metropolitan centers alone; smaller cities face them as well. If one were to look only at the headlines, one would have to conclude that our cities are dying, and that city government is at best a moribund holding action.

Walking down the streets of American cities, however, provides a much different picture, as does reading past the scare headlines into the back pages. It would be foolish to deny that there are major problems; after all, the riots, the crime, the strikes, and the breakdowns do occur. But our cities are not dying. The faces of New York, Chicago, Louisville, New Orleans, and many other American cities have been radically altered in recent years by the biggest building boom in history, and hardheaded businesses do not invest millions and billions of dollars in dying areas. Strikes and breakdowns are not solely urban problems, but affect our entire industrial society, while racism can hardly be located or blamed only on cities. Many neighborhoods have fallen apart, it is true; but many more seem to have been born, and in countless urban areas there are signs of physical and social regeneration. With the political impetus of local participation, new modes of providing *communitas* within the urban framework are being explored.

Now, as in the past, cities are the magnet to which the brightest, the most talented, and the most creative people are drawn. It is in cities, and only in cities, that the visual arts—theater, ballet, and opera—flourish, that great museums and concert halls thrive, and where our great universities are to be found. There, too, for better or for worse, our styles and trends are set. And there, too, extremes in poverty and wealth abide cheek by jowl. While our worst racial riots take place in city slums, and terrible examples of discrimination abound, it is also in the urbane cosmopolitanism of cities that the greatest integration and fullest opportunity exist.

The contributors to this volume were asked to look at certain facets of urban America. While they all reported that the problems they found were indeed Gargantuan in scope, they also noted many hopeful and innovative efforts to deal with them, especially on a local level. They found American cities confronted by seemingly insurmountable tasks, yet rather than collapsing, they found the cities still alive and vibrant, with at least a chance to solve these dilemmas.

The missing ingredient seems to be a national commitment to save our cities, to bail them out from under problems not of their own making. For racism, crime, education, and the environment—to name but a few—are certainly not urban problems alone, but problems of our total society, which, unfortunately, take their most visual and malignant forms in urban settings. There is no doubt that we as a nation have the wealth and the power to deal with these thorny issues. It is a matter of setting our priorities straight, of removing the burden of national problems from local governments. Cities are alive and capable of dealing with their own difficulties; they may yet flounder trying to solve those of the larger society. The depressing note that our contributors sound is that they have so far been unable to find any signs of a national commitment or leadership in this pressing task. In the long run, this would be the only problem that can really kill our cities.

MELVIN I. UROFSKY
*Allen Collegiate Center*
*State University of New York at Albany*

Thou hast heard men scorn the city, call her wild
Of counsel, mad; thou has seen the fire of morn
Flash from her eyes in answer to their scorn!
Come toil on toil, 'tis this that makes her grand.
Peril on peril! And common states that stand
In caution, twilight cities, dimly wise—
Ye know them; for no light is in their eyes!
Go forth, my son, and help.

—EURIPEDES, *The Suppliants*

# CHAPTER 1

# THE IDEA OF COMMUNITY IN THE CITY

## Paul Meadows

Urban life has long been considered by both laymen and sociologists as disruptive of those values and relationships essential in forming a sense of community among people. While city living is undeniably different from village life, Paul Meadows argues that it, too, is endowed with communal bonds as valid as those found in small towns. "Community in the city," he writes, "is a multanimity, not a unanimity, of values and controls, utilizing interactional processes of conflict, competition, accommodation, persuasion, manipulation and force as they are employed in a ceaseless flow of opinion and action." It is this vitality and diversity that is the hallmark of the urban community. Unfortunately, many of the efforts to deal with urban problems fail to recognize this, and are aimed at re-creating the city in the image of a nostalgic and mythical past; unless the city is seen and accepted and appreciated for what it is, these efforts will continue to fail.

Paul Meadows has for many years been concerned with the problems of *communitas;* he participated as a research associate in The Montana Study, as a member of the Nebraska University Council on the Community, as a board member of Family Services Association, Lincoln, and as a participant in minority group programs and civil rights activities. He has written extensively about the community and other problems of industrial society. He is former chairman and presently research professor, Department of Sociology, State University of New York at Albany.

*The conventional view of the community in the city has been handicapped by a romantic ideological bias and by a theoretical orientation to a limited range of empirical data and to macro-social interests. The community in the modern city is a sea of social life which needs better conceptual nets to capture the human phenomena of interaction and change which characterize the contemporary urban scene.*

IN ALL accounts of the community, of any type and by any skill of interpretation, the accent on community is an emphasis on those qualities and dimensions of human existence shared in common: literally the state or condition of commonalities. Basically a territorial or locality concept, "community" traditionally connotes a form or degree of human relationships characterized by interpersonal intimacy, emotional significance, moral bondedness, group cohesion, and persistence over time. Indeed, whenever sociologists have discussed the idea of "the social," their reference has been to the human phenomena of *communitas,* not *societas.*

## THE CITY AND THE COMMUNITY THEME

Historically, "community" has carried with it a sense of abiding involvement, though the forms of that involvement have taken different expression. The carriers of the common actions which express and form the community have been tightly knit kinship or ethnic groups, confessional associations of individual believers, contractual corporate bodies, aggregates of interest-bound or skill groups. The ties that bind have included religion, ethnicity, land, corporate charter, civic organization, market place, feudal administration, collective enterprise, and civil morality. Men have created community out of many different common bonds. Community is historically a pluri-bonded concept.

Defining the human community has been as varied a task as has been the formation of communities, for social reality tends to be a function of particular perspectives. Thus, the community may be viewed (1) as the place where people live, (2) as a spatial unity of human aggregation, (3) as a way of life, (4) as an area of human interaction, (5) as a time-binding and space-binding tradition, and (6) as a social system. One sociologist has, in fact, assembled some ninety-four different definitions of the community. Two thirds of them designate as fundamentally important three dimensions of human communities: interest, area, and common tie or ties. Seeking similarities in usages, another sociologist found in a study of definitions agreement on six distinguishing qualities: population, territory, interdependence of specialized parts, integrating culture and social system, consciousness of belongingness, and ability to act in a corporate fashion. His summarizing definition, therefore, is useful: the community is usually a spatial group wherein the effects of interdependence and integration are made evident by the community's consciousness of unity and its ability to exercise adequate control over social, cultural, and biotic processes within its boundaries. In fundamental terms, we may regard communities as those aggregates of social units and systems performing major social functions and solving those major social problems as sensed and felt in their particular locations.

It has been customary among sociologists to associate social phenomena with numbers of people and the scale of their interactions. Increase in the size and density of population have consequences for the quality and quantity of community life. The historical changes in social life in the community called *urbanization* add to locality and to similar or even dissimilar interests and problems the very strategic factors of both size and economic organization as community-generating processes.

The human community as a problem of existence and of action seems to be associated everywhere with the emergence of urbanism as a type or a phase of human settlement. This is not at all surprising. Communities of any size, type, and geographic or cultural location arise and function as organizations solving the problems and satisfying the social interests of a particular group or groups. Whatever changes the nature of these problems or interests will, of course, change the character of the relationships which constitute that community. Historically, urbanization has always had a profound impact on the nature of the human community.

It was this understanding which formed the background of the famous paper by Chicago sociologist Louis Wirth, "The Urban Way of Life." Wirth focused on the social relationships and behaviors in groups in the type of community setting called the city, a pattern of social life which, of course, does not confine itself to the physical limits of cities. He sought to isolate the distinctive factors which are responsible for the historic pattern of community existence called urbanism. He named three such variables: large size, extreme density, and heterogeneity of the residents. The interaction of these factors produces a society which is, in any given city, characterized by spatial segregation of individuals according to color, ethnic heritage, economic and social status, tastes and preferences. The high degree of in- and out-movement diminishes the bonds of kinship, of enduring neighborliness, and of all those sentiments which arise from people living together for generations. Competition and formal social control mechanisms substitute for the bonds of folk solidarity. Add to high mobility the fact of high specialization and division of labor and there emerges the view of the urban society as a fast-moving but shallow stream of social life.

Wirth's theme emphasized (1) secondary rather than primary interaction, (2) ecological segregation, (3) competition, (4) formal controls, and (5) segmentalization and mobility in human relationships. These aspects of urbanism have come to characterize much of the conventional view of community in the modern city, a view which has the enviable value of simultaneously explaining both the organizational and disorganizational, the functional and the dysfunctional aspects of the urban community.

One can argue that this view of the city deals not with urban *community* but with urban *society*. That is, it deals with the global, abstract qualities of a type of societal organization as distinct from real entities of human interaction in a given time and place. The "macro-social" approach is typified not only in Wirth's paper but also in Max Weber's *The City* and Ferdinand Tonnies' *Gemeinschaft und Gesellschaft,* both of them very influential in contemporary social science thinking about the city. A "micro-social" view is exemplified by the "Chicago School" with its famous studies of the Jewish ghetto, the Italian immigrant settlement, the Black Belt, crime neighborhoods, and hobohemia.

The micro-social approach to the city describes major urban impact on social institutions. It reports urban variations in age, sex, occupation, vital rates, life styles, and personality patterns and disorders. The macro-social approach portrays changes in the city as massive, unalterable, and total: e.g., shifts in the direction of class achievement, impersonality and anonymity, nationalism, cosmopolitanism. The micro-social approach portrays the city as a landscape of myriad empirical changes in the daily life of urban residents. Both approaches to community in the city are historical. The difference between them lies in the scale and span of study: global versus local, abstract versus empirical, meta-theoretical versus analytically inductive.

The conventional view of community in the city has been handicapped in two ways: by a romantic ideological bias and by a theoretical orientation to a limited range of empirical data and to macro-social interests. However, community in the modern city is a sea of social life which needs better conceptual nets to capture the rich and complex human phenomena of interaction and change which characterize the contemporary urban scene. One way of describing the newer approach, a counter-conventional approach, to community in the modern city is to say that the shift is necessarily from trait analysis to process studies. Such a change in community theory renders obsolete the older discussions of "rural and urban," "the urban way of life," and community as a "normative state" of social existence.

Concern with process was, of course, not absent from the conventional studies of the urban community, as witness the invaluable investigations of urban ecology done in the 1920s and 1930s and the regional economics of the 1940s to the present. The current interest in the urban environment as an "ecosystem" is reviving this important literature and is enriching it by the new disciplines of the environmental sciences. This newer orientation to process, moreover, is rooted in the significant work done decades ago on "patterns of social interaction," commonly called "social processes."

The turn to community as process is a response in great measure to the spreading concern with community development problems, with community planning, with the sociology of power regarded in terms of decision-making, with leadership conceived as social process, and with community as processes of participation. Above all, the turn to the community as process has its backgrounds in the multiple forces and problems generated by the elaboration of the industrial process. The dominant metaphor is that of machine process. Rationalization of human relationships is the counterpart of the mechanization of work. Bureaucratization of effort is the counterpart of the machine-discipline of energy. Social structures are linked organically with techno-economic processes. The conventional idea of the community process separated consumption and residence from production, social forms from economic actualities. Such a separation is not only obsolete in any realistic analysis of community in the industrial city; it is dangerous. The idea of community did not die in the industrial city; it has, on the contrary, taken on new forms, shows new faces, moves in new directions in the pluri-bonded community which we call the modern industrial city.

SOCIAL BONDS IN THE PLURAL COMMUNITY

The conventional view of community in the city has been nostalgic, a romantic yearning for the small town life of the preindustrial past. Life was then, it is said, simpler, quieter, slower, more personal, more democratic, closer to nature. "Democracy," opined H. G. Wells in a memorable judgment, "dies five miles from the parish pump." In that long-gone day custom was king, and tradition defined the collective actions for common ends. The effect of the city has been the fragmentation of human relationships, which become casual, mobile, impersonal. The closest thing in the city to this mythic agrarian paradise was thought to be the ethnic enclave, which has been from time to time the model of efforts at revival of a social order and social control thought to thrive in the setting of clan, tribe, family, or agricultural village. Examples of such efforts abound, from the folkic glorification of the Nation-State by Hitler to the separatism of the militant black community to the communes of the sixties. This ideological view of the community is basically psychological: sociologist Charles Cooley at the turn of the century described it in terms of wholeness or "we-ness." "One lives," he wrote, "in the feeling of the whole and finds the chief aim of his will in that feeling." In a similar vein, Jane Addams and Robert E. Park re-enforced this theme with their call for programs and services centering in settlement houses and in the multiplicity of vigorous primary groups.

There was a pronounced populism in the conventional view, but also a certain pragmatism. Thus, William James considered the big unit hollow and brutal and, as Morton White points out, Jane Addams sought to reconstruct localism in the city, with the schoolhouse and the settlement-house as urban surrogates for that lost paradise, the village. There was a pervasive hatred of industrialism. The city was attacked as the horrible embodiment of machine-dominated culture: mobile, spectatorial, depersonalized, artificial, and callously exploitive. The thrust against the industrial city was made, as White has concluded, by a double-edged sword: the city is overcivilized, it is under-civilized. In either case it is anathema, because it is in everything subversive of long-established human values.

In opposition to the conventional view of community in the city, I would suggest another approach to the problems of social integration and action confronting the urban community. It is an approach which emphasizes (1) the social bonds that integrate the multiplicity of human beings and groups living in the city; (2) the formation and protection of social processes and forms expressing a spreading spectrum of diverse social values; and (3) the development of mechanisms and forms of corporate action which seek the realization of the stubbornly differentiated interests and needs of people in the city.

Contrary to the agrarian-inspired discontent with urbanism, this view holds that the city has not been the grave-yard of primary integration and social identification. In fact, it has fostered both in a rich variety of new and un-expected ways. This fact has been demonstrated in two different sets of sociological studies. One set deals with primary group life in the city—families, neighborhoods, friend-ship cliques, social networks. These studies suggest that the conventional version of community in the city was actually reporting exceptions rather than the overwhelming rule. I refer here to the abundant generalizations about the pre-dominant anonymity, depersonalization, and rootlessness of city life. These studies conclude that the average city dweller maintains close relations with friends among either neighbors or with people in other parts of the urban area or with both. Mobility creates city-wide ties while residential stability fosters local ties; most city dwellers have both.

It is important to emphasize here that though occupa-tional and residential mobility and heterogeneity do indeed characterize the city, they are not necessarily disruptive. In a much-cited study of migration in Chicago from 1935–

1940 it was reported that some highly "disorganized" areas, those with large, diverse, foreign-born population with high insanity and delinquency rates, had low rates of mobility, while some stable, middle-class areas had high rates. Length of residence and improving social and economic status are essential to the strengthening of social ties in the city, not only of people as residents but also as workers. In a well-known study of "moral integration" in forty-three American cities it was similarly noted that mobility or heterogeneity had a very high negative correlation (−.79) with integration. There is no denying that the industrial city is still a world of strangers or that interpersonal relations continue to be dominantly "secondary." But the available studies do argue that the breakdown of primary groups and of informal social controls, widely proclaimed in the conventional literature, has not occurred on the scale or with the ultimate consequences stipulated by the conventional view.

This conclusion has been re-enforced by the growing literature on relationships formed by the still vigorous extended family in the city. It has also been strengthened by more recent work on the "slum" and the "ghetto." Notable instances are the field reports on the interplay effects of human relationships, social types, and communal functions in the modern city, which facilitate both "cultural" and "structural" assimilation and intensify the complexity of interpersonal and interethnic relations in the ghetto and in city slums.[1] Finally, the extensive literature on voluntary associations and citizen participation has emphasized the presence of strong integrating bonds in the American city.[2]

A second set of sociological studies, dealing with mass organizations in the city, suggests not only the continuing presence of informal and primary relations in the city but also that the clash of interests which they generate may have significant stabilizing effects. Thus, a California team of sociologists found in their study that half of the members

[1] See Chapter 4.
[2] See Chapter 6.

of formal organizations identified nine or more members as close personal friends; less than seventeen percent said they had no close personal friends in these organizations. These groups were also felt by their members to be sources of material benefit and social supports of various kinds. Noteworthy for communal ties and action is the fact that such secondary associations as the church, the trade union, the corporation, the political party, the professional association serve as great mixers of people.

The conventional view of community in the modern city has always been comfortable with a pattern of values and norms often summarized, perhaps unfairly, by the phrases "Puritan ethic," "work ethic," and "success ethic." The city has, of course, been regarded alternately as the product of that pattern of expectations and as its implacable if not deadly enemy. Both legitimate and extra-legitimate as well as illegitimate sanctions—that is, those of authority and power—have been put into play to safeguard as well as to promote this vaunted pattern. The relationships between these traditional values and norms, on the one hand, and the available authority and power, on the other, may be expressed in the following diagram.

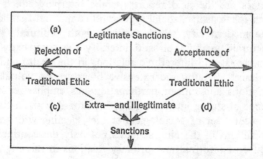

Thought of as a field of forces, the relationships between the vectors depicted in this diagram have a shifting pattern, but ordinarily responding to a pull toward values and norms generally accepted. However, at any time groups in the community operate at some times and in different ways in each of the sectors denoted a, b, c, and d. Community in the city, in other words, is a multanimity, not a unanimity, of values and controls, utilizing interactional processes such as conflict, competition, accommodation, persuasion, manipulation, and force as they are employed in a ceaseless flow of opinion and action.

There is, then, the conventional view with its assumption of a universal and homogeneous structure of community values and norms from which dissident or discontented individuals and groups deviate—and thus by definition (and subsequent sanction) engage in deviant behavior. The counter-conventional theme, however, underscores the manner in which collections of human beings select, organize, and rationalize a given set of values and norms (and with the appropriate set of sanctions). In so doing, they form a relatively tight, selectively homogeneous, and powerful unanimity that prescribes a pattern of conformity for their particular group.

The counter-conventional view talks about "contra-cultures" and "sub-cultures" operating in the community. It sees the community as a plurality of such cultures commanding the differential loyalties of different groups of members of the community. "Sub-cultures" refer to complexes of people, values, norms, and social roles operating in their own distinctive ways *within* an established system of community culture. "Contra-cultures" represent emergent and protestive complexes of people, values, norms, and roles *in conflict* at some decisive point or points, perhaps indeed in totality, with the established system of community culture.

Remembering that sanctions work within patterns of authority and power, this distinction makes it possible for us to identify community in the city as a system of *dominant, sub-dominant,* and *contra-dominant* complexes. As such, it forms in sum and in action a plural system of norms within which variation and novelty, individuality and conformity, freedom and organization maintain community in the city and also maintain it as a system of going concerns. It rejects the nostalgic and romantic view of the human community which is seen in terms of a leveling "normal" culture. It substitutes a more realistic view of community in the city as a field of viable options for living, in which groups of human beings find their own unity in community in that diversity of experience called the city.

Such a view underlines the need for another look at the community in terms of the concepts of *social bondedness* and of *deviancy*. From this view, deviancy is not a property inherent in any instance of behavior: it is a property conferred or imposed on an individual's behavior by others who do not share it. Normation is a universal and intrinsic property of social behavior; deviancy is a function of membership in another group of which some non-members disapprove. Any given community contains a wide radius of such normations. In fact, it needs such a radius as an essential part of its functioning as an on-going system of interactions. The city as a community of traits and purposes must thus be seen as a community in which the process of norm-making, norm-following, and norm-enforcing functions as an essential dimension of corporate action. It is a process of relatively uneasy, certainly of dynamic, equilibrium of plural patterns of conformity. From this counter-conventional view community in the city is seen not as an overriding and monolithic conformity but as a process of plural conformity.

The third problem confronting community in the modern city concerns the development of mechanisms and forms of corporate action seeking the realization of markedly differentiated needs and interests. This problem can be seen in two contexts, one of socio-economic status and community participation and one of socio-political power and community control.

In the conventional approach, locality groups have been assigned a central role in explaining the rise and decline of community in the city. Locality is, of course, a major distinguishing dimension of any community discussion. It follows that corporate action in and of the city must be considered in the context of local areas and local groups. In general, the conventional view has argued that because there is such a diversity of localities within the city, community of effort is simply not possible, at least not in terms of the older parochialism of the small-town version of community. However, in point of actual practice the political process in American cities has long since recognized ethnic neighborhoods and economic-function groups as dynamic, inescapable, and indeed very useful blocs of interests and pressures in the political representation and decision-making of the city.

A very large number of studies by social scientists has established that local areas are clearly important in the identification and action which dramatize community in the modern city. This fact by no means diminishes the role of powerful economic-function groups in the life of the city. Indeed, so much attention has been paid to them that it is easy to assume that merely to chronicle their existence and activities is to tell the whole story of community in the modern city. Such a version, however, does not do justice to the way in which locality and status mingle in the struggle for participation in and control of the modern city.

### STRUCTURES OF IDENTITY AND THE FUTURE OF COMMUNITY IN THE CITY

It has long been a major theme in the literature of American sociology that social life—and thus communal life—occurs and continues only in and through consensus made possible by communication. Social order is consensual order. However, a related theme stresses the role of co-ordination and integration. It is essential to bring these two themes together, for both consensus and co-ordination occur in the human community at different levels and in different forms. They are, moreover, dependent on one another. For example, consensus depends on the type and extent of co-ordination required among members of a group. Thus, in trying to visualize the relationship between consensus and co-ordination (integration) in the community, one arrives at the following representation:

CONSENSUAL MODEL OF SOCIAL INTEGRATION

| *Continuum of Consensus* | *Continuum of Social Integration* | |
|---|---|---|
| | Monolithic | Pluralistic |
| *Monolithic* | Unanimity | Dissension |
| *Pluralistic* | Contest | Cleavage |

The consensual idea is of primary importance for our understanding of community in the modern city. The counter-conventional view of the city, we have argued, stresses the positive potentiality of its pluralistic character: *the* "community" is a co-ordination of a plurality of "communities." That plurality may be portrayed in an ascending movement toward unanimity of consensus and toward an ultimate integration. The relationship between the two is depicted in the horizontal and vertical axes below.

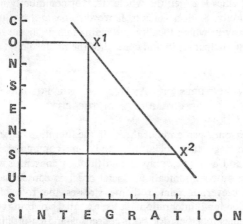

"Community" is any point of intersection between these two co-ordinates, such that it is possible to have high consensus and low integration, as in $x^1$, and low consensus and high integration, as in $x^2$. The conventional view of community has always dwelt on points of interaction which represent high consensus and (assumed) high integration, as in instances of kin groups, neighborhood groups, friendship cliques, "communes," cults, and informal primary groups such as development in major institutional contexts —churches, business forms, work places, social movements, and so on.

The problem of community, in this conventional view, lies in the emergence of conditions requiring more formalized, complex forms of integration, with attendant decline of consensus. The survival of community under such conditions is usually hailed as a triumph of the human spirit. (Note, however, that the systematic exploitation of a similar set of relationships by the Nazi regime in Germany, which formalized integration in the name of the unanimity of the national community—*Allheit, Gemeinschaft, Gleichschaltuung*—presents a severe problem of interpretation for supporters of this view, as genocidal gas chambers bear monumental if mute witness!) This last comment indeed raises a profoundly disturbing question about the still continuing yearning for minimal dissension, high homogeneity, and simplicity of organization among some adherents of the conventional conception of community. It is one of the troublesome legacies of Rousseauan contractualism.

The counter-conventional conception of community in the city addresses itself to the incredibly complicated question of preserving varieties of community within the city under conditions of plural combinations of consensus and integration. One major premise here is the inevitability of some form of organization of community under conditions of *pluralistic* consensus and *monolithic* integration. How essential this is can easily be understood when one thinks of the need for some kind of centralized administration and some concentration of power of the sprawling metropolis. At best unsatisfactory, because of its low level of consensus, this idea arouses comparable dissatisfaction from its formalization of efforts at co-ordination. One attractive alternative has been prompted by the many different partisans of the so-called "neighborhood formula." It is a compromise formula; its viability has yet to be demonstrated, a fact which the numerous critics of recent federal efforts at "maximum feasible participation" have been quick to emphasize. In retrospect, it appears that the full story of these efforts has yet to be written.

No less attractive, though for some more threatening, is the consensus—co-ordination formula offered by the partisans of social movements in the city—tenant strikes, welfare demonstrations, manifestoes, and citizen rallies of the sort urged, for example, by the late Saul Alinsky. The argument here is simple: really novel and corrective action comes only through crisis. These innovators of community organization have turned to the continuous production of crisis situations in the community. They hope in this way that they can intervene in the routines of community bureaucracies in behalf of their clients. "Community" in this view is to be found in crisis creation and management in behalf of client advocacy.

Closer to the other pole of integration and consensus are the innumerable voluntary civic organizations which dot the landscape of the average city today—councils of social agencies, community chest, community councils, community development or improvement associations, youth councils, and so on. Finally, at the extreme end of integration—as measured by formalization, with varying degrees and completeness of consensus—are the specialized public and private organizations of interest and power— Model Cities, urban renewal agencies, metropolitan authorities, chambers of commerce, associations of manufacturers, and so on.

Several values predominate in recent studies of consensus and co-ordination of community in the modern city. These values center in three interrelated questions: how to maintain and enhance community *autonomy;* how to continue and encourage community *viability;* and how to achieve and support a broad distribution of community-decision-making *power* among the constituent interest and power groups comprising the city.

These questions form the focus of the growing literature on community decision-making. That literature concerns itself largely with what sociologist Roland Warren has called "concerted decision-making," a process in which individual community decisions of two or more units are made on a more comprehensive and systematic level that includes these units. This more inclusive and intergroup approach to community theory makes it possible for us to state a number of propositions concerning the behavior of these units in any concert of decision-making. These propositions can be put in functional form, as follows:

(1) participation = $\int$(desire of units to preserve and expend their domains);

(2) concerted decision-making = $\int$(trade-off inducements, or of coercive power);

(3) concerted decision-making = $\int$(differential contexts of action of these units);

(4) concerted decision-making = $\int$(convergence or divergence of "issue outcome interest" of these units);

(5) involvement = $\int$(type of concerted action contemplated or initiated).

This last proposition refers to the fact that concert in decision-making assumes many different forms, which can be represented on a continuum, thus:

*Forms of Concerted Decision-making*

*Illustrative Type*

(1) unitary — City health department

(2) federative — Council of social agencies

(3) coalitions — Alliance of interest groups seeking to attract a new industry

(4) social choice — Alliance of interest groups around conflictive issues, such as welfare or desegregation

The relative importance of these various units involved in concerted decision-making has prompted the research activity of a large number of social scientists, who have studied the structure and dynamics of power in the contemporary city. These studies may be sorted out according to two perspectives, the "elitist" and the "pluralist" approaches. The first stresses the predominance in community life of a relatively small group of men with economic and political power to initiate, direct, and resolve decisions in the city. The second emphasizes the point that power is distributed among a number of organized community groups, their domination shifting according to community issues. The possibility and viability of democracy under either of these conditions are critical problems for community in the city. How critical may be seen in the suggestion by one political scientist that the prevailing pattern of American communities might be called one of "stable unrepresentation." Such an arrangement precludes or at least seriously inhibits the entry of new groupings into the organized power factions unless the new groups resort to a show of force or violent confrontation.

This concern with the concertedness of action in community decision-making, not merely with the presence of well-known individual leaders or groups, makes possible a very new and productive view of community power. By locating the "clusters" of organizations involved in the same issues confronting a community, social scientists have found that community issues thus reveal organizational participation "linking up" groups and issues into interorganizational networks shaping community decisions. Exploring this finding, more recent studies have found that it is not the potency of individual leaders or even groups but "the shape of the web," to use one suggested phrase, in which they are located which outlines the structure of persisting community power. The decisive variable is the involvement of a "resource network," not specific individuals or organizations, in particular situations of decision-making. This perspective on shared power obviously changes or at least challenges the conventional conception of community in the city. It also underlines the inadequacy of the romantic view of democracy in the city.

Access to and control over available resources are therefore strategically important for the patterns of concerted decision-making. They are even more crucial for the community values which are at the core of the idea of community in the modern city—the values of autonomy, viability, and equitable distribution of power of and among the constituent individuals and interest groups in the city.

An extensive literature on the community is developing around this problem of restricted access to community resources and on their inequitable distribution. One impressive theme dwells on the disturbing analogy between American relationships to its poor and the relationships of expanding European societies during the nineteenth and twentieth centuries to their "aboriginal" populations, which have in the last few decades successfully managed to complicate and disrupt the existence of colonizing Europeans. It is thus possible to talk about the emergence of urban "aborigines" in the American metropolitan community.

This analogy to colonialism has been the center of recent, widely read publications on urban discontent and violence in the United States during the decade of the sixties, publications which link "internal colonialism" and "ghetto revolt." Oriented largely to black protest as expressed in urban riots, cultural nationalism, and movements for ghetto control, these writers see these new community phenomena as collective responses to colonized conditions in American cities.

This perspective on the relationships between power and protest in the community clearly collides with the conventional conception of the community in the city. Indeed, conventional theorists have sought to defuse the explosive meaning of this protest by absorbing its significance within the traditional assimilation-integration philosophy of the conventional view. It seems plain that these new collective behaviors belong to that most primitive dimension of the human community—the assertion of claim to territoriality. The increasing proportion of depressed-income populations, both black and white, in the central areas of American cities lends dramatic if not indeed ominous significance to the emerging structures of identity and power in the American community.

It is tempting to view community in the modern city in the disillusioning light of failure—the failure of established forms of collective action, the failure of consensus (at least in the conventional sense of that word), even failure of the idea of community itself. A more realistic view, certainly one that is more challenging and viable, turns to the idea that problems of the city are not problems of decadence and failure but of growth, indeed of vigorous vitality. The conventional view, which tends to equate truth with continuity and comfort, makes people unhappy with novelty, particularly with unexpected and uncontrolled novelty. There is, however, a fast-growing body of literature on the community which concerns itself not only with innovation—that is, with the appearance of new strategies and tactics for dealing with collective problems, with new institutional contexts and agencies for urban action—but also with the measurement of effectiveness and with the factors which determine success or failure.

Thus, one team of social scientists, exploring relationships between forms of co-ordination and the degree of innovativeness in the city, concluded from an examination of the experience with urban renewal programs of 582 cities of 20,000 or more population that innovation is positively correlated with three things. It is correlated with (1) structural differentiation within the city (that is, populational and institutional differences), (2) accumulation of experience and information over a period of time, and (3) the stability and extent of interorganizational networks. This finding is important for the idea of community in the city. It points to the fact that the greater the number of "centers of power" in a community, the more pervasive and encompassing the "interfaces" (i.e., the links between these centers of power), the higher the probability of innovativeness in the community. In a similar vein, a West Coast sociologist studied the relationships between the number of national business headquarters in a city (as a measure of a city's organizational integration into the broader national society), on the one hand, and the flow of poverty funds from federal agencies to and among organizations within 130 of our largest American cities, on the other hand. He found that the "extra-local integration" proved capable of predicting the activity level of a new interorganizational network which is characterized by both local and "extra-local" elements. The "idea" of community has thus been given a new organizational form.

In the conventional conception of community, the city was strongly permeated by a powerful nostalgic populism with its fear of bigness and its love of the small scale. This yearning still clings to popular modes of planned change in the community, models such as community conflict or community development. The pluralistic character of the counter-conventional view envisions a plurality of change strategies—e.g., collaboration, campaigns, contest, confrontation, demonstration—working through interorganizational networks of power. Planned change is apparently the only route to the enhancement of the nuclear values of community existence, today as in the past. As such, it is linked to consensus. However, it is important to emphasize that we are talking here about the goal orientations of groups *in* the city, not *of* the city itself. For goal-orientation is not an inherent property of community at any level of definition, certainly not at the level of the modern metropolis. The accent of community theory must increasingly be placed on the search for viable combinations of consensus and co-ordination. Such a stress also means that formalization of community organization must more and more come to carry the load of community action.

## FOR FURTHER READING

Aiken, M., and R. R. Alford. "Community Structure and Innovativeness: The Case of Urban Renewal." *American Sociological Review,* 35 (August 1970), 650–54.

Babchuck, N., and A. Booth. "Voluntary Association Membership: A Longitudinal Analysis." *American Sociological Review,* 34 (February 1969), 31–45.

Bernard, Jesse. *American Community Behavior.* New York: Dryden Press, 1949.

Brownell, Baker. *The Human Community.* New York: Harper & Row, 1950.

Clark, Kenneth. *Dark Ghetto: Dilemmas of Social Power.* New York: College and University Press, 1963.

Gans, Herbert. *The Urban Villages.* New York: The Free Press, 1962.

Mangin, William. *Peasants in Cities.* New York: Houghton Mifflin, 1970.

Meadows, Paul. *The Many Faces of Change.* Cambridge: Schenkman, 1971.

———, and E. H. Mizruchi. *Urbanization, Urbanism and Change.* Reading, Massachusetts: Addison, Wesley, 1969.

Moynihan, Daniel Patrick. *Maximum Feasible Misunderstanding.* New York: The Free Press, 1969.

Perucci, R., and M. Pilisuk. "Leaders and Ruling Elites: The Interorganizational Bases of Community Power." *American Sociological Review,* 35 (December 1970), 1040–57.

Reissman, L. *The Urban Process: Cities in Industrial Societies.* New York: The Free Press, 1964.

Suttles, Gerald D. *The Social Order of the Slum: Ethnicity and Territoriality in the Inner City.* Chicago: University of Chicago Press, 1968.

Sweetser, F. L., Jr. *Neighborhood Acquaintance and Association: A Study of Personal Neighborhood.* New York: Columbia University Press, 1941.

Warren, Roland. *Perspectives on the American Community.* Chicago: Rand, McNally, 1966.

White, Morton and Lucia. *The Intellectual versus the City.* New York: Mentor, 1964.

Wilensky, H. L., and Charles N. Lebeaux. *Industrial Society and Social Welfare.* New York: Russell Sage, 1958.

# CHAPTER 2

# THE FRONTIER HERITAGE OF
# URBAN AMERICA

## C. W. Griffin

The frontier has been the great mythic force in American history, shaping our attitudes and actions, our thoughts and deeds. We have become a nation of city dwellers, however, and a frontier ethos based on wide-open spaces and unlimited natural resources has wreaked havoc with the growth of metropolitan areas. In a sardonic attack on this frontier heritage, C. W. Griffin pleads for a realization that in the twentieth century we need a modern philosophy and sensitivity to such urban problems as land use, mass transit, and waste disposal. It is time, he declares, for Americans to grow out of an archaic adolescence, and to stop viewing "progress" as the ultimate desideratum, and to reject the simple-minded notion that "more is better."

C. W. Griffin is a professional engineer and planner, and former editor of *Engineering News-Record*. He has written on numerous aspects of the discrepancy between our past and present, and his work frequently appears in popular magazines.

SEVERAL years ago, in a magazine article ominously entitled *Is Your Right to Drive in Danger?*, former Secretary of Commerce Luther Hodges denounced mass-transit boosters who want frontier Americans to stop driving their motorized steeds to work and ride the stagecoach with the dudes. "Fuzzy-minded theorists," reacting to spreading traffic jams, have proposed imposition of rush-hour tolls to reduce traffic volume on major urban highways and a cutback in the urban freeway-building program, warned Mr. Hodges. Such proposals, he said, threaten "our right to come and go as we please . . . a heritage from frontier days."

Nostalgia for frontier freedoms is manifest in almost every facet of American life—from the popularity of Wild West paperbacks, screen plays, and television shows, to the economic "rugged individualism" extolled by businessmen living off cost-plus government contracts. The vicarious reliving of frontier days is both psychological escape and protest against the increasing frictions and collisions accompanying urban growth.

Many public issues reveal the depth of the pioneer strain. Obscured by campus protests and civil rights battles, less dramatic struggles to retain pioneer freedoms vent the irritations of urban Americans. In 1963, the citizens of Phoenix, Arizona, repealed a "socialistic" housing code that required slum landlords to furnish tenants with toilets, running water, and other decadent luxuries. Blissfully oblivious of their downstream neighbors, the citizens of frontier-fabled St. Joseph, Missouri, fought for the right to discharge raw sewage into the Missouri River. After voting down two sewage-treatment bond issues, they abandoned their struggle only after the federal government instituted court action against their city. In June 1955, against the orders of the Los Angeles County Air Pollution Control District, the citizens fought to retain their forefathers' right to burn trash in back-yard incinerators rather than accept the imposition of a municipal trash collection system. The exercise of this right released some five hundred tons of contaminants into Los Angeles' smog-polluted atmosphere every day. But that fact meant little compared with the historic freedom to burn trash.

Even more passionate in defending frontier freedoms are the gun enthusiasts parroting the propaganda of the National Rifle Association and the profiteers in gun traffic. At the primitive level of frontier civilization, vigilantism and widespread gun ownership were perhaps a partially rational adaptation to that lawless society. But today, in the tension-stressed, crowded cities of modern America, resurgence of the gun mentality is a dangerous, infantile regression. Contemporary frontier outposts, such as Dallas, proportionately produce one hundred to two hundred times as many gun killings alone as such gun-controlled nations as Great Britain.

THE FILTHY FREEDOMS

Expressing frontier freedoms in a less lethal, but more visible way, the trash-littered streets of American cities are their most immediately apparent contrast with European cities. Yet this still potent American talent for fouling the urban environment is merely a pallid vestige of the frontiersmen's talent. Everett Dick's book *The Sodhouse Frontier: 1854–1890* depicts the stark historical facts. In Wichita, Kansas, a typical frontier town, the ground at the hitching post was a stinking, fly-infested cesspool. Superimposed on this heady odor was the stench of outhouses, pigpens, and garbage tossed into the street or left at the doorstep by these pristine rugged individualists. The artfully blended aroma inspired the Wichita *Eagle's* fastidious editor, a nineteenth-century precursor of the "fuzzy-minded theorists and wild-eyed planners" denounced by latter-day frontiersmen, to advocate controls that must have seemed socialistic:

A fair example of what we may expect in the way of variety and kinds of smell, and the different thicknesses of the strata, was given last Saturday, when it was a little warmer than any previous day this spring, with a stiff breeze blowing from the south. Pedestrians on Main, Market and Water Streets, any- where north of Douglas Avenue, were regaled with oleaginous olefiant, concentrated and moist, with the quintessence of putre- faction. Oh! was the exclamation of those who, according to size, had their olfactories saluted while plodding nose high in the different stratifications. Many differed as to the resemblances but a tall man who was sitting on the sidewalk said, as he got up and passed through them with his nose, that there were two hundred and forty distinct and odd smells prevailing there and then; this confirmed all dissenting reports. All, however, agree that some sanitary measures are needed, and heavy fines should be imposed on those who will throw slops, old meats, and de- caying vegetable matter at their doors or on the street.

The price paid for these filthy freedoms only began with the stench. Spread by disease-bearing flies that fed on the filth of outhouses and streets, typhoid epidemics sometimes swept through entire towns. Cholera, smallpox, and diphtheria were also epidemic. During the 1850s, Lawrence, Kansas, became a vast hospital. The primitive frontier technology made adequate sanitation difficult, and frontier medicine was just this side of witchcraft. But the mentally muscle-bound individualism of the frontier, with its contempt for public sanitation, extorted a graver price than was necessary. Even the almost instinctively visual- ized picture of vigorous, ruddy-faced pioneers was largely a myth. Disembarking from trains arriving in these frontier towns, visiting easterners were often struck with the na- tives' sallow complexions, a consequence of the prairie's most common disease, the ague.

TOWNS ON THE MOVE

Town-building in frontier America often entailed an incredibly crude combination of greed and chicanery, while federal policy encouraged the destructive work of land speculators. To qualify for purchase of a 160-acre quarter section at a bargain price, a frontier land pre-emptor merely had to produce a witness to swear that the land was cultivated and improved with a "habitable dwelling," twelve feet square in plan. Among the ruses used to circumvent the law was a house on wheels (the archetypal trailer!), rented for five dollars a day and moved from claim to claim. Another was a house erected by railroad agents at the intersection of four lots, with one corner in each of the four 160-acre plots.

Railroad towns exhibited the "impatience, the speculative greed and the lack of taste which characterized the founders," according to planner John W. Reps. Existing towns, hoping to become important cities, fought fiercely for the railroad. But the railroads sometimes bypassed towns that refused to pay the required tribute and built their own. Railroad town-building was often ludicrous. West of the Mississippi, seeking access to newly opened markets, some railroad towns literally moved as track construction proceeded westward. As terminal depot for one rail line, Cheyenne, Wyoming, was augmented by an erstwhile eastward town. According to a witness, a train arrived laden with frame-house lumber, furniture, palings, old tents, and other paraphernalia. A train guard called out, "Gentlemen, here's Julesburg."

Even under the normal conditions of frontier town development, the transience of population worked against cultivation of the civic spirit that inspires the stable populations of old European cities to preserve and enhance the beauty and amenity of their urban environment. Migration became a way of life for many Midwesterners. In his famous essay *The Significance of the Frontier in American History,* historian Frederick Jackson Turner tells of hundreds of men, less than fifty years old, who had re-settled five or six times.

Capitalists instituted a civilizing process when they bought out the original settlers of small villages. Following traders, ranchers, miners, and farmers, this last wave of settlers transformed the frontier from villages of rough-hewn log houses to towns of respectable brick structures.

But the farmers' practice of depleting the soil and moving on to exhaust new virgin tracts of prairie land nourished the frontier attitude of anarchic, anti-social individualism. With El Dorado always beckoning from beyond the western horizon, the migrant frontiersmen cared little for their present surroundings. Their attitude survives in today's mobile Americans who have learned well their forefathers' lesson to hold private goods higher than public values.

### THE REVOLTING REVOLUTION

What little justification was retained by the frontier ethic disappeared with the advent of the industrial revolution and accelerated growth of American cities. The United States was not alone in creating hellish urban landscapes. The Coketowns of Dickens' day, with their soot-blackened buildings, crowded tenements, smoke-poisoned air, and foul-gray rivers, were models for their American counterparts. But America's frontier ethic reinforced the warped, utilitarian philosophy of the new industrialists and produced more uniformly desolate cities than Europe's. The older European cities generally had a form and a tradition that resisted the depredations of the capitalists. But nineteenth-century Americans lacked the architectural splendors of Venice's Piazzo San Marco or London's magnificent system of parks to inspire and educate them. They had no tradition of city planning or land-use control.

A subtler, but no less potent factor in shaping American attitudes toward cities was our city-hating intellectual tradition, expressed most violently by Thomas Jefferson: "The mobs of great cities add just so much to the support of pure government as sores do to the strength of the human body." Jefferson was repelled by the merging industrial cities of Europe, with their exploited proletariat living in dehumanized conditions on a scale unknown in the American cities of Jefferson's day. Overwhelmed by the horrors of what he saw, he leaped to the conclusion that freedom would be cherished best by sturdy, independent farmers. Falsely generalizing from his own life as an aristocratic gentleman farmer, he forgot the facts of rural life.

At best, life in farm villages has always been a dull, plodding, intellectually torpid existence dominated by a deadly, ancestrally prescribed routine. At worst, it is a crucible for cruel superstitions and perdurable prejudices. Despite his admiration for the classic Greeks, Jefferson, along with Thoreau, Emerson, Howells, Melville, Poe, Hawthorne, and other American writers, seemed to forget that democracy was born in a city named Athens.

At bottom, Jefferson confused *physical* freedom with *political* freedom. Breathing the pure air, enjoying the scenic pleasures at Monticello, Jefferson apparently concluded that such a salubrious environment must produce better men than the teeming, noxious cities. But as contemporary America so vividly demonstrates, political freedom gets its intellectual nutrients only from urban soil. In place of the virtuous individualists visualized by Jefferson, we find human sheep grazing in the American countryside, easy prey for racists, Cold Warriors, and press censors.

In his famous Cross of Gold speech, which won him the 1896 Democratic party presidential nomination, young William Jennings Bryan expressed the durable anti-urban sentiments on the political level. He eulogized the rural descendants of the frontiersmen at the expense of the rising urban industrial class:

The hardy pioneers who have braved all the dangers of the wilderness, who have made the desert to blossom as the rose— the pioneers . . . who rear their children near to nature's heart, where they can mingle their voices with the voices of the birds . . . where they have erected schoolhouses for the education of their young, churches where they praise their Creator, and cemeteries where rest the ashes of their dead—these people, we say, are as deserving of the consideration of our party as any people in this country.

Later in the speech, Bryan reiterated what Jane Jacobs calls "The Myth of Agricultural Primacy":

You come to tell us that the great cities are in favor of the gold standard; we reply that the great cities rest upon our broad and fertile prairies. Burn down your cities and leave our farms, and your cities will spring up again as if by magic; but destroy our farms and the grass will grow in the streets of every city in the country.

American literature has historically praised rural innocence and the ideal of small-town farm life as superior to life in the wicked cities. Frank Norris' novel *McTeague* reeks of this rural sentimentality. After escaping the corrupting complexities of life in San Francisco, McTeague, the giant protagonist, finds temporary joy on his return to a mining camp. There "the still, colossal mountains took him back again like a returning prodigal and vaguely, without knowing why, he yielded to their influence—their immensity, their enormous power, crude and blind, reflecting themselves in his own nature, huge, strong, brutal in its simplicity." Throughout the book, crude symbols of gold denote the avarice of the city. As an implied counterpoint, the mining camp became an eleemosynary institution operated for the psychological rehabilitation of urban misfits.

Imbued with this national contempt for urban values, Americans designed their cities with the same sensitivity used on barnyards. River fronts were sacrificed to factories, warehouses, and wharves, with no concession to the citizens' need for recreational park sites. Sprawling railroad yards blighted vast areas adjacent to the central business districts. Soot-belching engines chugged through the densest urban districts, in contrast with the European example of banning railroads from the urban core. In New York's most thickly settled slums, people were packed into six-story tenements at densities unequaled elsewhere in the Western world.

Yet despite the desolation of these bleak monuments to greed, urban growth continued for a century or so without major breakdown. White immigrants, sustained by the American dream, accepted their start in the urban slums. Successful urbanites, retreating before the advancing immigrants throughout most of our history, deserted the Commons in Boston, the Independence Hall area in Philadelphia, and Astor Place in New York. In Henry James's novel *Washington Square* (1881), a character described the strategy: "At the end of three or four years we'll move. That's the way we live in New York . . . Then you always get the last thing." Fueled by the immigrants' hope of upward economic mobility and the middle-class hope of outward physical mobility, the urbanizing process kept going, despite the increasing frictions of accelerated urban growth.

Today, however, as hostility supplants hope in the central city ghettos, the old urbanizing mechanism threatens to break down. The earlier Italian, German, Irish, and Jewish newcomers never had to contend with the race prejudice that helps keep Negro migrants trapped in the ghettos. Like the earlier immigrants, urban Negroes occupy the lowest rung of the ladder to success. But for them the higher rungs have been sawed off, and the old American dream inspired by hope has yielded to escapist delusions inspired by dope.

Prosperous Americans' dreams of continual escape, if not shattered, are fading. Slums, with their accompanying crime and other social diseases, are spreading outward through the old suburbs and even into newer ones, continuing the historic trend. Present housing policies offer no hope of eliminating the slum racket. It remains the last vestige of primitive nineteenth-century capitalism, subsidized by ludicrously generous federal depreciation formulas, archaic local tax-assessing policies, and slumlord-favoring, condemnation-pricing procedures. So long as they are profitable (and possibly even after they aren't), slums will endure. Unlike the more civilized European nations that have eradicated slums, the United States has no national commitment to do so.

The white retreat from the spreading blight, through suburbia and exurbia, cannot continue indefinitely. The rising costs of land and public services and the ordeal of intra-urban transportation are curtailing the sprawling development that has spread recklessly over the countryside throughout the past two decades. The carving of white commuters' freeways through black neighborhoods is meeting stronger resistance. Decaying central cities, spreading traffic jams, smog, polluted water, and vanishing recreational space have become the norm. Intensive planning and control on a regional basis, a subjugation of anarchic individual and local prerogatives to over-all community interests, offer the only hope of creating a decent urban environment, or even halting the deterioration of our present environment.

WAR AGAINST NATURE

The idea of planning and conservation hits American traditions broadside. The successive waves of pioneers and farmers who rolled westward across the continent were as oblivious of their impact as the breakers that crash on the beach, shift the sands, and bend the coast line. Less innocent but more destructive, the industrial pirates who followed the pioneers plundered the resources and fouled the natural beauty of this continent, to the applause of

Congress. Not until the timber raiders had left trails of blackened woods and stripped hillsides, demonstrating to all but the willfully blind that our resources were not inexhaustible, did Congress reluctantly enact conservation legislation.

The most zealous nineteenth-century preachers of the frontier ethic glorified timber thieves as public benefactors, persecuted by an oppressive government enforcing outrageous trespass laws. In a speech delivered in 1852 to the House of Representatives, Henry Hastings Sibley, delegate from the Wisconsin Territory, denounced the federal trespass laws as "a disgrace to the country and to the nineteenth century." Delegate Sibley extolled the virtuous victims of the law in ringing phrases:

Especially is he pursued with unrelenting severity, who has dared to break the silence of the primeval forest by the blows of the American ax. The hardy lumberman who has penetrated to the remotest wilds of the Northwest, to drag from their recesses the materials for building up towns and cities in the great valley of the Mississippi, has been particularly marked out as a victim. After enduring all the privations and subjecting himself to all the perils incident to his vocation—when he has toiled for months to add by his honest labor to the comfort of his fellow men, and to the aggregate wealth of the nation, he finds himself suddenly in the clutches of the law for trespassing on the public domain. The proceeds of his long winter's work are reft from him, and exposed to public sale for the benefit of his paternal government . . . and the object of this oppression and wrong is further harassed by vexatious law proceedings against him.

As evidence that praise for timber thieves was eminently respectable, Frederick Jackson Turner cites the lack of protest from other congressmen and the subsequent success of Delegate Sibley. He became Minnesota's first governor, a regent of its university, president of its historical society, and received a doctor of laws from Princeton University—an exquisitely polished pillar of society. Turner concluded: "Thus many of the pioneers, following the ideal of the right of the individual to rise, subordinated the rights of the nation and posterity to the desire that the country should be 'developed' and that the individual should advance with as little interference as possible. Squatter doctrines and individualism have left deep traces upon American conceptions."

Today, well over half a century since Turner wrote this passage, those "deep traces" remain disgracefully deep. Contemporary industrial polluters who recklessly poison the nation's air and water secretly agree with Delegate Sibley, but they can no longer openly defend lawbreaking without staining their image. The contemptuous, plundering spirit of nineteenth-century capitalism lives on today in industrial polluters, highway-building lobbyists, land speculators, slumlords, and investment builders. Unlike the Swedes, who have accepted city planning and public land controls for centuries, we subsidize the destruction of our urban environment. That is why our disordered, traffic-plagued metropolises are such a contrast with Stockholm's well-planned open space and co-ordinated rapid transit system.

### MYTH V. REALITY

More than any other major American city, Los Angeles illustrates the ludicrous conflict between frontier mythology and contemporary reality. The frontier mystique survives in almost pristine purity in America's Southwest. As described by the late Christopher Rand in *Los Angeles: The Ultimate City,* the "short-range jet set," shuttling between the southern California beaches and the Texas oil fields, lives a luxurious imitation frontier life—camping, hunting, fishing, and ranching. Inspired by such political heroes as Governor Ronald Reagan and Arizona senator Barry Goldwater, Los Angeles' make-believe frontiersmen still preach *laissez-faire* rugged individualism, despite their city's desperate economic dependence on federal war production.

More ominous for their city's future, these latter-day Babbitts still preach the provincial frontier virtues that obstruct Los Angeles' orderly transition into a super-metropolis. Before the year 2000, the Los Angeles region's projected thirty-two million population should overtake New York as the nation's largest urbanized area. Yet the transplanted, small-town Midwesterners who had dominated Los Angeles' stream of immigrants have never really accepted their new home as a city.

A few decades after American ranchers took over the sleepy Spanish pueblo, following Mexico's cession of California in 1848, Los Angeles' citizens began promoting their cow town, in one early visitor's words, ". . . as the choicest part of the earth." A national promotional campaign to lure immigrants to the "land of perpetual spring" has continued ever since, powered by American optimism in a bigger and necessarily better future, but pervaded with rural nostalgia. Los Angeles' citizens never wanted a cosmopolitan city; they wanted a gigantic collection of villages. Their spirit was embodied in the Reverend Dana W. Bartlett, a minister born in Maine and reared in Iowa (Los Angeles' chief source of immigrants). Reverend Bartlett attributed urban blight to ethnic ghettos and congestion. His prescription for curing urban ills, written in 1907, is still the watchword for Los Angeles and the modern advocates of sprawl: "Ruralize the city; urbanize the country."

Los Angeles' physical form expresses this paradox of small-town people congregating in a big city. Its sprawling, unplanned development has spawned a host of social ills. Rather than patrolling their beats on foot, Los Angeles' policemen patrol the city's sprawling precincts in radio cars, remote and alienated from the citizens. With its characteristic contempt for public services, Los Angeles long ago taxed its rail transit service to death to build competing highways. Having abandoned the rail network, which could have promoted orderly development and conserved open space, the city delivered itself almost totally to the cult of the automobile, thereby encouraging sprawl. Commuters forced to drive in the frenzied traffic made Los Angeles the photo-chemical smog capital of the world. The lack of public transportation also aggravated the isolation of the Watts ghetto, severely limiting access to the city's widely scattered centers of employment.

Los Angeles' obsession with the private side of life is expressed in other ways. Its zoning ordinances favor the single-family house as the most morally exalted form of human habitation, isolated from corrupting contact with residential apartments or commercial development. This policy promotes a more rigorous racial segregation than could possibly be achieved in a city like New York, with its greater mingling of land uses and its greater reliance on public facilities.

The city has squandered countless opportunities to build public parks and preserve open space. Despite the unequaled resource of twenty-five square miles of wild land within its city limits, Los Angeles has no counterpart to New York's Central Park or San Francisco's equally remarkable Golden Gate Park.

The private developers' bulldozed desecration of the Santa Monica Mountains recalls the depredations of the nineteenth-century miners, who washed away hillsides, silted streams, and ruined fertile valleys in their frantic search for gold. The conservationists' failure to preserve these mountains for public use is another reminder of Los Angeles' frontier ethos. Los Angeles land speculators pursue their desperate quest for private wealth in a desert of public poverty.

THE MORE THE MERRIER

The naïve frontier spirit still pervades American attitudes toward the growth of its largest metropolises and even toward population growth. Fortunately, the pioneer worship of big families has declined, but not enough to assure progress toward the zero population growth that must ultimately become national policy if we are to avert ecological calamity. In adapting to this discipline of urban life, America lags behind other industrial democracies, whose citizens express their preference for smaller families both in public opinion polls and in lower, virtually stabilized reproduction rates. As latter-day devotees of the frontier faith in limitless resources, the American masses see only a dim connection between their presumed absolute right to have three, four, or five children and the inexorably rising toll of pollution, congestion, crime, and social friction. Though less zealously than their pioneer ancestors, contemporary Americans still practice Jehovah's pristine commandment, "Be fruitful and multiply, and replenish the earth, and subdue it . . ." with emphasis on "multiply" and "subdue."

But the starkest contrast between the United States and other industrialized nations concerns the official attitude toward urban growth. Chiefly because of their superior economic opportunities, cities all over the globe naturally attract population, but, unlike other Western industrial democracies, America cheers growth. Great Britain, The Netherlands, Denmark, France, and Sweden have all adopted governmental policies aimed at discouraging growth in their largest metropolises. To limit the growth of its capital, the world's third-largest city, the British government has virtually banned commercial construction in London's core and severely limited all construction in an 850-square-mile green belt surrounding the city. A law enacted by Parliament in 1938 forbids the sprawling development that chokes most American metropolises. Since the end of World War II, Britain's new-towns program has settled some two million Britons, about three per cent of the population, in small cities separated from major metropolitan centers such as Edinburgh, Manchester, and Leeds, as well as London.

In the United States, the opposite policy is pressed at all levels of government. Despite the rising toll of congestion in the nation's two most populous metropolitan regions, government at all levels cheers and even subsidizes the growth of these areas. Population projections indicate more than thirty million inhabitants for both the New York and Greater Los Angeles metropolitan regions before the year 2000. Yet no federal, state, or city official has audibly challenged the notion that bigger is necessarily better.

The federal government has, in fact, collaborated with Los Angeles in promoting growth. Through the years Los Angeles and its southern California neighbors have plotted to bring water from other regions to the arid metropolis. Without advanced water management, the fantastic growth in southern California's semi-desert would have stopped at a tiny fraction of Greater Los Angeles' present thirteen million. A series of aqueducts, reaching ever farther, brings most of the Rocky Mountain watershed to Los Angeles. In the 1920s, the United States Reclamation Service backed Los Angeles' acquisition of the Owens River Valley supply, 225 miles to the north, against outraged protests of the local citizens; in 1935, Congress authorized diversion of the Colorado River to Los Angeles. A later Congress voted some federal funds for projects included in the tremendous $2.8 billion California Water Project, which will divert waters to Los Angeles from some 700 miles away in northern California.

In justifying the vast expense of this project, financed by California taxpayers, and to a minor degree by all U.S. taxpayers, the California Department of Water Resources goes metaphysical: "The main problem in California is that nature has not provided the right amount of water in the right places at the right times. More than 70% of our water originates in the northern third of the state, while 77% of the need is in the southern two-thirds." The Creator, it appears, failed to consult with the Los Angeles Chamber of Commerce before designing the state's ecology, and the citizens of northern California must bear their share of rectifying His extravagant mistake. To suggest that perhaps population growth could be better distributed between northern and southern California, that there is no urgent need to create the world's most populous metropolitan region in southern California's semi-desert, might open one to the charge of serving God instead of Mammon.

A similar drive to increase the population of a much older and still much bigger metropolis underlies the perennial campaign to build a fourth jetport in the New York metropolitan region. For nearly a decade, the Port of New York Authority, a bistate agency created in 1921 to coordinate transportation in the northern New Jersey-New York metropolitan region, attempted to force an unwanted jetport on the citizens of Morris County, New Jersey. In its report urging construction of the jetport, the Port Authority warned: "If the New Jersey-New York area is to grow and thrive, it is absolutely essential that adequate air transportation facilities be provided to serve the people of the region."

At bottom, the controversy over the fourth New York jetport pits the convenience of a few thousand elite air travelers, whose private planes crowd the skies at peak hours, against the environmental amenities of millions in the larger community. (By totally banning the highly disruptive operations of lightly loaded private planes and air taxis at the three major airports, the Port Authority could accommodate essential commercial flights with no additional jetport at least until 1980.)

But the most fantastic thing about the controversy is the universal acceptance of the Port Authority's reasons for pushing the fourth jetport—the warning that without it the New York area would not "grow and thrive." Common sense alone would suggest restraint in deliberately accelerating the growth of the world's largest metropolis. If the present trend is any indication, the New York metropolitan region must cease to grow before it can thrive, and if it continues to grow in the present way, it cannot thrive. Yet the Federal Aviation Agency joins the Port Authority, the two state governors, senators, and other dignitaries dedicated to a continued search for a new jetport site so the "area can grow and thrive."

A major concern to all, including the federal officials, is the threat of diverting some international flights to other cities' jetports. That the diversion of a few international flights to other cities, transferring the stimulus for industrial growth and consequent population growth to smaller cities, might be the best resolution of the problem was, of course, never suggested by anyone that counts.

In its proposal to build the Morris County jetport, the Port Authority's banker-dominated board of directors predictably, and understandably, ignored the interests of millions in preserving what little tranquillity remains in northern New Jersey, where frantically built, unplanned residential tracts, shopping centers, and neon-lit commercial strips are recklessly consuming open space desperately needed for recreational escape from the teeming population centers. Construction of a jetport, with its economic stimulus and construction truck traffic on the packed highways, would accelerate the environmental deterioration. But there are no spokesmen of authority with the temerity to question PROGRESS. Responding to the jetport threat, Morris County and state officials never seized the reason advanced for the jetport's construction as a good reason not to build it. They merely said, "Not here!"

Despite its acceptance in most advanced European nations, government policy deliberately designed to discourage growth, even in an area suffering the advanced stages of urban elephantiasis, is a heresy few Americans publicly advocate. The land speculator's freedom to build whenever and wherever he pleases, regardless of the social and ecological consequences, is virtually absolute. One grotesque exception is the use of local zoning power to ban apartments and low- or even moderately-priced housing, and their poor or even middle-class residents, from a community seeking to minimize taxes. But land control on the regional or metropolitan European scale, to assure city dwellers' access to open recreational space, or to protect green oases from the onslaught of bulldozers and the spreading concrete crust, is an alien concept in this country. The land speculator's right to exploit growth, and to be taxed at favored capital gains rates as a reward for his anti-social profiteering, expresses the frontier philosophy of private gain over public welfare. Today's land speculators are merely subtler contemporary models of the nineteenth century's plundering industrial pirates.

The throat-catching rhetoric of frontier freedom still stirs Americans, but at best the frontier ethic was only a partially valid response to the challenge of the wilderness. It has lasted at least a century past its time, and many of its values appear corrupt in retrospect. Today, even in its less objectionable aspects, the anarchic individualism of the frontier is as outmoded as the prairie schooner. What has survived is not true rugged individualism, but its ugly residue—the obsession with private goods. To accommodate 100 million additional Americans destined to descend on our cities and suburbs over the next three decades, we must reject the insipid dream of a tamed frontier transformed into a semi-rural, suburban arcadia. There is no place to hide from the stark realities of our crowded, city-centered society with its inevitable frictions, conflict, and turmoil. As pioneers on the urban frontier, can we outgrow the values of our rural ancestors and adapt to civilized urban life?

## FOR FURTHER READING

Dick, Everett. *The Sodhouse Frontier, 1854–1890*. New York: D. Appleton-Century, 1937.

Fogelson, Robert M. *The Fragmented Metropolis, Los Angeles 1850–1930*. Cambridge, Massachusetts: Harvard University Press, 1967.

Griffin, C. W. *Frontier Freedoms and Space Age Cities*. New York: Pitman, 1971.

Handlin, Oscar. *The Newcomers.* Cambridge, Massachusetts: Harvard University Press, 1959.

Jacobs, Jane. *The Economy of Cities.* New York: Random House, 1969.

Mumford, Lewis. *The City in History.* New York: Harcourt, Brace & World, 1961.

Rand, Christopher. *Los Angeles: The Ultimate City.* New York: Oxford University Press, 1967.

Reps, John W. *The Making of Urban America.* Princeton: Princeton University Press, 1965.

Schneider, Wolf. *Babylon Is Everywhere.* New York: McGraw-Hill, 1963.

Turner, Frederick Jackson. *The Frontier in American History.* New York: Holt, Rinehart & Winston, 1962.

White, Morton and Lucia. *The Intellectual vs. the City: From Thomas Jefferson to Frank Lloyd Wright.* Cambridge, Massachusetts: Harvard University Press, 1962.

# CHAPTER 3

# THE IMMIGRANT AND THE URBAN MELTING POT

## *Francis X. Femminella*

Not only are we a nation of immigrants, but our cities have been the magnets which attracted and held millions of newcomers. Certainly the diversity created by the "Little Italies" and "Little Polands" in numerous cities contributed greatly to the vitality and growth of cosmopolitan centers. New York, Chicago, New Orleans, and San Francisco would be dreary places without their ethnic colonies. Yet, given the unfamiliar manners and languages of the immigrants, as well as the rural distrust of cities, it was inevitable that immigrants and cities became the target of nativist attacks. As Frank Femminella points out, a number of ideologies on immigration and assimilation were propounded to satisfy the current worries about the newcomers, and, manifestly, these theories rarely came to grips with reality. While the immigrants were being Americanized, they were also affecting and changing American society, and the chief beneficiaries of this transformation were the cities.

A former social worker, Francis X. Femminella is currently professor of sociology and education at the State University of New York at Albany, with a special interest in ethnicity, about which he has written a number of pieces. In addition, he has served as special consultant to a Model Cities Program, to the Teacher Corps, and in the training of federal desegregation specialists.

*There she lies, the great Melting Pot—listen! Can't you hear the roaring and the bubbling? There gapes her mouth—the harbour where a thousand mammoth feeders come from the ends of the world, to pour in their human freight. . . . Celt and Latin, Slav and Teuton, Greek and Syrian, Jew and Gentile. . . . what is the glory of Rome and Jerusalem where all nations come to worship and look back, compared with the glory of America, where all races and nations come to labour and look forward!*

—Israel Zangwill, *The Melting Pot*

THE UNITED STATES is one of those nations in the world which got a good deal more out of its immigrations than just people. No nation gets *only* people—that is, population statistics—but America received much more; it acquired an "immigrant culture." What this means and how it happened can be understood by exploring the fascinating interconnections between a number of ideas—ideas concerning immigration, concerning intergroup processes, and concerning cities.

THE SOCIAL USES OF THEORY

Certain salient ideas have a multiplicity of statuses and functions. To illustrate briefly what this implies, we can take the idea of the "melting pot" as an obvious example. In this country, the melting pot idea can be categorized in a number of ways. First, it represents a belief, a hope, and a symbol for allaying fears; it is thus a collective *ideology*. Next, it is a description and explanation of social events and processes, and serves as a kind of *social theory*. Finally, this idea can be seen as one of those historical fictions and myths whose function was to stabilize the social order, or what Karl Mannheim referred to as a "utopian wish image."[1]

The very mention of the terms "immigrants" and "cities" stimulates in some people images which are ideologically colored and which have in the past generated feelings of strangeness and prejudice. Judgments were made regarding reasons for immigration, city life, and the "types" of people who moved to cities, largely apart from either empirical or historical reference. To say that man migrates because he is by nature nomadic is one thing. To point to man's migrations as "proof" of this theorem is circular reasoning. For our purposes, it ought to be enough simply to assert that from prehistoric times, some men have migrated over long distances presumably to better their life chances; they settled in large numbers in areas where their life chances were enhanced or where they were forced to stay, and certain of these settlements developed into cities. The most usual pattern in the United States was for immigrants to settle in cities; and one can hardly understand either immigration or cities in the United States without taking the developmental dynamics of both into account. These assertions are not enough, however, since they fail to provide adequate methodological or theoretical direction for finding important distinctions in the various immigrations to the United States or migration within the states, or for understanding the implications of these differences. William Petersen's typology may help us out of this prob-

---

[1] *Ideology* will be used to refer to an individual's or group's coherent body of ideas, values, beliefs, and ways of perceiving as these are determined by the social and historical context in which they live, and which provide them with a sense of direction in life. *Social theory* will be used to refer to a formal explanation of any social event, social process, or of relationships between social phenomena. As we shall see, too often the social theories which explained certain events have followed and fit too perfectly the social and political ideologies of the day. When this occurs, we cannot help but suspect that these ideological projections have fostered, if not conscious falsification, then at least unconscious self-deception. The projection of these values and beliefs have had not only scientific but political and social consequences as well.

lem. He distinguishes between the 1] *Primitive* (Wandering, Ranging; and Flight from the Land) migrations which result from ecological necessity; 2] *Forced* (Displacement; and Slave Trade); 3] *Impelled* (Flight; and Coolie Trade) migrations resulting from the pressure of social institutions; 4] *Free* (Group; and Pioneer) migrations which result from social norms and man's higher aspiration; and 5] *Mass* (Settlement; and Urbanization) migrations resulting from social momentum and which are examples of collective behavior. In this classification scheme, the first parenthetical term of each class of migration represents what Petersen calls a *Conservative* type of migration, in that persons move geographically in order to retain as much else of their former life as possible; and the second term of the parenthesis represents an *Innovating* type of migration in that persons move in order to achieve something new. The immigrations to the United States during the nineteenth century changed in character from Free to Mass migrations and, toward the end of the century, at nearly the same time that our economy was shifting from an agrarian to an industrial base, the migrations shifted from a Conservative Settlement type of migration to an Innovating Urbanizing type of migration. Industrialism, urbanization, and immigration became tied to one another at the same time that the United States was becoming a very changed nation. Initially, the interconnection of economy, ecology, and demography was grossly misunderstood, and popular interpretations of the meaning of these social processes were largely ideological. In the mind of nativist and immigrant alike the problems generated by one process became confused with the problems generated by others.

From ancient times, however, men *have* linked notions regarding the evolution of culture, the attainment of freedom, and the growth of cities. Cities, meaning buildings and streets (*urbs*), and cities, meaning a community of citizens (*civitas*), began to develop in prehistoric times. The classical philosophers of Greece and Rome, and social thinkers even to the eighteenth and nineteenth centuries, recognized that the lives of urbanites were different from the lives of farm and village people; and they defended the city as a "natural" development. As the intensity of tribal systems diminished, as man became "civilized," cities provided the harmonious mediation required for systematic social and cultural change. New economic, religious, and civil institutions, reflecting changing economic, religious, and political philosophies and beliefs were generated. Cities were thought of as micro-images of society itself. The industrial cities of the eighteenth and nineteenth centuries exhibited a complexity and entanglement of social structures and an increase in the *scale* of society, that is, an increase in the scope and range of human interactions as the population increased, and a correlative change in the patterns of mutual dependency. Poverty, overcrowding, lack of sanitation, merciless child labor practices, exploitation, and other human indignities were social problems which arose or expanded in these changing cities. These conditions were understood and explained as being concomitant dimensions of a society whose members were in continuous economic competition. They were accepted as implacably emanating out of the human market place, a characteristic of social life. Here again, however, the ideological projections of the writers of the period must be taken into account. Artists and thinkers first saw the cities of Europe during the eighteenth and nineteenth centuries as essentially a new *good* thing. Later, they began to describe the city as an *evil* thing, and finally, as *neither* virtue nor vice in itself.

Twentieth-century social theorists, finding the earlier economic determinist descriptions and explanations of these phenomena oversimplified, developed a broader view of urbanism and a new approach to the study of cities. In the first place, they recognized that non-economic variables also contributed to the complexity of urban social structures and were in turn shaped by conditions uniquely urban. Secondly, they saw urban settlements as places which

originally grew as the result of the movement of persons
from the countryside into the town. Next, they recognized the characteristics of heterogeneity of human kinds
and of human activities, of anonymity, of large impersonal
bureaucracies, of superficiality and lack of warmth in interpersonal relations, of often times inhumane rationality—all
of which they identified as aspects of urban culture. Finally, they saw cities as integrated social forms which could
be analyzed and contrasted with other social forms.

If urbanism was problematic for European social thinkers, how much more so it must have been for thinkers in
the United States who were witnessing the development of
the largest urban centers in the world. The immensity of
the immigrations that took place during the years before
World War I was unparalleled in history. This was already
the beginning of the age of the "super-city." The slums
and the "sins" of crowded cities had been described and
analyzed from as early as 1840, largely by reformers of
various types who, while occasionally contributing to the
passage of effective reform legislation, more often revealed
little or no understanding of the forces which generated
the evils that shocked them. After World War I, however,
the new ecological approach to urban studies was begun.
Robert E. Park, Roderick D. McKenzie, and Ernest W.
Burgess analyzed the internal structure of the city, emphasizing the relationship of the parts to one another and to
the whole. Using analogies from plant and animal ecology,
they introduced the concepts of "competition," "dominance," "accommodation," and "invasion and succession"
into sociological thinking. They interpreted the city as a
vital product of human nature; and they assumed that by
studying it, they could learn about human nature and the
evolution of culture. Their notions were infused with
"American," more properly—"United-Statesian" ideology.
The idea of "the American promise," of America as "a
cornucopia of well-being and freedom" is there. The dominant traits of the early citizens of the United States as
they were described by Hector de St. John Crèvecoeur,

Alexis de Tocqueville, Harriet Martineau, and James Lord Bryce, stressing equality, freedom, individualism, practicality, success, and concern for the opinion of others, were also there, and underlie the works of those urbanologists who focused their attention on minority groups and city life.

If we accept the anthropological truism that cultures are integrated, then there is an apparent contradiction in placing high value on both conformity with concern for the opinion of others, on the one hand, and nonconformity and individuality, on the other; between equality for all with racial heterogeneity (the "melting pot") and disdain and distrust of foreigners with feelings of superiority over them. These important paradoxes are supported by a kind of logic which emanates out of the ideologies of the group. Thus, there is no contradiction in a group's "strain for consistency" with its consequent imposition of uniformities, and its stress on personal competition for economic advantage. Immigrants residing in the cities were a locus where these contradictory forces came together. As foreigners, they had to learn the meaning and the manners of society, at first for sheer survival; then after some initial success they were impelled, seemingly by some inner human dynamic, to participate in the great American dream. In practice, this meant they entered into the life of the city—and especially the action of the market —learning to compete. Once this happened, the "race relations cycle" began. When an immigrant retained his foreign ways, the competition became racial and impersonal and conflict followed; but when he obliterated the external differences, personal competition ensued, and people attained positions they were "best fitted to fill," out of which developed friendships and ultimately assimilation.

In time it became a basic tenet of belief that cities served as the primary agency for the assimilation of foreign groups. Robert E. Park wrote: "Great cities have always been the melting pots of races and of cultures. Out of the vivid and subtle interactions of which they have been the centers, there have come the newer breeds and the newer social types." The inference that, to a very large extent, immigrant groups in the United States were not assimilating on the farms and the villages, would have to be denied, although there is some truth to it. First, however, a question must be raised about the meaning of "assimilation."

Park used the term "assimilation" to refer to that social process whereby people of different races and cultures are drawn into "the ever narrowing circle of a common life." This meant the erasing of external differences, the development of superficial uniformities particularly in manners and fashion but also in language, which enabled newcomers to participate in the new life, in a "practical working arrangement," so that like-mindedness in individual opinions, sentiments, and beliefs could eventually accrue. H. P. Fairchild, on the other hand, wrote: "The process by which a nationality preserves its unity while admitting representatives of outside nationalities, is properly termed 'assimilation.'"

Two important points are raised by these definitions. First, the difference in the direction of change should be noted in those two conceptions. For Park, assimilation denoted change on the part of the alien, but it also implied change on the part of the host society, in compromises and accommodations. Accommodation always preceded assimilation; secondary relationships based on interests inevitably engendered personal intercourse and friendship, based on sentiment, which would break down social distance between people. Fairchild, on the other hand, placed the burden of change on the immigrant: "It is he who must undergo the entire transformation; the true member of the American nationality is not called upon to change in the least. . . . There is no 'give and take' in assimilation."

A second important point raised by these definitions is the distinction between "cultural" assimilation and "social" assimilation. While the newcomer may indeed acquire the behavioral patterns of the host society, that is, be acculturated, he may not as yet be admitted, as Milton M. Gordon points out, to the "cliques, clubs and institutions of the host society on a primary group level," that is, he may be *culturally* but not *structurally* assimilated. Structural assimilation precedes marital amalgamation, which is followed by the development of a unifying sense of peoplehood based exclusively on the host society. More interpenetrating aspects of unification follow wherein prejudice, discrimination, and value and power conflicts are all absent. While the melting pot refers to assimilation of peoples, we now see two areas of inquiry. First, which "direction of change"—change of immigrant, change of host society, or some combination of both—does the melting pot imply? Second, does this idea refer to cultural assimilation or to structural assimilation and deeper levels of unity?

## A NATION OF IMMIGRANTS

The melting pot idea, with its profound influence on United States history, is best analyzed in its socio-historical context as it related to the peopling of the country and the development of a culture. The union of the people of the United States has been legally defined, and it has been defended with bloodshed, but with all this the meaning of union is variegated. The early colonists distrusted governments, but were beginning to establish a sense of themselves as a united group whose elusive nature was yet to be determined. Were they to be a people, a nation, a civilization, or some combination of these? It must be remembered that the United States is a nation which originated among immigrants and had, for its first hundred years as a republic, a policy of open migration. In all, from the initial colonization of America by northern Europeans to the present, nearly fifty million immigrants have come to these shores. Although immigration statistics were not kept before 1820, it is estimated that during the first century of the republic, nine and a half million persons entered the country. While the numbers are significant in themselves, they do not tell the whole story. What is even more meaningful is the cultural diversity of these millions of people and the fact that they poured in over the nation like huge waves crashing over a sea wall. The influence this had on the nation was put poetically by Oscar Handlin in the introduction to his Pulitzer prize-winning *The Uprooted:* "Once I thought to write a history of the immigrants in America. Then I discovered that the immigrants *were* American history." Historians have vividly described the migration of foreigners from England, Scotland, Wales, Ireland, Germany, Scandinavia, The Netherlands, France, and Africa. Jews from all over Europe, but particularly from Germany and Poland, came to the United States, and by the middle of the nineteenth century, a small number of Italians had already arrived. In addition, a limited migration from the Orient is also recorded. This intermingling of cultural groups was early observed and extolled by Crèvecoeur, who wrote, "The Americans were once scattered all over Europe, here they are incorporated into one of the finest systems of population which has ever appeared." Crèvecoeur seems to have been one of the earliest writers, if not the first, to herald the melting pot idea, and it is worth recalling his classic description:

. . . whence came all those people? They are a mixture of English, Scotch, Irish, French, Dutch, Germans, and Swedes. From this promiscuous breed, that race now called Americans has risen.

. . . What then is the American, this new man? He is either a European, or the descendant of a European, hence that strange mixture of blood, which you will find in no other country. I could point out to you a family whose grandfather was an Englishman, whose wife was Dutch, whose son married a French woman, and whose present four sons have now four wives of different nations. *He* is an American who, leaving behind him all his ancient prejudices and manners, receives new ones from the new mode of life he has embraced, the new government he obeys and the new rank he holds. He becomes an American by being received in the broad lap of our great

*Alma Mater.* Here individuals of all nations are melted into a new race of men, whose labours and posterity will one day cause great changes in the world.

The evidence, however, seems rather to indicate that this intermixing was not as general as Crèvecoeur made it out to be, and one can document the failure of assimilation among the Germans, the Dutch, the Irish, the Scots, and the French during the years 1789 to 1829. Indeed, in reviewing the literature of the period it seems clear that English immigrants arrived in sufficient numbers and exhibited sufficient aggressiveness and strength to impose their standards on all of their co-settlers and among the native inhabitants as well. By the close of the colonial period, white, Anglo-Saxon, Protestant standards dominated. Because the growth of the nation required more manpower, free immigration was allowed, regulated only by the states. Nevertheless, critical attitudes toward non-English immigrants developed early, with some states taxing non-English and non-Welsh immigrants, and abusive treatment was accorded the German and Scotch-Irish immigrants of that time. Their attempts at, or resistance to, becoming anglicized over the next three or four generations, and the success of some, particularly in Pennsylvania, at maintaining their own language and customs seemed to presage the ethnic struggles of our history. Far worse than this was the pernicious torment the colonists inflicted upon Indians and Africans in their midst, whom they used. That the melting pot idea was not understood, or rather was interpreted differently at different times according to prevailing ideologies, is seen in the arguments for and against free immigration which began early in our history and still go on today.

In some of these early arguments one can discern the distinctively bourgeois characteristics of the emerging middle class beginning to crystallize. The "Native American" and the "Know-Nothing" movements in the mid-nineteenth century developed out of antipathy for alien ways and what was taken to be a threat of "take over" by foreign kings, socialists, and papists. "America for the Americans" was the motto they proclaimed. White, Anglo-Saxon, middle-class, Protestant United-Statesians, and also those others who had shed all vestiges of their former heritage, exhibited fear and hostility equally toward immigrants and toward those fellow-citizens who refused or were unable to be anglicized. For these Anglo-Americans, whether consciously or not, the melting pot had a very distinct meaning: it meant the dissolution of all non-English ways. Pride in the product—a free, democratic, egalitarian, successful, non-urban people, the new superior "American"—prevented them from seeing either any inconsistencies in their beliefs or any good in cultural diversity. Robert Louis Stevenson's poem "Foreign Children," written in the latter part of the nineteenth century, expressed the theme well.

Little Indian, Sioux or Crow,
Little frosty Eskimo,
Little Turk or Japanee,
O! don't you wish that you were me?

You have seen the scarlet trees
And the lions overseas;
You have eaten ostrich eggs,
And turned the turtles off their legs.

Such a life is very fine,
But it's not so nice as mine:
You must often, as you trod,
Have wearied, *not* to be abroad.

You have curious things to eat,
I am fed on proper meat;
You must dwell beyond the foam,
But I am safe and live at home.

Little Indian, Sioux or Crow,
Little frosty Eskimo,
Little Turk or Japanee,
O! don't you wish that you were me?

As the country expanded, the need for manpower both for the frontier and for industry continued, and so did free migration. But the xenophobic forces opposed to open migration kept at their work, too. In March 1875, the first restrictive federal legislation was passed, prohibiting the admittance of felons and prostitutes into the country. In May 1882, the first racial restriction was legislated—Chinese laborers were denied entry—and in August of that year "convicts," "idiots," "lunatics," and potential paupers were rejected. In subsequent acts, the list of restricted persons gradually lengthened, and eventually quotas for the admittance of selected immigrants were established in May 1921.

This and the even more prejudicial amended Quota Act of 1924 grew out of a race ideology synthesizing beliefs in 1) the superiority of Anglo-Saxon people; 2) the right of Anglo-Americans to set behavioral and cultural standards for all the citizens of the United States; and 3) the formation of an "American" race. In the decades prior to the passage of the first Quota Act, Anglo-American ethnocentrism sometimes took extreme forms. The Tomkins Square police riot of 1874, the Molly Maguires arrests of 1875, the convictions following the Haymarket Affair in 1887, the Lawrence, Massachusetts, textile workers' strike of 1912, the Palmer "Red Raids" of 1919, and the Sacco and Vanzetti case of 1920 were all characterized by the interconnection of these xenophobic elements: 1) an irrational anti-foreign sentiment; 2) strong rejection of any form of socialist or other "radical" philosophy; 3) an identification of 1 with 2 and vice versa; and 4) excessive self-righteousness. In June 1952 a completely revised law relating to immigration and naturalization was enacted; and the persistence of the Anglo-Saxon superiority myth was evident both in the congressional debate before enactment and in the law itself. In addition, the restrictive aspects of the law were made more stringent, under the guise of protecting the national interest against anarchy, communism, and other "foreign" political doctrines. In October 1965

a new Immigration Act was signed into law, whose purpose
was to rid the law of race prejudice and discrimination.
The quota system was abolished, although immigration reform continued. Still unresolved, however, is the meaning
of the "melting pot."


THE MELTING POT


The last decades of the nineteenth century have been
called an era of upheaval. They were a time of tumultuous
change in the economic history of the country—mass industrialization, paralyzing depressions, the organization of
labor. As the new century began, cities bulged with newcomers from the farms of this country and from foreign
lands. The immigrants themselves were different, coming
not from Northern and Western Europe but from Southern
and Eastern Europe. They were Italians, Greeks, Poles,
Jews, Russians, and Slavs; and each year sufficient numbers
of them came to populate a good-size city. And indeed, it
was to the cities that they came rather than to the farms
or the frontier. Nativists could now link their anti-
newcomer, anti-Catholic, and anti-Semitic sentiments to
their anti-urban sentiments. "During this period, it would
seem that rural-agrarian and urban-industrial life are sym-
bolically antithetical," wrote Paul Charosh in his moving
study of songs about "home." The distinctive institutions
and social organization which developed in the United
States and which reflected the goals of democracy and free
enterprise seemed threatened. Israel Zangwill's play *The
Melting Pot* was produced at this time (1909) and served
as oil poured on troubled waters. It projected a new image
of the teeming-with-immigrants city, presenting it as a seeth-
ing cauldron into which have been poured people from all
the nations and all the races of mankind, and out of which
comes a new unified super-being, the "American." The
"melting pot" became, for a while, a popular symbol of

hope for the future unity and homogeneity of the country and of its people.

The melting pot ideas of Crèvecoeur and Zangwill predicted change in the immigrants and change in the host society as well, leading to total assimilation. There are some differences, however, that should be noted. First, the "ingredients" that went into Crèvecoeur's pot were (excepting Africans and Indians) homogeneous in race and religion, and the majority were of the same national origin. Zangwill's pot contained far more heterogeneity in race, national origin, and religion. Next, there were important differences between the two in reasons for migrating. The Zangwill immigrants were for the most part a mass urbanization migration; Crèvecoeur's migrants came for varied reasons. Another salient difference between Crèvecoeur and Zangwill is the migrant's response to the social and cultural condition of the host society. Crèvecoeur's immigrants regarded the Indian tribes and nations as savages to be Christianized. When the Indians resisted further encroachment of their lands they were callously ejected or destroyed. Zangwill's migrants sought with dignity to become a vital working part of the strange culture they encountered, and to share in the "American dream" of freedom and prosperity.

Finally, the product which supposedly emerged from the melting pot of Crèvecoeur was the rural, Protestant, Anglo-American. But what could emerge from the pot of Zangwill? Certainly if we take the analogy seriously we can expect that a new "American," not an Anglo-American will emerge. And his destiny will be tied to an *urban,* not a rural way of life. Zangwill's view was that a superman would be produced. The Anglo-American view around the turn of the century was that if immigration were unchecked, the great American race would be diluted, its strength dissipated, its worth spent, its future one of decadence. The Quota Acts of 1921 and 1924, following this view, severely restricted non-Nordic peoples. Of course, not everyone felt this way. Emma Lazarus wrote:

Not like the brazen giants of Greek fame,
With conquering limbs astride from land to land
Here at our sea-washed, sunset gates shall stand
A mighty woman with a torch, whose flame
Is the imprisoned lightning and her name
Mother of Exiles. From her beacon-hand
Glows world-wide welcome; her mild eyes command
The air-bridged harbor that twin cities frame.
"Keep, ancient lands, your storied pomp!" cries she
With silent lips. "Give me your tired, your poor
Your huddled masses yearning to breathe free,
The wretched refuse of your teeming shore,
Send these, the homeless, tempest-tossed to me,
I lift my lamp beside the golden door!"

John F. Kennedy, long interested in immigration problems, wrote that in view of the Immigration Act of 1952, "there should be added: 'as long as they come from northern Europe, are not too tired or too poor or slightly ill, never stole a loaf of bread, never joined any questionable organization, and can document their activities for the past two years.'" The 1965 Immigration Act, managed through the floor of the U. S. Senate by Senator Edward Kennedy, partially changed this situation.

## CULTURAL PLURALISM

The law can do a good deal to shape the minds and hearts of men, but it must work indirectly. It can set the stage, as it were, but the drama must be played by actors. It can throw open the "Golden Door," but then the real people must deal with one another. If the law allows, the people together will make their culture; they'll make themselves. The immigrants came to the cities of the United States; they made the cities; and the cities made them urban United-Statesians. As we review the recent studies of these groups, however, we find that they have not "melted." These Germans, Italians, Irish, Jews, Poles, Africans, Japanese, and others have in so many ways not become Anglo-Americans, and indeed, they seem not to *want* to be Anglo-Americans. They want to be German-Americans, Italian-Americans, Irish-Americans, Jewish-Americans, Polish-Americans, African-Americans, Japanese-Americans, and so on. In view of this, we must move along two avenues of inquiry. First, how is this hyphenated form of group adjustment and assimilation to be explained? Secondly, what does this signify about "American," that is, United States culture?

Briefly, theories explaining assimilation in the United States followed closely the ideologies respecting immigration. Initially, it was thought that all immigrants would, after two, three, or at most four generations, become Anglo-Americans or conform as closely as possible to this model. When it became apparent that not all immigrants were conforming (the Irish and Germans were especially noticeable) a new explanation was sought, and for some, the melting pot idea later popularized by Zangwill served the purpose. The fires of deeply felt hatreds, however, are not extinguished by popular slogans. The re-establishment of the Ku Klux Klan in 1915 and the "Red Raids" following World War I were part of a new revival of nativism which took the view that the melting pot idea was a mistake, that the only way to save America from the foreign peril was to Americanize the aliens in our midst, and forestall the entry of new ones. The immigrant communities found in every large city were too numerous and too conspicuous to be ignored. The supporters of the Americanization movement explained these immigrant colonies as temporary formations which would eventually disappear. Through education in the public schools, through the teaching of the English language and United States civics and history, the foreigner would be Americanized. The restrictionists, nativists such as Fairchild, who did not believe Americanization could work, ridiculed the effort and called upon immigrants individually to renounce the foreign colonies, explaining that only by disassociating oneself from the foreign element could one acquire the true American sentiments.

Even after passage of the Quota Acts, new little worlds grew up in the cities. Migrations from rural areas to cities went on. In the next decade or so, the rural-urban trek was made by ever increasing numbers of persons. From the South, both whites and blacks moved into northern and western cities and they established colonies. Mexicans and Canadians, not restricted by the law, moved into the United States. Even casual observers of cities recognized that neither the "Anglo-conformity" nor the "melting pot" nor the "Americanization" concepts explained either the characteristics of the population or the processes that produced them. Real cities in this country were not monocultural fields. On the contrary, they reflected the "nation of nations" that the United States was becoming. Cultural pluralism, a concept first introduced by Horace Kallen in 1915, was revived in the late thirties and early forties both as an ideology and as an explanation of the observed behavior. Briefly, it implies that each ethnic group can, should, and does maintain itself as a "community" with its distinctive culture, even while its members become citizens and participate in the politics and economy of the wider society. We could call this kind of behavior "structural pluralism" with each group exhibiting some degree of cultural assimilation. A clear example of non-assimilation in this society is the adherence to various religious institutions found here. For the cultural pluralist, democracy guarantees the right of these groups to remain structurally separate, and it prohibits discrimination based on religious affiliation. That ethnic groups in the cities of the United States have shown some degree of assimilation is as obvious from what has been said as the fact that they have not been totally assimilated. They, as groups, have learned to communicate in English, become citizens, acquire the values of success and upward mobility, and so on. In a word, they have moved in the direction of the Anglo-American.

The Anglo-American cultural system was predominant

at the time of the founding of the nation and it remains the core of our society. Anglo-American is essentially English, but English modified by the experience of crossing an ocean, of settling in a virgin territory, of clearing land, building homes, and of taming a frontier. The social experience of the colonists matched for novelty their ecological experience. The English engaged in social contact with peoples of different races and cultures. They united and led the insurrection against their English motherland, and they began a political and economic revolution based upon a non-English ideology leading to the creation of a new nation. To be Anglo-American is not to be English-American. But being Anglo-American does, more often than not, mean being white, Anglo-Saxon, and Protestant. Because Anglo-Americans placed such high value on their own ways and excessively low value on other cultures, and because they feared and even hated, without reason, those who looked or acted in ways unfamiliar to them, Anglo-Americans did what had to be done to keep people believing that they were the only "real" or "true" United-Statesians. White, Anglo-Saxon, Protestants, however, are now seen not as the model to which all other groups must necessarily conform but rather as the most successful fellow-United-Statesian group, with whom one must deal. What this means is that WASP-Americans are entering, consciously or unconsciously, willingly or unwillingly, into accommodation patterns with the ethnic communities around them; and particularly in the cities, they have recognized that structural pluralism is a salient aspect of United States culture. Assimilation, then, must be seen as having two directions—toward the core culture and then back to the ethnic sub-culture. In this sense, the culture of the United States may be described as a fluctuating "emerging culture." Change itself is the most salient characteristic of this life. Ethnic groups in this culture are not to be thought of as merely unassimilated holdouts left over from the earlier immigrations which will disappear in time.

Rather they have become a fundamental part of United-Statesian social structure and they are most evident in the cities.

IMPACT-INTEGRATION

Finally, in discussing this form of group adjustment and assimilation, we may use the idea of "impact-integration." The more familiar term integration was taken over from mathematics and was apparently first used by Nathan Glazer as a neutral substitute for such words as assimilation and acculturation. For Glazer, immigrants are integrated with Americans when: 1) they no longer present any special social problem; 2) their old-nation political interests are subordinate to United States interests; and 3) when, in the United-Statesian culture which they have changed, they as well as old United-Statesians are at home. William S. Bernard, in using the term, wrote as follows: "Our immigrant stock and our so called 'native' stock have each integrated with the other. That is to say that each element has been changed by association with the other, without complete loss of its own cultural identity, and with a change in the resultant cultural amalgam, or civilization if you will, that is vital, vigorous, and an advance beyond its previous level. Without becoming metaphysical, let us say that the whole is greater than the sum of its parts, and the parts, while affected by interaction with each other, nevertheless, remain complementary but individual." "Integration" as used here is located in the tradition of cultural pluralism, and it describes a dimension of emerging culture. "Impact" refers to certain aspects of the *coming together* of ethnic groups. The term rings with a negative, destructive tone in that it suggests a *booming collision* resulting in a violent fusion, a forced entanglement.

It is important to recognize the underlying forces, that is, the complex dynamic of this collision. The core of the dominant ethnic group of a society reacts territorially to the immigration of a large number of newcomers. It observes the different, sometimes mutually exclusive, cultural systems of the migrants, and perceives them, ideologically, as adversaries. This "boundary crisis" may be heightened if there is competition for limited rewards, otherwise absorption may be facilitated. Territorial defensiveness takes various forms and goes on in many ways. There are, for example, a whole set of behaviors for emphasizing priority, and there are the many ways, with varying degrees of subtlety, of pressing one's own appropriateness to the country. Some of the more obvious aspects of "institutional racism" include: economic and political exploitation, negative discrimination in job and career opportunities, involuntary segregation and poor housing, exclusion from viable education, inequality before the law, a denial of the freedom to choose, especially to choose to do things differently, legalized harassment, to say nothing of the infliction of outright violent assault and destruction. The song of the dominant group is: "We belong to the land; and the land we belong to is . . . ours!" Deprecating the newcomers, and negating their attempts at "making something of themselves," the core group generates its polar opposite—the estranged intruder.

In the conflict that ensues the price demanded of the immigrant to legitimize his presence is social, economic, and cultural subordination and submission. But healthy men, who have grown stronger by the choice they made to migrate, do not submit so easily. For them, freedom is too attractive a treasure to surrender. The empirical evidence seems to indicate that no ethnic group in the United States has ever totally submitted. Race and ethnic conflicts have been and are still a very real and important part of our history; for it is out of this impacting that new syntheses evolve. The conflict is resolved in a cultural integration that changes not only the persons involved, nor even also their groups, but the whole society itself. One sees this best in the cities, where, as Michael Parenti has shown, ethnic colonies persist. But it can be seen, too, in the suburbs where voluntary segregation along ethnic as well as social class lines has developed.

Impacting also changes the people in the society; the immigrants are changed most of all, but so are the earlier residents. Sociologists have provided us with general descriptions about these changes in the newcomers. They have described the confusion, the alienation, and the fears that the immigrant experiences when first settling and the comfort and security he derived from moving into close physical proximity to friends and relatives. These are the immigrant communities, the foreign colonies about which we have heard. Second-generation ethnics, the United States-born children of immigrants, ashamed of the foreign behavior of their parents, often rejected their ancestry; others, as a defense against the overt cruel acts of prejudice directed toward them, overidentified with the old culture of their parents. Many of this generation felt the pain of marginality, not knowing whether they were United-Statesians or foreigners. In the third generation and beyond, the immigrants' progeny have felt more secure in their belongingness, in their "United Statesness." As they become young adults, they are able, in assessing their own self-resources, to ask about their distinctive backgrounds and develop new interest in their ancestral heritage. The process of coming to feel at home in the United States has, for most ethnic groups, been a work of generations.

These changes are not just atavistic, but are facilitated by the simultaneous changes which have been occurring in the core culture as well. Earlier residents, expanding the boundaries of United States culture and society, accept its realities; and as a result of the confrontation they, too, have experienced ideological reorientation. Many have found that they are able not only to maintain their link with the older United States heritage but can also achieve a unity in a new emerging United States culture, which, as we began this paper, we called an immigrant culture. Immigrants have always been people who "looked to the future"; action- and doing-oriented, they were sometimes accused of being too ruggedly individualistic; believing in God, they believed He helped those who helped themselves, and their aim was to conquer nature. These will be recognized as the value traits often ascribed to Americans; these are also the value traits of immigrants. The decision to migrate is a decision to leave home ground, a fixed point which enables us to understand things in a traditional way and to accept change. Change and diversity is the immigrant's cloak; it is the central characteristic of urban United States.

## FOR FURTHER READING

Alloway, David N. and Francesco Cordasco. *Minorities and the American City.* New York: David McKay, 1970.

Bailey, Harry A., Jr., and Ellis Katz (eds.). *Ethnic Group Politics.* Columbus, Ohio: Charles E. Merrill, 1969.

Banton, Michael. *Race Relations.* New York: Basic Books, Inc., 1967.

Dinnerstein, Leonard and Frederic Copla Jaher (eds.). *The Aliens.* New York: Meredith, 1970.

Glazer, Nathan and Daniel Patrick Moynihan. *Beyond the Melting Pot.* Cambridge, Massachusetts: Massachusetts Institute of Technology Press and Harvard University Press, 1963.

Gordon, Milton M. *Assimilation in American Life.* New York: Oxford University Press, 1964.

Handlin, Oscar. *The Uprooted.* Boston: Little, Brown, 1951.

Hansen, Marcus Lee. *The Atlantic Migration 1607–1860.* New York: Harper & Row, 1961.

———, *The Immigrant in American History.* New York: Harper & Row, 1964.

Kennedy, John F. *A Nation of Immigrants.* New York: Anti-Defamation League of B'nai B'rith, 1963.

Lieberson, Stanley. *Ethnic Patterns in American Cities.* New York: The Free Press, 1963.

# CHAPTER 4

# PSYCHOLOGICAL PROBLEMS OF THE URBAN POOR

## *Ross A. Evans*

While there have always been problems of poverty in cities, the normal attitude for many centuries reflected the biblical view that "the poor you shall always have with ye." Cities since antiquity contained large pockets of disease-ridden slums, populated by slaves and the dregs of society, and only in the last century has there been any concern about alleviating this condition. In the United States, progressive reformers at the turn of the century attempted to awaken the country's conscience to the problems of the poor in the cities, and set forth various remedies they hoped would help the poor to rise above their environment.

Unfortunately, at the very time when social critics were examining these problems, the massive influx of immigrants caused by industrialization expanded the slum areas by a massive factor. Between the wars, a large influx of blacks from the rural South introduced the complicating tensions of racial animosities and prejudices. Gigantic problems, instead of being met by a concerted drive, were attacked piecemeal by proponents of various panaceas, each of whom was convinced that he alone had the right answer.

In the last decade it has become obvious that the problems, instead of being solved, are growing, and a society that has seemingly lost its internal sense of direction has tended to blame the poor for the conditions of which they are the prime victims. In this essay, Professor Evans attacks those who would blame the poor for their misery, and explicitly argues that for all the middle-class fears of crime in the streets and terrible cities, it is the poor urban slum dweller who suffers the most.

Ross A. Evans is currently director of the Research and Demonstration Center for the Education of Handicapped Children at Teachers College, Columbia. He has written widely on learning disabilities, and on the special social handicaps faced by black people.

*What happens to a dream deferred?*

*Does it dry up*
  *like a raisin in the sun?*
*Or fester like a sore—*
  *and then run?*
*Does it stink*
  *like rotten meat?*
*Or crust and sugar over—*
  *like a syrupy sweet?*

*Maybe it just hangs*
  *like a heavy load.*

*Or does it explode?*

—LANGSTON HUGHES

THERE are shared human problems for individuals no matter where they live. The problem of securing adequate health care services, for example, is shared by urbanite, the suburbanite, and the rural American—albeit in varying degrees. But what, one might ask, causes a particular problem to become primarily identified with *urban* areas? What makes problems of urban education distinctive from general education? Similarly, when do urban mental health problems become sufficiently unique to warrant separate consideration? When are the urban problems of New York City and St. Louis, Missouri, reduced to a common denominator? When does an individual or family fall below the poverty line? Are there absolute criteria, or is being poor relative to the over-all economic condition of the country, state, or municipality? Does low income alone provide an adequate barometer for the degree of economic deprivation suffered by the poverty-stricken?

Consideration of these questions occupies substantial space in the social science literature on poverty, since one must agree on the definition of a concept before it can be discussed intelligently. And yet there is something very pathetic about our attempts to convert human misery and suffering to percentages and ratios. It is widely agreed that our affluent American society possesses the economic resources to alleviate completely the burden of poverty which has befallen between sixteen to thirty-six per cent of its population (depending on the definition employed). Certainly, the best strategy for the reallocation of vital resources does not enjoy such widespread agreement. But this is another matter. *First,* there must be a firm commitment to the goal; only then can the question of strategy become more than an academic exercise.

The literature on the poor has undergone considerable proliferation since President John Kennedy declared and President Lyndon Johnson attempted to implement an unconditional war on poverty in the early 1960s. Invidious comparisons between the victims of today's poverty and the poverty-stricken of the late nineteenth and early twentieth centuries and the depression years have been plethoric. A sort of naïve romanticism has been reconstructed regarding the poverty of the earlier days, portraying the former urban inhabitants as vigorous, spirited souls, who forthrightly struggled to overcome the encumbrances of economic impoverishment. At the same time, today's urban poor are frequently stereotyped as lazy, unmotivated, largely rural in-migrants, whose own lack of ingenuity and self-respect are basically responsible for their economic plight. Moreover, child-rearing practices and parental (largely maternal) attitudes are said to perpetuate a "culture of poverty" that is transmitted to future generations, further militating against upward social and economic mobility.

The concept of a "culture of poverty" is quite a convenient invention, for it allows one to explain the problem by merely describing it. It is, in effect, equivalent to the pronouncement that a child's failure to learn in the classroom is due to the fact that he is stupid, or that he has a learning disability. The question as to the nature of his "learning handicap" remains unanswered.

The concept of a "culture of poverty" has additional drawbacks with respect to our attempts to understand chronic intergenerational economic impoverishment. Foremost, it diverts our attention from inequities in our social and economic policies, whose correction could be instrumental in admitting the economic "underclass" into the mainstream of American life. Moreover, it provides the more privileged classes a convenient catch phrase with which further to stigmatize the poor for their inability to "make it" in the system. Finally, the notion of intergenerational transmission of a "culture" (or more precisely social class behaviors) implicitly or explicitly suggests the operation of immutable hereditary factors, reminiscent of the moral degeneration theory of old. Such postures have invariably led to "do nothing" policies with respect to the elimination of poverty and slum conditions at best, and to callous and inhumane eugenics programs at worst. (One has only to read of the activities of the prominent psychologist H. H. Goddard, who, around the turn of the century, administered intelligence tests to newly arrived immigrants at Ellis Island. This was done in order to ascertain whether the admission of these poor immigrants would likely dilute the intellectual vitality of the Anglo-American stock. Without taking language problems into account, Goddard concluded that forty per cent of the immigrants were feeble-minded.) Thus, in sum, the concept of a "culture of poverty" has little scientific heuristic value; and due to its global and diffuse nature, it has less practical utility.

Charles Valentine graphically reinforces this point in his excellent publication, *Culture and Poverty*. Valentine contends that the expositors of the culture of poverty seem to suggest that the solutions "to the basic bioeconomic problem of survival"

. . . are part of the lower-class "design for living" in the sense that they are supported by subcultural values and attitudes and perpetuated by personality traits that result from lower-class socialization patterns. The alternative interpretation is that lack of work, lack of income, and the rest pose conditions to which the poor must adapt through whatever sociocultural resources they control. That is, these conditions are phenomena of the environment in which the lower-class lives, determined not so much by behaviors and values of the poor as by the structure of the total social system.

By adopting this position, Valentine suggests that we may then "view behaviors and values peculiar to the poor as responses to the experience of their special socioeconomic environment and as adaptations to this environment."

## A BEHAVIORAL FORMULATION

When a collection of individuals becomes identified as constituting a social problem, their unique individual modes of behavior are responded to in a compartmentalized fashion. Consequently, their intra-group similarities tend to be overemphasized, while their individual differences are minimized. Correspondingly, great effort is made in an attempt to demonstrate the many discrepancies between their behaviors, values, and attitudes, and the characteristics of non-problem groups. Such has indeed been the case with psychological, sociological, and anthropological studies of the economically disadvantaged. Ostensibly, the rationale for the investigations is to provide a basis for the development of social interventional programs designed to remedy the problems of the underprivileged. In actuality, the disadvantaged group is indicted for causing the problem. A cogent analysis of this process has been captured by William Ryan in his insightful book *Blaming the Victim*. Ryan points out that:

All of this (victim blaming) happens so smoothly that it seems downright rational. First, identify a social problem. Second, study those affected by the problem and discover in what ways they are different from the rest of us as a consequence of deprivation and injustice. Third, define the differences as the cause of the social problem itself. Finally, of course, assign a government bureaucrat to invent a humanitarian action program to correct the differences.

As we can plainly see, the circular reasoning underlying this problem-solving approach hardly enables one to progress toward a better understanding of the problem condition and its behavioral consequences. Guided by this rationale, it is of little wonder that so many widespread stereotypes about the poor have been perpetuated; also, it is understandable why so little *useful* behavioral research has been conducted with this group.

It is indeed shameful that social science researchers have approached the psychological difficulties of the poor (especially the black poor) with such a dearth of insight and plain common sense. How easy it is to forget that the major characteristic of poverty is a lack of money and the despair of not knowing how to get any. And yet, behavioral research remains preoccupied with the intra-psychic problems of the poor—those problems, for example, emanating from defective child-rearing practices—in lieu of those resulting from the constant psychological stress which accompanies their state of economic impoverishment. Perhaps, in this sense, behavioral scientists, following the reasoning of conventional wisdom, have failed to appreciate the scientific necessity of differentiating between *cause* and *history*. Kurt Lewin, in his *Principles of Topological Psychology*, makes the importance of this distinction abundantly clear. In Lewin's words:

I am sitting in the rain under a tree whose leaves keep me from getting wet. I ask: "Why don't I get wet?" It is possible to answer this question by finding out the direction and velocity of the falling drops, the position of the leaves, my own position, etc. In short one can represent the present situation and, by applying the laws of mechanics or other relevant laws, derive what events must occur in such a situation. But the answer to this question could also be as follows: It is thanks to your grandfather who planted this tree that you do not get wet. To be sure the soil is not very good right here, but your grandfather took special care of the tree during its first years. Yet if the plan for the new state road had gone through last year the tree would already have been cut down and you couldn't sit here without getting wet.

While Lewin acknowledged that history is very important in its contribution to the characteristics of a given individual in a given situation, his point was that the mere occurrence of an event in the past did not mean that it automatically had implication for the contemporary situation.

More recently another psychologist, Julian Rotter, has developed a social-learning theory which is consonant with Lewin's philosophy of science and psychological theory construction. Several characteristics of Rotter's theory render it particularly appropriate for analyzing the psychological problems of the poor. First, the theory is intrinsically parsimonious, notably devoid of vaguely defined hypothetical constructs. Second, it is designed to predict overt human behavior in social situations. Third, it recognizes the importance of *social learning* in the acquisition of behavior. Finally (and perhaps most appealing), it is based on the proposition that all behavior, *irrespective* of its consequences, attempts to be adaptive. Anecdotally, a psychologist friend of mine had a standard answer whenever he was asked the reason for choosing an alternative which did not particularly work out. "Well," he would reply, "it sort of seemed like the thing to do at the time." My psychologist friend, in his characteristically homey fashion, was basically summarizing the central theme of Rotter's social-learning theory.

### SOCIAL-LEARNING THEORY AND THE PSYCHOLOGICAL IMPACT OF URBAN POVERTY

The opening lyric of an old blues song advises:

> *Them that's got shall get*
> *Them that's not shall lose*
> *So the Bible said*
> *And it still is news.*

Within the framework of social-learning theory, it is possible to understand why throughout history, "them that's not got" typically lose. Having previously rejected the value of the "culture of poverty" explanation as a useful scientific construct, we must turn to the contemporary events in the lives of the urban poor to understand their dilemma.

The concept of *expectancy* is one of the most important constructs in Rotter's social-learning theory. In addition, it perhaps has the most relevance for understanding the psychological problems of the urban poor. Expectancy is the perceived likelihood that a given behavior will lead to a reinforcement (positive outcome) of a given value in a particular situation. In everyday parlance, the probability that a person will behave in a given manner depends to a large extent on how much conviction he has that the behavior under consideration will lead to a pay-off. A poor slum dweller with a fourth-grade education is unlikely to apply for a variety of high-paying jobs *not* because he is lazy, or that he does not value the high income or prestige. On the contrary, he may be burning with desire for the reinforcements associated with the higher level occupations, but he has ascertained that there is *no way* that he will be granted one of those jobs. Therefore, he stops filling out applications. As children we used to have a jingle with which to taunt our playmates, much as the affluence of our society taunts the poor: "Your eyes may shine and your teeth may grit, but none of *my* goodies will you get." (Incidentally, they did the same to us when they were in the advantaged position.)

Another boyhood memory may also be relevant here. My older sister, in an effort to earn a little money to help defray forthcoming college expenses, had begun baby-sitting for a rather affluent family (the owners of a major furniture store in my home town). On several occasions, I had the opportunity to accompany my parents as they drove my sister from our modest neighborhood to the exclusive section where her employers resided. Indeed, how my eyes did shine—nose pressed against the car window —as I gazed upon the expensive houses, beautifully manicured lawns, and residents, dressed in Bermuda shorts and colorful sport shirts. The mix of emotion I experienced on those occasions is hard to describe. But certainly, prominent among them were feelings of sheer awe and amazement at the splendor of such affluence. Another element, I must admit, was a bit of depression—not resentment— which resulted from the "realization" that I (a plain black boy) would never enjoy those luxuries. I simply did not expect it.

During this general period of my life, I had another experience which also pertains here—an experience that left an indelible impression on my young mind. My father was the head scoutmaster of our local Boy Scout troop. Every Christmas, all of the boys in the troop would bring various items of food (mostly canned food) to our December meetings, the adult leaders would contribute a few major items (perhaps a roast or ham), and suddenly we would have our annual Christmas charity "basket." A civic organization would distribute a list of the most needy families, and by some mechanism, our leaders would select one of these. On Christmas Eve, it was the duty of my father, as scoutmaster, to deliver the package, and I was always taken along.

I remember one of these occasions quite vividly. The family selected lived in the heart of the city's worst black slum, in an overcrowded second-floor apartment. A young child afflicted with polio (at that time called infantile paralysis) lay in a crib which was much too small for his twisted body. The father, mother, and elderly grandmother who received our package were all taken by surprise. The women cried from gratitude, while the father tried to find enough space to offer us a place to sit. Everyone was extremely grateful for the food, which certainly could not last for more than two or three weeks. I wondered what they would do when it was gone, and in general, how they existed from day to day. They seemed to expect so little from life, and this is exactly what they received. Expectancy for reinforcement obviously exerts a powerful influence over behavior at every socio-economic level. Thus, it is readily understandable that Rotter selected this as his most fundamental construct.

The first important thing to remember about expectancies is that they are *learned*. After numerous attempts to achieve a goal have met with consistent failure, one begins to get the message that the probability of the behavior in question leading to satisfaction is not particularly high. Let me stress that what has changed in this hypothetical situation is *not* the person's "level of aspiration" or "achievement"; neither has the value of the reinforcement been lowered. The person has merely reduced the subjective probability of his expectancy for success in the particular circumstance. This is a cognitive process, which unfortunately is often confused with lack of motivation.

The second important thing to know about expectancies is that they can be increased and maintained via reinforcement. In this connection, the statement that "nothing succeeds like success" becomes more than a cliché. However, the type of reward system called for here is not the non-contingent reinforcement of behaviors which relieve economic stress on an unpredictable basis, such as the present degrading welfare system. Reinforcement of this nature fails to strengthen the poverty-stricken individual's perception that the "locus of control" for achieving satisfaction resides (to some degree) within his own person, i.e., that he can "make it happen." Income distribution policies must be organized in such a manner that the poor person is able to discern the functional relationship between his effort and its consequences.

The essence of this distinction undergirds a major proposal for reducing poverty offered by Charles Valentine in *Culture and Poverty*. Valentine states:

The key to this proposal is to place substantial new economic, social, and political resources under the control of the poor so that they will have the power to act in such a way as to reduce their inequality significantly. Reducing inequality does not mean what has come to be called "equal opportunity." It means equitability of results in the sense of achievement, fulfillment, and enjoyment of the rewards and satisfactions already generally available to citizens outside disadvantaged groups.

Expectancies may be rather specific or they may be generalized. That is, a person may have a low expectancy for success in one domain, or in a wide range of situations. In the latter case, the person is considered to have limited "freedom of movement," i.e., he is able to perceive few alternative avenues by which he expects to achieve reinforcement. As Rotter uses the term, freedom of movement bears similarity to certain clinical concepts, such as anxiety and psychological stress. Hans Selyve, in *The Stress of Life,* offers a casual definition of stress which is very appropriate for the present discussion. Selyve states that: "Stress is essentially the rate of wear and tear caused by life."

Owing to the overabundance of wear and tear on the urban poor, their lives are relentlessly stressful. Some attempt to cope with these pressures through the use of drugs and alcohol. Others escape by mentally detaching themselves from their grim worlds of reality. They, too, had aspirations, but they found life unaccommodating; so in order to elude failure, they opted to ignore success.

Fortunately, the proportion of the chronic poor (old and young, black and white, men and women) who have completely given up is relatively few, when compared with the so-called stable poor. Many of the former can be found on the street corners of Harlem or the Bowery in the bitter cold of winter or the stifling heat of summer. Michael Harrington, in *The Other America,* describes his experiences while working with alcoholics in the Bowery, which led to his vow never again to refer to anyone as a bum. In Harrington's words:

During 1951 and 1952, I lived on Chrystie Street, one block from the Bowery in New York. I was a member of the Catholic Worker group that had a house there. Beds were given out on a "first-come, first-served" basis; we had a bread line in the early morning that provided coffee and rich brown bread, and a soup line at noon; and hand-me-down clothes that readers of the newspaper sent in were distributed. Those of us who came to live at the Worker house accepted a philosophy of voluntary poverty. We had no money and received no pay. We shared the living conditions of the people whom we were helping: alcoholics and the mentally ill. We did not participate in the living hell of that area, for we were not tortured by alcoholism and we had chosen our lot. But we were close, very close, to that world. We could see its horror every day.

Harrington goes on to describe how the smell of urine hung over the living quarters of the men; and how they sometimes passed out drunk in the snow during winter. He graphically recalls the filthy, putrid, ill-fitting clothing of the men; and he describes the looks on their pathetic faces, often "caked with blood after a particularly terrible drunk." These were frightened, defeated men, for whom life, as they knew it, had simply been unyielding. Occasionally, in moments of sobriety, they wondered aloud why anyone of sound mind would want to care for them.

It is regrettable that when one speaks of the *urban* poor, the image conveyed is usually that of unstable or pathological individuals, such as the alcoholics and other societal deviates. Too often are the stable poor (the "copers") overlooked. In this category, we find numerous black and white elderly individuals, who simply try to "make do" on their inadequate fixed incomes, which confine them to the oldest sections of the inner city. These "senior citizens" have long led lives characterized by high standards of personal, familial, and societal responsibility. Ironically, a great many people are thus "recruited to poverty" after relatively long lives of economic productivity.

According to the 1958 census, slightly less than sixty per cent of the elderly—persons over sixty-five—had an income of under $1,000 a year. Over one half of these people were dependent on some sort of federal assistance, which in 1959 averaged about $70 a month. Of these individuals, approximately twenty-five per cent had no savings at all and over fifty per cent had assets of less than $1,000. Thus, it is not surprising that a 1960 Senate report indicated that ". . . at least one-half of the aged— approximately eight million people—cannot afford decent housing, proper nutrition, adequate medical care, or recreation." Worst of all, there is little reason to assume that this state of affairs has undergone substantial improvement over the past decade.

Also, a considerable number of black families are of the stable poor. These are the families whose poverty is a direct result of institutional racism and job discrimination: The family in which the father and mother worry every day of the year about making ends meet, but who always seem to "figure out a way" to work Mary's birthday present into the budget; the family who never fails to send an occasional "care package" to their son attending college on a partial athletic scholarship; or the family in which the father seeks a solution to his financial dilemma by applying for an additional night job. It is for these struggling black people that Langston Hughes wrote his "Little Lyric (Of Great Importance)":[1]

> *I wish the rent*
> *was heaven sent.*

The rent, however, never seems to arrive from heaven. So the stable poor continue to scrape and save, cutting corners which have already been cut, in order to meet this obligation. The landlord, as the piper, must be paid.

[1] As Webster Smalley wrote about Hughes, "He prefers to write about those of his race who live constantly on the edge of financial disaster, who are used to living precariously, occasionally falling over the edge and crawling back up, and who have no time to be pretentious." Webster Smalley, "Introduction," *Five Plays by Langston Hughes* (Bloomington: University of Indiana Press, 1963), p. vii.

One might wonder why this group of urban poor persists in this struggle, since they receive so little return on their investment. But for complex reasons, which psychologists should better understand, their survival instincts and expectancy for a better life have been remarkably resistant to extermination.

The survival instincts of the urban poor are all the more remarkable in view of the fact that they are exploited and discriminated against in virtually every aspect of daily living. David Caplovitz hits the nail squarely on the head in the title of his book *The Poor Pay More*. First, the working poor contribute a greater proportion of their income to public taxes, as difficult as *this* is to believe. (And the situation is growing more traumatic in view of the fact that city revenues are becoming increasingly dependent on property tax, extracted from those with insufficient resources to flee to the suburbs.)

The poor also pay a greater proportion of their disposable income for housing—often because of, rather than in spite of, urban renewal (sometimes referred to as "black removal") programs. As Herbert Gans points out:

Real estate economists argue that families should pay about 20 percent of their income for housing, but what is manageable for middle-income people is a burden to those with low incomes who pay a higher share of their earnings for food and other necessities. Yet even so, low-income Negroes generally have to devote about 30 percent of their income to housing, and a Chicago study cited by Hartmen reports that among nonwhite families earning less than $3,000 a year, median rent rose from 35 percent of income before relocation to 46 percent afterward.

Think of it. The average family paid about one half of their total income on housing! As for the myth of widespread sub-standard rents paid by the urban poor, Gans asserts that "these are factual in only a small proportion of cases, and then mostly among whites."

As if the above inequities were not enough, the urban poor comprise the single most exploited consumer group in the nation. The basic problem is that the low-income consumers are unable to make major purchases on a cash basis either from large department stores or less expensive discount houses. Moreover, because they are considered poor credit risks by the larger chain department stores, they are forced to turn to exploitative "easy credit" neighborhood stores, or to marginally ethical, door-to-door peddlers. (Hustlers is perhaps the more accurate term.) These tendencies among the urban poor simply cannot be taken as examples of unsophisticated consumer practices. Due to the fact that the credit needs of the poor are not currently being met by legitimate enterprises, families with limited resources must turn to establishments which employ questionable ethical practices. Thus, as Caplovitz so aptly summarized the circumstance, "society now virtually offers the poor risks with twin options: of foregoing major purchases or of being exploited."

Caplovitz's *The Poor Pay More* presents many graphic illustrations of the high-pressure tactics of salesmen, the frequent practice of merchandise substitution, the exorbitant prices, and the incredible interest rates that are "commonplace" on the low-income market. With great sensitivity, he describes how low-income consumers are sold reconditioned appliances as new; how door-to-door peddlers sell installment contracts to high-risk finance companies with astronomical interest rates; how economically marginal families have major appliances repossessed because of a missed payment, only to discover later that they are still responsible for a sizable debt from accumulated interest; and on and on. But what is most saddening is that the majority of the low-income consumers do nothing to rectify the unethical and/or illegal practices, simply because they know of no "meaningful courses of action . . . to take in the face of unresponsive and frequently powerless community agencies."

Pursuing our application of Rotter's social-learning theory to the problem of urban poverty and its behavioral impact, we should next turn our attention to the concept of *reinforcement value*. By reinforcement value, we are referring to the average "preference value of one set of reinforcements over another set of reinforcements, when expectancy is held constant." In terms of poverty, we ask how much do the urban poor desire the "worldly and psychic goods" provided [to some] by our American system, as compared with the supposed uncomplicated life of the complacent impoverished. This, of course, may determine how hard they are willing to work to achieve the former. Reinforcement value, thus, is an incentive construct.

One of the problems often associated with the economically impoverished is that many of them have *learned* to be satisfied with reinforcements of relatively low value. To a poor person who has only achieved the bare essentials for existence, a quite modest increase in the quality of his life may be highly valued. To the more well-to-do individual, the subsistence-level attainments of his less fortunate counterpart may possess little reinforcement value.

Let me point out here that what I am referring to is not diminished motivation, nor am I speaking of low expectancy for success. What I am saying is that the poor, because of their barren reinforcement histories, have tended to establish deflated "minimal goal levels." The minimal goal level, as Rotter has defined it, is ". . . the lowest level in a continuum of potential reinforcements for some life situation or situations which will be perceived as a satisfaction." Reinforcement value and minimal goal levels are both experientially determined, and thus are heuristically more valuable than global explanations such as "lack of motivation."

The last of the social-learning theory concepts which we will consider is that of the *psychological situation*. The importance of this construct is aptly summarized by Rotter:

It is presumed that the manner in which a person perceives a given situation will determine for him which behaviors are likely to have reasonable probability or the highest probabilities of leading to satisfaction . . . should his perception of the situation change, the expectancy that given behaviors will lead to satisfaction will change markedly. In some instances the value of a given reinforcement will change if the situation is recategorized.

Thus, while a reclassification of the psychological situation does not greatly affect the value of a reinforcement as such, it does alter the specific expectancies that certain behaviors will lead to certain reinforcements. For example, the passage of a succession of civil rights and anti-discrimination employment acts during the fifties and sixties led to a reclassification of the personal psychological situation for a great many people. More simply put, opportunities which were heretofore off limits for many, suddenly became realistic possibilities. The black postal employee who for years "knew" that he would never rise above the level of a clerk or letter carrier could now aspire to a supervisory position by virtue of newly instituted anti-discrimination civil service examinations. Now, overnight, black men (and more recently, women) eagerly submitted applications for the higher paying and more prestigious positions. The reinforcement value associated with the supervisory positions had not changed one iota. The psychological situation had simply been reclassified, which resulted in a concomitant change in the expectancy that the behavior of filing an application could lead to a satisfactory result.

The phenomenon which has been unfortunately termed "the revolution of rising expectations" (suggesting that the more poor black people get, the greedier they become) may be more accurately interpreted as a reclassification of the psychological situation. It indeed seems ludicrous to assume that the underprivileged black classes never really wanted a slice of the "good life" simply because they had never tasted it. Poor black people have been the greatest pretenders in the world, as Langston Hughes portrayed in much of his poetry.

POVERTY AND THE RACIAL OVERLAY

In the words of George Bernard Shaw, "The greatest of evils and the worst of crimes is poverty." One might add that being both poor and black is to compound the hideous felony. While whites constitute the majority of the urban poor in absolute numbers, the proportion of blacks who fall below the poverty line is incredible, with many estimates as high as fifty per cent. The other low-income related statistics on black people are equally mind-boggling. But these statistics, as alarming as they are, do not deliver the impact and sense of despair as well as do the words of Michael Harrington. Harrington states:

If all the discriminatory laws in the United States were immediately repealed, race would still remain as one of the most pressing moral and political problems in the nation. Negroes and other minorities are not simply the victims of a series of iniquitous statutes. The American economy, the American society, the American unconscious are all racist. If all the laws were framed to provide equal opportunity, a majority of the Negroes would not be able to take full advantage of the change. There would still be a vast, silent, and automatic system directed against men and women of color.

Yet, all the while black people are being blamed for the urban crisis. They are blamed for being the perpetrators of crime, without adequate recognition that they are also by far the greatest victims of crime. More than anyone, blacks need adequate police protection and safety in the streets. In a recent magazine article, a confessed mugger indicated that the ideal target for a "hit" was an elderly black woman on her ghetto street or in the hallways of her ghetto apartment building, during daylight hours.

But why all this mugging and burglary in the inner city? In a word, narcotics—mainly heroin. (Narcotics have always existed in the ghetto. However, they were never really considered a problem until they spread to the suburbs.) It has been estimated that an unemployed heroin addict, with a moderately large habit, would have to steal approximately seven hundred dollars' worth of merchandise daily in order to maintain that habit. (This is due to the greatly diminished resale value of the goods.) This is why most addicts, who are forced to steal or mug, prefer cold hard cash—although most will take what they can get.

And who profits from the misery of both the drug addict and his prey? Quite plainly, *white* organized crime, which is allowed to exist because of lax multi-level governmental policies. Yet, very few campaigns are based on the promise to stamp out *organized* crime, even though the President's Crime Commission reported that it "takes in about twice as much money . . . as the total income from all other kinds of criminal activities combined." On the contrary, the typical politician passionately declares his intention to eliminate "crime in the streets" (which in the minds of the masses can mean anything from assault and murder to an orderly but vociferous demonstration by black and Puerto Rican welfare mothers). The strategy, obviously, is designed to appeal to the anti-minority sentiments of the white electorate. Ironically, it would be the ghetto residents who would receive proportionately greater peace of mind if street crimes were in fact reduced.

And then there is the question of rape. Contrary to the impression one would get from the news media, black women are far more often victims of rape than their white counterparts. A recent study of *reported* rapes conducted in Philadelphia revealed that the largest per cent (about three fourths) of the rape victims were black women. Of the white victims, the great majority of them were raped by white men. There were very few interracial rapes reported, and they were equally distributed between black men who raped white women and white men who raped black women. This is a small concession, but it just might enable a few to breathe a bit easier.

Next, let us turn our attention to the proposition of the so-called social pathology of the black community. William Ryan makes an excellent observation when he asserts that social pathology and human distress "are the same thing defined from different standpoints." The unemployment rate in Harlem, for example, is two to three times higher than that for New York City as a whole. But this is not due to apathy, or lack of motivation, as some have suggested. A moderately aware black social scientist would quickly discard this notion simply by listening quietly as he gets a haircut on 125th Street near Amsterdam Avenue.

As regards living conditions in Harlem, it is instructive to note that the 1959 Civil Rights Commission calculated that "if the population density in some of Harlem's worst blocks obtained in the rest of New York City, the entire population of the United States could fit into three of New York's boroughs." It is this tremendous human density problem, along with the alleged poor sanitation habits of recent black rural in-migrants, which has led some to accuse the blacks of increasing the need for municipal services, thereby creating the urban fiscal crisis. (To use William Ryan's metaphor, this is a case of blaming the victim squared!) However, as Frances Fox Piven has cogently argued, "the urban crisis is not a crisis of rising needs, but a crisis of rising demands." Not the rising demands of blacks, mind you, but the rising salary and other job-benefit demands of "organized provider groups," such as teachers, sanitation workers, health care professionals, policemen, and others. Thus, as Professor Piven notes, "the average pay raises for city employees in New York averaged 12 percent each year in 1967, '68 and '69." And the state and local governments, angered by this escalation, responded by threatening to cut back welfare benefits!

Finally, let us consider what progress the black worker has made in the meantime. The evidence is clear that the income gap between blacks and whites has been widening rather than decreasing. One sociologist, using 1960 census data and employing sophisticated quantitative formulas, estimated that after correcting for education, family background, occupation, and region of residence, the average *cost* of being black is roughly $1,000 per year in salary. In 1960, 20 per cent of whites and 9 per cent of blacks held high-skill industrial jobs; conversely, 48 per cent of black males and 25.3 per cent of white males were semi-skilled workers and laborers. As regards black women, who suffer double discrimination, over one third in the labor force were employed as domestics. Add to this the fact that health problems are far more prevalent among blacks in every index from infant mortality to life expectancy and one can readily appreciate the passion of James Baldwin's now classic statement that "To be a Negro in this country and to be relatively conscious is to be in rage almost all of the time."

Summing up the general state of affairs, we find that because of long-standing institutional racism, a staggering proportion of blacks (as compared with whites) are poorer, have less education, have more health problems, receive less adequate health care and pay a greater proportion of their income for it, have less adequate housing and pay substantially more than it's worth, have a higher crime rate *but* are also more victimized by crime, have shorter life expectancies, and on and on we could go.

All this constitutes a very serious problem. But the solution will not be achieved by ritualistic head-shaking, historical explanations of the problem, or massive psychotherapy to blacks. The problem will only be eradicated when the wider society finally decides to attack the *contemporary* socio-environmental conditions which perpetuate this grievous dilemma.

PROSPECTS FOR CHANGE

One of the major contentions of the present chapter is
that traditional ritualistic approaches to the problem of
poverty—such as victim-blaming—have militated against
substantial progress in this area. Obviously, more "action-
oriented" programs are needed if the problem is to be
meaningfully attacked. Unfortunately, as in most cases,
there are no simple and sovereign solutions to the poverty
dilemma. However, Charles Valentine has suggested three
basic conceptual models of poverty, each of which leads
to different courses of action.

*Model 1:* Self-perpetuating Sub-society with a Defective,
Unhealthy Sub-culture (The Sub-cultural Deviance
Model).

The model assumes that the lower classes possess a distinct sub-culture, which is characterized by a distorted, disorganized, pathological or incomplete version of the mainstream middle-class culture. One of the major expositors
of this model is Daniel Patrick Moynihan, a principal archi-
tect of President Lyndon Johnson's "War on Poverty"
legislation of 1964. Moynihan's views on race and poverty
have been widely publicized; i.e., that the pathological
conditions of the black poor are capable of perpetuating
themselves without any assistance from the white world
whatsoever. Thus, this model leads to the position that the
poverty sub-culture must be eliminated, and the poor assimilated into the middle-class or working-class cultures.
This is to be brought about by "directed culture change
through social work, psychiatry, and education." Essentially, the poor are to be operated *upon*. The participation
of the poor themselves is not deemed essential.[2]

*Model 2:* Externally Suppressed Sub-society with an

[2] The provision for the "maximum feasible participation" of the
poor in the Economic Opportunity Act was included at the insistence
of Robert F. Kennedy, who was Attorney General at that time.

Imposed, Exploited Sub-culture (The Sub-cultural Colonization Model).

This model is very popular among the radical left, and found its initial contemporary expression in Stokely Carmichael and Charles V. Hamilton's *Black Power: The Politics of Liberation in America*. This model holds that the structure of the whole society must be radically altered, accompanied by a total redistribution of resources, in order for poverty to be eliminated. Further, "these changes can come about only through a revolutionary accession to power by representatives of the poor."

*Model 3:* Heterogeneous Sub-society with Variable, Adaptive Sub-cultures (The Sub-culture Difference Model).

This model, which Valentine prefers, attempts to take into account both the strengths and weaknesses of the poor. It attempts to incorporate the best features of Models 1 and 2. In order for poverty to be eliminated, there must be (a) increases in the resources actually available to the poor; (b) alterations of the total social structure with additional power to the poor; and (c) changes in some sub-cultural patterns.

While Model 3 has great surface appeal, it leaves numerous questions on vital issues unapproached. For example, how does one go about redistributing resources? By what mechanisms are the poor to be given more power? Precisely, which low-income sub-cultural patterns are to be altered—and who is to make this decision? But there is a far more urgent question which each of us must seriously consider: What *does* happen to a dream deferred?


FOR FURTHER READING

Caplovitz, David. *The Poor Pay More*. New York: The Free Press, 1967.

Donovan, James C. *The Politics of Poverty*. New York: Western Publishing, 1967.

Harrington, Michael. *The Other America: Poverty in the United States.* Baltimore: Penguin Books, Inc., 1971.

Rotter, J. B. *Social Learning and Clinical Psychology.* Englewood Cliffs, New Jersey: Prentice-Hall, 1954.

——, J. Chance, and E. J. Phares. *Applications of a Social Learning Theory of Personality.* New York: Holt, Rinehart & Winston, 1971.

Ryan, William. *Blaming the Victim.* New York: Pantheon Books, 1971.

Valentine, C. A. *Culture and Poverty: Critique and Counter-Proposals.* Chicago: University of Chicago Press, 1968.

# CHAPTER 5

# THE WHITE PROBLEM OF THE CITIES

## Charles E. Wilson

Certainly the major demographic factor in recent urban history has been the influx of millions of blacks from southern rural areas to northern cities. Poor, unskilled, and uneducated, many of them have found that the dreams they had of living in decent homes, sending their children to good schools, and of being treated without prejudice have turned to dross. Blacks have been packed into slums, seen social and educational services deteriorate, been locked out of good jobs, and have found anti-black prejudice, if less open, just as pervasive as it is in the South. In turn, northern whites have blamed blacks for the deterioration of the inner city, the rising crime rate, higher taxes to pay for welfare—in fact, blacks have been accused of causing nearly all of our current urban problems.

In an angry accusation of his own, Charles Wilson claims that it is not blacks who have caused these problems, but whites, whose prejudices have forced minority groups to live a life of crushed dreams and oppression. While white men proclaim a doctrine of equality and fairness, they hypocritically treat blacks unfairly, and when blacks, unable to cast off this burden, fail to achieve unrealistic goals, whites blame it on the nature of the blacks (see preceding chapter). Unless white men face up to their own problem, he warns, the ills now besetting the cities will soon overcome the entire society.

Charles E. Wilson has long worked to improve the fortunes of the black community, and was the administrator of the I.S.-201 project in New York. A contributor to many radical and black journals, he is now a special assistant to the president of the Bank Street College of Education.

> "... the attempt to relate prejudice to the specific nature of its object is a cunning projection of the prejudice of the dominant group; cunning because it passes as scientific curiosity. As long as the majority can pretend that the source of prejudice inheres in the nature of the victim, social action can be indefinitely postponed, there is always still another investigation which must be made."
>
> —CAREY MCWILLIAMS, *Brothers Under the Skin*

THE mounting problems of America's large cities are steadily driving the already distracted members of the American community to the verge of insanity.

Urbanologists, writers, and scholars have all taken their turns at describing and diagnosing the ills besetting the cities, especially in terms of the issues related to race. For some observers, the coming of the "black hordes" to the fair northern and western cities has been taken as a sure sign of the Armageddon, while for others the striking increase in the black population of the cities has been taken as a sign that America has lost her special place by the side of the Deity.

Many "experts" have "objectively" proposed that the source of the current urban troubles lies within the black folks and the poor folks themselves—within their unwillingness or inability to work their way up from the bottom; within their self-destructive life styles; within their underdeveloped family structure; within their limited communal framework; within their strong criminal propensities; within their attachment to the glamorous aspects of the poverty cycle; or within their defective gene pools. In order to meet these deficiencies, skeletal programs have been initiated on the federal, state, and local levels—started, stuck in, and then phased out. The Model Cities program is a shining example of this gambit. That these programs have had such a small impact does not seem to phase the experts, for they either propose that the poor should be left alone altogether (as in Banfield's *The Un-Heavenly City*) or that larger and still larger programs of uncertain value should be mounted.

Why must the black and the poor be blamed for this crisis of urban areas? In a white, middle-class dominated society, the dispossessed are hardly the movers or the shakers; to a great degree these groups are hardly part of the society's traditional political processes at all. To make matters worse, these groups are supposed *to agree* with the white definitions and assessment of the basis of the urban problems.

Blacks are expected to have but one "civilized" response. They are expected to marshal facts as if the truth alone will reduce oppression and exploitation, which has become institutionalized. And, of course, they are expected to remain objective in spite of Franz Fanon's famous admonition that every native soon learns that the objectivity of the majority will always be used against him. But the fool's errand of objectivity and the entire repertoire of sophisticated attempts to reduce the anger of the blacks are just some ways that rage of the oppressed is channeled through cultural processes.

For in America, topics of racial and class matter are seldom called by their right names. Many items are deliberately mislabeled and misplaced in order to protect certain economic and social interests and ensure the acceptance of certain myths. In addition, Americans do not want to be characterized or grouped, nor do they wish to be held individually responsible for their part in collective actions which have plainly negative consequences. With these notions in mind, the sources of the urban difficulty may indeed not lie within black folks. The sources may instead lie within the basic structure of the American system—its outlook, its practices, its mindless, preconscious conceptions, and its very patterns of intergroup relations. The trouble may lie in:

— the American psychology, with its basic antipathy toward the cities as places in which people reside

— the unrelenting character of racism in the American system

— the change in the character and organization of the employment picture so that blacks and newcomers to the cities cannot work their way up the antiquated institutional fabric of the society

Yes, the trouble lies within the very bone and marrow of this most opulent of all European plunderings. The trouble lies within white America. For the crisis of the cities is a crisis of European-Americans, and it is up to them to grasp the core issues, to seek the help of others in this task, and, more importantly, to set about saving themselves from their own worst impulses.

### CITIES AND THE AMERICAN PSYCHE

While three out of four Americans now reside in cities, American history offers evidence that, as a people, Americans have not liked cities. In fact, they have suspected cities as the very "bastions of corruption."

European cities from the fourteenth through the seventeenth centuries offered many examples of the corruption and degradation of the city life, and the experiences of workers during early European industrialization did little to reduce this impression. The industrial centers of the European continent and British Isles were the prototypes of American industrial slums. Anxiety about the nature of cities influenced early colonists such as William Penn to plan Philadelphia as a "holy city" with sufficient light and space between dwellings to avoid the population density of Europe. Urbophobia led Thomas Jefferson to perceive America's greatest strength as her agricultural population and her vast vacant land. It was simply an article of faith to the Founding Fathers that the city was just no place for a respectable American.

This same doubt about cities was transmitted to visitors and critics of this "Great Experiment" in government in the New World. Alexis de Tocqueville, for example, wrote: "I look upon American cities, and especially on the nature of their population, as a real danger which threatens the future security of the New World." Rapid industrialization, wars, periodic investigations of political corruption, epidemics within the overcrowded large cities, and the exposure of urban despair and poverty in the nineteenth century did little to shift these anti-urban prejudices. In fact, each new occurrence had a tendency to confirm, in the minds of "the people on the farm," that the American city was itself a place of indecency. The eastern cities were continually pictured as cesspools of vice and degradation. Ethnic groups that resided in the cities were tainted by the alleged exposure, subject to castigation and characterization as criminal and undesirable—guilt by residence.

As immigrants flocked to cities and brought new life and vitality to them, commentators predicted all sorts of dire consequences for the American Dream[1] as a result of this migration of cheap labor to of all places, the cities. Even when a writer of that period was optimistic about the eventual outcome of the migration to the city he still had a low opinion of the migrants. Jessup Scott wrote: "A large influx of these laborers, though it may lower the average character of our people, will, it is hoped in a greater degree elevate theirs."

While the pull of the cities could not be denied, the transfer of political hegemony from rural areas to the cities was effectively stymied. Rural political domination of the more populated urban areas was defended on the basis of the tendency of urban areas toward indecency. During New York State's 1890 Constitutional Convention, a rural delegate went so far as to suggest that the rural areas were "wiser, more virtuous, and more moral than the decadent city" and, therefore, the rural residents should

[1] See Chapter 3.

receive a disproportionate weighing in political representation.

From that time until the Supreme Court's one man—one vote ruling, cities have been denied fair representation in state legislatures and, of course, in Congress. The political significance of urban underrepresentation should not be overlooked, for it has meant that social legislation, taxation formulas, labor laws, public welfare mandates, and aid to education have all been shaped by rurally dominated legislatures in whose constituencies the crush of urban life was *not* being felt. The legislators were in fact making the laws governing the very life of the cities from the safety of their rural seats.

It would be naïve to suggest that men thought consciously of the city as the hotbed of evil and they (the representatives of the *real* people) would not help city people. The basis for the reaction was probably more subtle, less direct, but its long-term effect could hardly have been more deleterious to the cities. From 1890 to the Great Depression, urban problems were largely neglected. After World War II, federal housing legislation subsidized low-interest mortgages so that Americans might build and purchase homes in the near green areas about the cities. The availability of homesites, the dream home in the suburbs, changed the American's dream of a castle into an actual possibility. Visions of "one's castle, green grass for the kids, trees, shrubs, and space" were brought within the reach of the white middle-income and working class, and they began to abandon the cities. In New York City alone, the decade of the 1960s saw some 800,000 mainly white, middle-income dwellers flee the city.

The flight to the suburbs and beyond has been made possible by the collaboration of government, business, and industry. The production of millions of housing units in the suburbs was made possible by federal aid and FITA guarantees. But Congress did not see fit to make equivalent money available for the renovation of city neighborhoods.

Already severely tested by the emergence of the autonomy-withdrawal syndrome,[2] a phenomenon of mass urban life today, fearing the continued loss of status in a mass technologically advanced society, the working class (middle-class professional and white-collar workers as well as the middle-income artisans and blue-collar skilled tradesmen) has taken refuge in the suburbs, hoping to escape the misery and madness of city life.

With their flight to the suburbs, the former city dwellers have come to adopt a new hostility toward the cities. Although many of their number still are dependent upon the city for their income, recreation, arts, and pleasures, they profess a disdain for the city, its taxes, its way of life. The hostility to the city of the present is neither without instrumentation from social forces and cultural leaders nor without real pay-offs. The pay-offs emerge in various forms, such as job security and guaranteed pensions for municipal civil service personnel, who work in the cities and live in the suburbs, and in reduced taxes for suburban social welfare services. Pay-offs are available in political forms as well, for the suburbs represent a new electorate seeking state support for a number of projects and these new enclaves are in direct competition with the cities for the not too abundant state fiscal support. The shift of middle-income populations (largely white) to the suburbs has tended to consolidate and enhance the political power of small-town and rural interests in the political system. Neither protest nor urban riots seem able to slow the pay-offs nor affect the political union.

What we are dealing with then is a historic phenomena, the antipathy to cities, reinforced today by grim economic and political necessity. The anti-urbanism of today, however, differs from that of previous eras. In former times,

[2] The syndrome can best be described in terms of stress which pushes people to withdraw to themselves; while a sense of autonomy pulls them to this separateness and autonomy. Pushed and pulled, people build a private world about themselves, a world with a minimum of genuine intimacy, contact, feeling, or concern for others.

an anti-urban bias was based upon the notions of the
Founding Fathers and Europe's industrialization experience. Today's anti-urbanism seems to have roots in a bias
manipulated by those interests who wish to sell the suburbs,
to sell exclusively, to induce and to glorify the moral
passivity that permits willful indifference or even hostility
to programs aimed at eradicating conditions of poverty
in the city. The hostility permits the city to be impoverished
from within and strangled from without, and contributes
to a real paradox: A nation of cities is dominated by
interests opposed to the current city dwellers. Frightened
by the prospect of transferring power to undesirables within
the cities, society proposes not to face its fears but to
retreat to a "safe distance," there to exploit and strangle
the present urban environs and start the process of what
it calls "city building" again, on a smaller scale.

### RACISM—A CHANGE IN FORM BUT A RETENTION OF SUBSTANCE

The crisis of the cities is a consequence of the white
man's racial problem. This problem and its burden of consequences falls smack on the backs of minority folks. Truly,
the white man's burden is the black man's load. It is ironic
that this society, obsessed and haunted by race, finds the
drama of its racism and its resistance to governmental
innovation played out in its very centers of life and culture, the cities. For American society may be, at one and
the same time, the most race conscious and the most
racist.

America's racism is of a special variety that has endured throughout its history. Its racism is in fact: A SIN-
ISTER BOURGEOIS RACISM OF CONTEMPT. *Sinister*
in its false offer of a real chance to achieve full humanity
to the members of its minorities—if they conform; *bourgeois* in that it hypocritically proclaims fair play, human

dignity, and equality as central concerns; and *contemptuous* because it minimizes and devalues the people that it hates. To characterize America's racism in such terms raises the hackles of European-Americans (whites), especially the liberals who demand that "objective scientific data" be provided to support such contentions. As if any ruling majority would ever allow the subservient minority to learn that the basis for their exploitation and privilege was not "deserved."

If one questions the sinister quality of this system, then ask this question: Do non-whites possess a real chance in this society? The recent Department of Commerce reports suggest that Negroes (as they refer to them) made substantial economic and social gains during the decade of the sixties. Yet, despite all the progress, Negroes find themselves behind whites in most economic and social categories, and with few prospects of equality. Thomas Pettigrew, a distinguished Harvard social psychologist, once offered this estimate of the years when parity in different fields of employment might be achieved:

| | |
|---|---|
| skilled jobs | 2005 |
| professional jobs | 2017 |
| sales workers | 2114 |
| business managers and proprietors | 2730 |

This professional estimate mocks those who talk of incremental progress within this system. And, perhaps more mocking, is Murray Kempton's statement: "There are few Negroes who really know what is being done *to* them."

What can be more widespread and more frequently repeated than this society's talk of fair play and human dignity? Then why, one hundred years after the end of slavery, almost twenty years after the Supreme Court decision of 1954, does a pattern of social and legal restraints persist designed to impose an odium of inferiority on the cast-out group? Nationwide patterns of residential segregation have not been significantly weakened despite federal statutes and municipal ordinances to the contrary, and we face continuing conflict over residential segregation.

And then there is Attica, the Soledad Brothers of San Quentin, the system of imprisonment and punishment, the entire morass of law, law enforcement, parole, and probation. Before this monument to callousness, who knows what is "human dignity"? Having been arrested in a community demonstration, this author goes so far as to say that no questionnaire will ever capture the mindless, faceless, brutality of this system as it is visited on non-whites. Nor for that matter was there any questionnaire or poll of the German people under Nazism that could uncover the systematic brutality of that highly organized cabal of thugs.

The talk of human dignity obscures the daily reality of the most vulnerable segment of minority groups, and the covert brutality which is not purposeless. Sheldon Levy suggests that systematic punishment leads to a reduction in political activity as well as behavioral and psychological rigidity. That rigidity leads to anxiety in complex situations, increased dependency, and subsequent identification with authority in order to reduce anxiety. The dependency and identification in turn endorse the official use of force.

Is there a real question that the racism is a racism of contempt? The current language of America *alone* betrays the contempt—"Nigger," "coon," "spook," "shine," "uppity," "they are going too far," "culturally deprived," "lazy,"—and efforts to prove blacks less intelligent than whites also suggest a grim disdain. There are the official explanations for the actions of the system's functionaries in defending the system in racial conflict situations. Do these explanations reflect anything but a contempt for human intelligence? Attica, Jackson State, San Quentin, the Algiers Motel incident, raids on local Panther party headquarters, Watts, and Newark, all should raise serious questions about whether blacks are even considered citizens.

But what must be appreciated besides the character of the racism is the "functional" nature of that racism.

From the first, America's brand of racism possessed two important qualities that may account for its durability: It was *adaptable* as an article of faith and it was *environmentally* appropriate. In the southern colonies, slavery based on racism was a matter of grim economic and political necessity. Its deterministic assumptions were based on supposed psycho-genetic factors, factors which have lost some of the support of science as genetics gave way to sociology. The present supportive assumptions are based on notions of environmental determinism buttressed by a firm sense that *"all"* people are free to do as they will, that in this society it is solely a question of motivation. Caught in the traffic of their own lives, perceiving the world from their own limited and highly personalized perspectives, and largely ignorant of the extent to which public institutions affect the lives of black people, the rank and file of Americans proceed along, blaming the victims for the inadequacies of an antiquated social system.

But racism is functional, especially in this matter of cities. It is the basis of a psychic reward to those whites who possess little else but the power to identify with their European *Herrenvolk;* it is the yardstick for exclusion in the housing market and at the workbench. Racism provides an acceptable explanation for what would normally be an unacceptable level of repression. Tom Wicker depicts a number of strategies based on a group of beliefs and assumptions which support a strong, firm posture of repression.

(1) Straw Man Strategy: snipers, revolutionaries
(2) Scare Stories: rumor of black invasions
(3) The Conspiracy: outside agitators
(4) Getting Tough: maximum fire power
(5) Lawbreaking: necessity of getting tough
(6) Black v. White: *they* are getting out of hand and we got to stop 'em.

Racism provides profits in employment, in the housing market, and in every sector of American industrial life, and racism also preserves the governance system. In the skin-color game, the inadequacies of the system can be overlooked, institutions can be rigidified, and brutal procedures can be defended. Uncaring police, inept city services, and restrictive unions are the vehicles for ethnic segregation which must be defended.

Racism is the creed of today's urban *status quo*. Racism is a multi-headed Hydra that separates man from his fellows. Racism will not be killed by individual frontal attacks or by the minor collective flurries that characterized the 1960s, though these attacks and flurries are important. For racism is not a blemish or imperfection on an otherwise well-oiled modern governance apparatus; rather, it is a symptom of Western man's deep-seated but profitable irrationalities.

## THINGS AIN'T WHAT THEY USED TO BE

Changes in the quality and character of America have gone unnoticed by a large number of the people. The reorganization of the employment picture is so sweeping that common sense is just inadequate in coping with the realities. The industrial economy has shifted from one of labor scarcity, which existed prior to the 1930s, to one that does not require the skill-less. Gone are the low-skill entry jobs and the days of railroads and heavy industry as major employers of job entrants. Going, going, gone are the major factories from the cities themselves, and more important, gone is the confidence that there is a rational connection between jobs as they exist and the present ways that preparation for work occurs. There is a heavy overdose of credentialism which affects the work field; the nature of work is increasingly technically oriented and sophisticated; and "career" jobs are located further away from the central city core.

It becomes a matter of ignorance, arrogance, or rank dishonesty to suggest that blacks retrace the route to middle-income security trod by earlier immigrant groups. For those very routes have been closed. The new routes will demand an open, discriminationless system in which a high level of training is required. The relative decline of farming, mining, and manufacturing industries as sources for employment has reduced the opportunities for the uneducated, the unskilled, and the marginally adapted, and all indicators point to a further decline of employment for the unskilled and the uneducated. Moreover, the shift of employment opportunities from the central cities to new growth industries located in suburban areas may work severe hardships on those blacks who have migrated to the cities in search of economic salvation.

The shift of employment opportunities is indeed striking. With blacks flocking to the cities in unprecedented numbers, almost two thirds of the industrial construction and one half of the mercantile construction is to be found outside of downtown areas. The flight of business from the cities now includes a growing number of white-collar firms, central office banking, and insurance firms. Just recently New York City (1971) was threatened by the loss of its garment industry as a number of factories are being located in the surrounding suburban industrial parks. Raymond Vernon explains this movement in terms of the strong parallel between location of jobs and residence. The real question is: "Whose residence?"

The 1970 census reports clearly document the connection between black urban wage opportunities on the one hand and the jobs and industries where Negroes are concentrated.

The chart does show a heavy concentration of blacks in private households, non-farm laborers, and service but it fails to show the disproportionate share in the lower-paid, less-skilled jobs when they are compared to white workers. Nor can this single chart reveal what the Equal Employment Opportunity Commission found in an investi-

Negro and Other Races as a Per Cent of All Workers
in Selected Occupations: 1960 and 1970[3]

| Occupation | 1960 | 1970 |
|---|---|---|
| Total, employed | 11 | 11 |
| Professional and technical | 4 | 7 |
| Medical and other health | 4 | 8 |
| Teachers, except college | 7 | 10 |
| Managers, officials, and proprietors | 3 | 4 |
| Clerical | 5 | 8 |
| Sales | 2 | 4 |
| Craftsmen and foremen | 5 | 7 |
| Construction craftsmen | 7 | 7 |
| Machinists, job-setters, and other metal craftsmen | 4 | 6 |
| Foremen | 2 | 5 |
| Operatives | 12 | 14 |
| Durable goods | 10 | 14 |
| Non-durable goods | 9 | 15 |
| Non-farm laborers | 27 | 23 |
| Private household workers | 50 | 42 |
| Other service workers | 20 | 19 |
| Protective service | 5 | 8 |
| Waiters, cooks, and bartenders | 15 | 13 |
| Farmers and farm workers | 16 | 11 |

gation of the high-wage industries. Blacks comprise but eight per cent of the total number found in employment there, but a piddling one per cent of the professional, technical, or managerial jobs of those industries; that within those same high-wage industries blacks possessed but five per cent of the craftsmen jobs and eleven per cent of the middle-level jobs. Blacks had a *smaller proportion* of the high-paying jobs in industries with high earnings than in the total reporting for all industries.

Even when blacks and whites are found in the same occupations blacks earn less money.

[3] Source: United States Department of Labor, Bureau of Labor Statistics.

| Occupation | % of White Earnings |
|---|---|
| Craftsmen-foremen | 68–81% |
| Service workers | 66–75% |

Increasingly in such a situation blacks have turned to government for employment where they take their place on the bottom of promotion-by-testing ascent systems or at the top in the highly visible appointive roles. Still others have sought quick returns in poverty program roles. What many people will not face, as they are unwilling to face a host of aspects of the urban crisis, is that the employment picture for young people and for black people *will be even bleaker without Vietnam.*

To complicate matters further, there is the reality of racial discrimination in employment. Herbert Hill of the NAACP reports that unionized white workers felt that the black workers should wait for desirable jobs until there was full employment of all white union members, at some indefinite future date. Hill suggested that this union position about "full employment" was shared by some of the very public officials who are called upon to enforce the federal statutes barring discrimination.

Thus while employment discrimination remains constant, jobs are moving one way while blacks are going another. Increasingly, however, blacks are defining for themselves the meaning of the words a "decent job." Many blacks have tried the rags to riches route and have learned that for them the trail from rags leads to still more rags. Under this new notion, a decent job becomes one which does more than just pay an adequate level of income; it must include opportunity, some sense of work enjoyment, and some potential for a promotion or a career. Since the economic situation is different from that of years ago, people's ideas about employment should also be different.

Change has come as well to the very agencies and segments who are supposed to smooth the adjustment of individuals to this complex technologically advanced society. The system of public and human services has deteriorated to a point where continuance of this present level seriously threatens both the economic structure of the cities and the peace of the American community. What must be recognized is that the rapid, explosive increase in the number of public assistance recipients is not merely a function of laziness or corruption but a by-product of the massive social, political, and economic shifts of this era and a function of the pathological bureaucratization of the so-called "helping agencies."

Pathological bureaucracies are units which have displaced service to society as their main function and have adopted courses of action designed to meet the opinions, concerns, and special competencies of the bureaucrats. Urban school systems, for example, steeped in their traditions are one kind of example of these "dysfunctional" service units, while the penal system is another. Two weeks after the catastrophic outburst at the Attica State prison in New York, for example, prison guards in the state were threatening a work disruption (lock-in) to reinforce their demands, not for prison reform, but for more guards.

In the hands of welfare bureaucracies, no matter how well meaning, welfare programs have deteriorated to the point of national scandal. At the operational level, the welfare recipient is led by the nose through a labyrinth of forms, regulations, and service inequities which lock the client into a system that indeed keeps him alive, but barely so, and which at the same time shrivels and destroys his human fiber and whatever incentive he may have. Increasingly, top officials are unable to control these bureaucracies, especially the pathological variety. Their growth in size and the strength of the job protections to incumbent, elected officials make it easier not to raise the crucial questions.

It is important to recognize three central concepts. First, a major change in the employment market and the focus of the human services areas have markedly altered the outlook and the prospects for the minority groups. Second, that common sense and personal observation do not provide a sufficient number of clues to grasp the meaning of the complex racial-class conflicts. Finally, that both of these two central concepts have direct consequences on the nature and quality of life in the cities.

### WHOSE PROBLEM?

The urban crisis then is the umbrella term for a host of separate problems which have emerged from the assumptions about cities, from the contradictions in the system of a democratic society with a racist institutional fabric, and from the very nature of societal change. Fortunately (or unfortunately), the racial aspects of these problems preserve the social order from drastic overhaul.

The combination of urban problems falls disproportionately on the black man's shoulders, but the resources for grappling with these problems are being wrenched from his hands and redirected to suburban and rural interests. So it is fair to ask: "Whose problem is this anyway?"

If the American psyche and its antipathy toward cities is appreciated, then need we ask questions of black people? If the unrelenting character of the bourgeois racism of contempt is recognized, need there be more rummaging through the psyches of minority groups, more questionnaires and more studies of their attitudes toward whites? And what if the extent and nature of change in the employment market, the consequences of the shift of jobs were accepted? Would there not be a ground swell of sentiment favoring a national full-employment-for-everyone strategy?

While the racism of today may be different in its capacity or willingness to act itself out as it once did in the not too distant past, the belief system is still there, the bend toward rationalizing inequities is still there, the grim determination to avoid righting the inequities is still there, and most beguiling is the wish to deny that skin-color privilege has provided whites an unmerited head start in the race for substance and status.

The crisis of the cities is a crisis of people—white and black. And unless people—white and black—seek to escape the fears and prejudices of the past and grapple with the reality of the present, then our urban crisis will soon overwhelm our entire society.

## FOR FURTHER READING

Hicks, Charles, with William Gaines and Charles Glatt. "Black Ghettos and Uncertain Futures." *Faculty Research Journal* (of St. Augustine College) (January 1971), 18–25.

Jacobs, Jane. *The Economy of Cities.* New York: Vintage Books, 1971.

Levy, Sheldon. "The Psychology of Political Activity." *Annals of the American Academy of Political and Social Science,* 391 (September 1970), 83–96.

Pettigrew, Thomas. *Profile of the Negro American.* Princeton: Van Nostrand, 1964.

Powdermaker, Hortense. "Channeling of Negro Aggression by Cultural Process." *American Journal of Sociology,* 48 (May 1943), 750–58.

Schuman, Howard. "Sociological Racism." *Transaction,* 7 (December 1969), 44–48.

United States Department of Commerce. *Social and Economic Status of Negroes in the United States—1970.* Washington, D.C.: United States Government Printing Office, 1970.

Waldhorn, Steven Arthur. "Government Lawlessness in America," in Theodore L. Becker and Vernon C. Murray (eds.), *Pathological Bureaucracies.* New York: Oxford University Press, 1971.

# CHAPTER 6

# CITIZEN PARTICIPATION: FEDERAL POLICY

*Melvin B. Mogulof*

In the 1960s, one of the main themes of American politics was that of citizen participation, of involving individuals in the decision-making that would affect their lives. Certainly no other groups were as disconnected from the political process as the urban poor and minority groups. In response, the federal government established a number of programs which required "maximum feasible involvement" of community residents in areas affected by federal projects. As the decade wore on, the nature of this participation changed, and what might have begun as token conciliation rapidly assumed larger dimensions, and aroused the fears and resentments of a number of middle-class groups.

In analyzing the effect of federal policies, Melvin Mogulof concludes that despite a number of problems, citizen participation has worked, and moreover, it has worked within the traditional American political experience of accommodation and conciliation. What is now needed is not more experimentation, but firm leadership to carry out this policy, which may be the only hope that we have to save our historic political systems within the cities.

In addition to academic training in social welfare planning, Melvin B. Mogulof has had experience as a regional director of both the OEO Community Action Program and the HUD Model Cities Program. He is currently a staff associate at the Urban Institute in Washington.

*"Citizen participation is needed at all stages of the planning process . . . lines of communication should . . . demonstrate to them in ways they understand that their views receive full and sincere consideration."*

—Federal Highway Administration, 1969

THE reader may discern condescension in this excerpt from a 1969 Federal Highway Administration policy guideline; he may sense that the word "them" is a euphemism for those who are of color and/or poor; and if he reads carefully he will note that "them" are being asked for advice not consent in the process of community decision-making. But the same reader must note that this policy guideline emanates from a federal agency not known for its efforts to include citizen participants, in the early days of a new national administration not exactly elected with a mandate to broaden the participation of "them" in the politics of road building. These federal guidelines when seen in the context of numerous similar federal pronouncements suggest that as we ended the decade of the sixties, participation as a concept was no longer controversial—it belonged to everyone (at least in concept).

The issue of participation may be as much characteristic of the sixties as any other factor. The impetus for participation rested largely in the new expectations which the black revolution created.[1] And the fulfillment of these expectations was strongly abetted in a series of federal program efforts aimed at "them." The evolution of these efforts began with the demonstration program sponsored by the President's Committee on Juvenile Delinquency, continued through the Office of Economic Opportunity's Community Action Program, and ended with the still current Model Cities Program.

[1] This argument is not to deny the critical role in this movement played by the young and not so young from every sector of American life who were seeking their individuality in an increasingly "mass society." Rather, I am primarily concerned about the interaction of federal influence and the rising expectations for participation of those who are poor and/or of visible minority status.

## CITIZENS

Federal interest in citizen participation began long before the language of the Economic Opportunity Act of 1964, which called for "maximum feasible participation." A variety of federal policies and guidelines had evolved relative to citizen participation without any agreement as to what is meant by the term or what the purposes of participation are. Actually the issue of citizen participation in federal social programs emerged to prominence in the nineteen-fifties and the early sixties as part of federal efforts in housing, urban renewal, delinquency prevention, manpower and economic development. In addition, citizen participation has been an important part of many Department of Agriculture programs, and it has been a distinctive feature of the Selective Service local draft board system. And viewed even more broadly, efforts at citizen participation have been a central theme in our national history, including the Woman's Suffrage Movement, the abolition of the poll tax, and governance of local school districts as well as current efforts to ensure the franchise for those who are literate in languages other than English.

It is not intended to discuss the issue of citizen participation as if it is focused on "everyman." The citizen in mind is one who is better captured by the term "them" used in the Federal Highway Administration guideline. This "citizen" is one whose current condition makes him the subject for federal (or other) efforts at resource distribution. He can also be defined as someone who might be potentially disadvantaged as a result of the use of federal resources, a person who, upon closer inspection, turn out to be largely poor, largely minority group, and often largely both.

For the purposes of meeting many federal guidelines there would appear to be less desirable and more desirable citizens. Most desirable would be the combined charac-

teristics of black or brown and poor. If one of these qualities had to be surrendered it would generally be that of
poverty. In return for this, some agencies would then define an acceptable citizen as one of visible minority status
who appears to have some bona fide connection to those
who are both poor and black or brown. The least desirable
person from the point of how well he fits this notion of
citizen would be one who is simply poor without being of
color. The ideal citizen from a federal point of view seems
one who is both disadvantaged and disconnected from (or
inadequately connected to) our major institutions.

The reader may find these definitions of "citizens" very
fluid and unsatisfactory. Partially it is a result of refusing
to settle for a definition of citizen which is so inclusive as
to be meaningless. It has been noted that the citizen who
is the target of federal involvement efforts is *not* everyman.
He is a specific segment of the population whose participation can be instrumental in achieving certain purposes.
Based upon an analysis by Daniel Fox the purposes of
citizen participation may be described as seeking to: (a)
decrease alienation, (b) engage the "sick" individual
(rather than the "sick" society), (c) create an organized
societal force capable of protecting aggrieved groups and
winning for them a fairer share of resources, and (d) develop a constituency and engineer its consent.

In this kind of purposeful world where people are used
as instruments, and not because their involvement is intrinsically to be valued, it is no accident that the citizen
who emerges as the target of federal participation policies
is one who is of minority status or poor or, ideally, both.
Not surprisingly, he is the very citizen who in the past
has shown the least likelihood for involvement in the organized life of his community. Whether his lack of prior
involvement in communal life is a symbol of his difficulties
or a cause of his difficulties is not at issue here. Rather, it
seems that if federal policy did not define the disadvantaged
and disconnected as the specific citizens they were interested
in, federal efforts at citizen involvement would be likely
to emerge with the same participant who has for so long

populated the world of voluntary social welfare—the white, the affluent, and the well-born.[2]

## PARTICIPATION

The location of citizen participants vis-à-vis those who make organizational decisions sets the condition for participation. The fact that the Federal Highway Administration assigns an "advisory" location to citizen participants does not inevitably mean that they will be confined to advice-giving. In the same way OEO's injunction for "maximum feasible participation" does not necessarily guarantee more "intensive" citizen participation, or a greater potential for influence and authority than the advice-giving role of the highway program. In looking at the development of participation, there appear to be three major patterns (in addition to that of non-participation). These patterns may be graphically captured in the following manner:

*Figure 1*

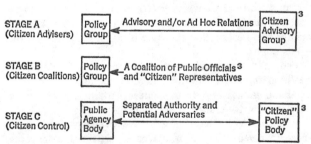

[2] Obviously this definition of a "citizen" should not be inverted to imply that anybody should be deprived of his citizenship rights because he is not poor, black, brown, or otherwise conceived to be disadvantaged. On the contrary, it is assumed that those not included are in a better position to assert their rights and will continue to do so through various political, economic, and social channels.

[3] The "citizens" in each of these three models may range from community "elites" to the black/brown/poor. Since citizen participation has had its greatest development in programs affecting the black/brown/poor, therefore the "citizens" in these models are most apt to be of that status.

Coalition policy groups, as represented in Stage B of Figure 1, may be a coalition of individuals representing different points of view or a more formal coalition of different interest groups (e.g., public agencies, the citizenry affected by a program and general public interests). Such coalitions are distinguished by the fact that control over a program rests with the coalition's policy group. Stage C (citizen control) reflects a situation where a body dominated by citizen representatives has certain final or preliminary authority. In the case of final authority, it would be the citizen-dominated body that makes program policy. In the case of preliminary authority, a public body would be unable to act on a policy decision until approval has been received from the citizen body. In this instance, the citizen body and the public body become potential adversaries in that each body possesses separate policy authority and neither body can act without the other. Stage A (advisory group) may reflect the highway program where there is an organized citizenry to serve as an advisory group. In these cases, the most "intense" forms of participation were of the adversary (control) variety. Moreover, analysts found a close match to the rhetoric of black leadership, who declare that the issue is no longer participation --it is control.

Federally supported programs seem more amenable to coalition forms of participation than to those of control. Coalition bodies *appear* to achieve certain key purposes; they *appear* to reduce the alienation of those involved; they *appear* to increase the competence and well-being of those involved (to the point where participation in community decision-making has provided an important job ladder for Negro participants) and they *appear* to ease the problems of winning consent for programs. In effect, participation in councils and policy bodies appears to "cool out" and connect those involved in precisely the way they were supposed to. The literature of citizen participation is filled with references to Pygmalion-like stories of black and brown leadership; in fact much of this literature winds up with a caveat that participation which creates connection to the "establishment" can at the same time disconnect the participant from the community he is supposed to represent. The above correlates of participation may underlie the apparent willingness of some programs to foster participation but they also emphasize the search by the minority communities for mechanisms by which to control their citizen representatives.

It is likely that in the past few years both federal officials and "citizen" leaders have become far more sensitive to the prerogatives involved in different types of participation. Outside of the Community Action and Model Cities programs, most participation is of the advisory-consultative variety. This seems particularly so when the local grantee is a public agency such as a school system, an employment service, a department of welfare, etc. However, there is some evidence that advisory groups composed solely of citizen types (such as an Urban Renewal Project Area Committee, or a Public Housing Tenants Council) can be at least as effective in pressing for change as neighborhood representatives participating in coalition bodies. Thus the effectiveness of influence does not necessarily move in a linear fashion from advisory relationships, to shared policy functions, to control. In its capacity to hold to a neighborhood (or "citizen") point of view, the all-"citizen" advisory group may be more effective than policy-making coalitions which include a minority of "citizen" interests.

A last comment on this issue of participation concerns the question of its quality. Community observation indicates that the actual state of participation is different from its public image. Participation tends to be sporadic and the participants often willing to leave policy-making to agency professionals. In this respect participation among minority groups and poor people may differ little from what we have known about participation by other segments of our population.[4] In fact, it could be argued that the

---

[4] A well-known statistic from Saul Alinsky's *Reveille for Radicals* describing his back-of-the-yards experience in Chicago indicated that at no time was more than two per cent of the community involved with the action program.

importance of participation rests less in its practice than in the *option* for its practice by formerly disconnected population groups.

The notion that client participation is a crucial factor in healing is central to many individually oriented therapies. Stress on client participation can also be seen as ideologically close to the idea that the poor are to blame for their misfortunes. The argument could read: "If we could only engage the poor man in desiring a better lot for himself,[5] he would learn to make better use of available resources, and his poverty would soon come to an end." A different view holds that the conditions of the poor, especially the poor who are black, stem from a misallocation of resources away from the poor. Further, even resources that are allocated to the poor are delivered through organizations controlled by middle-class whites in ways that sustain white middle-class interests. To those who see the problem in this light, the purpose of participation is either to win control of the resource-allocating mechanisms or to establish effective pressure points in order to change the ways in which resources are delivered to poor people.

Many leaders of black and other minority group poor, however, see sickness in society's controlling elements.[6] When the problem is so defined, the purpose of participation becomes the wresting of power from such controlling elements or, at the very least, forcing them to new kinds of accommodations affecting poor people and the black community.

Three federal programs have provided testing grounds for the evolution of the foregoing ideas of participation: the Juvenile Delinquency Demonstration Projects sponsored by the President's Committee on Juvenile Delinquency in the Kennedy administration; OEO's Community Action Program; and HUD's Model Cities Program. The developments in these programs have been influenced by—

[5] See Chapter 4.
[6] See Chapter 5.

and have influenced—a parallel black community movement away from integration toward a focus on independent black community development.

Though they developed sequentially, the Delinquency, Community Action, and Model Cities programs display a number of common features:

Establishment of local organizations to define the nature of the problems prior to organized intervention. Proposed intervention must have been able to stand the test of "comprehensiveness." In effect, action was to be preceded by planning.

Emphasis on local program development to meet assumed local differences about the problem.

Designation of a clearly defined population or area of service. In the Community Action Program it is interesting to note that the legislative phrase, "maximum feasible involvement of groups and areas to be served," is generally perverted to "maximum feasible involvement of the poor."

Predomination of programs in neighborhoods occupied by the black poor.

Formation by the local sponsoring agent of a policy-making coalition composed of representatives from some or all of the following sectors: public governing bodies (city, county, schools, state); community elites; voluntary agency representatives; the organized middle-class minority community; the poor and their selected representatives.

Encouragement of a "coming together" of the affected citizenry at the neighborhood level.

### THE DELINQUENCY DEMONSTRATION PROGRAM

The federal policy guide to the presentation of proposals for funding the Juvenile Delinquency Act said nothing about the composition of the governing body of a Delinquency Demonstration effort. But what this guide did say about neighborhood organization represented a bold conception that the strength or weakness of a community can itself be a factor in whether its children fall victim to the label of "delinquent." The guide suggested that a major outcome would be the "process by which the competence of local community residents is increased so that they become a more potent factor in the lives of their youth." To facilitate this outcome, the policy guide, in discussing criteria for intervention, noted the following: "In a project's consideration of means of intervention, evidence must be shown that careful thought was given to plans for increasing the competence of target area residents and organizations. Such competence will be expected to increase the capacity to participate more effectively in decisions affecting their welfare and that of their youth. In all likelihood, such a capacity would facilitate the attainment of the project's goals." Here, in specific and clear form, is the assumption that involvement of an affected community can be an instrument toward the achievement of a goal such as the prevention and control of delinquent behavior.

*Policy Participation.* While all of the federally supported delinquency projects sought, in some fashion, to involve affected populations in policy formulation, such involvement was more frequently in an advisory rather than a decision-making capacity. Further, the selection of such representatives was always at the discretion of the local sponsoring agent, with no formal attempt to have the affected neighborhood select its own representatives. Of the three programs under examination, it was only in the delinquency program that there could be found governing coalitions which include *no* significant representation from the neighborhood. The following appear to have been the dominant modes of policy-making coalitions in the delinquency projects:

*Strong mayor:* The policy board was appointed by and was advisory to the mayor. The strong mayor coalition generally included "elite" leadership from the voluntary welfare sector plus representatives from agencies whose resources might be central to development and implementation of the plan.

*Government-centered coalition:* The policy board was a coalition of independent units of government. Such units were most likely the city, the county, and the school district, sometimes supplemented by state representatives.

*Voluntary-public coalition:* Such coalitions were generally incorporated outside of government. They included community leadership oriented to the problems of delinquency as well as representatives from public and voluntary agencies who were seen as controlling critical resources.

In none of these policy-making coalitions in the juvenile delinquency program did the participation of neighborhood representatives approximate more than ten per cent of the governing body. In all cases, such representatives were selected by the coalition's sponsor—sometimes in consultation with community civil rights groups.

The above kinds of governing boards were often new *ad hoc* arrangements with ill-defined authority and a frail legitimacy. The delinquency demonstration projects needed a constituency if they were to be able to influence existing agencies to attempt new programs. In the search for a constituency, the affected neighborhood became a likely resource. This involvement of neighborhoods was abetted when project staff were from a profession which prized the client's participation in decision-making as a goal in itself (for example, social workers). In addition to the neighborhood, many projects found a powerful ally in the civil rights movement.

In perspective the quality and quantity of neighborhood involvement in juvenile delinquency policy-making seem at best minimal. Yet they were important steps, clearly linked in sequence to the quasi-governmental units which were later to emerge in various black communities as part of the Model Cities effort. Many of the factors that made the delinquency projects sensitive to the issue of neighborhood involvement continued and intensified in the Community Action and Model Cities programs.

*Neighborhood Organization.* In retrospect, it seems far-sighted that the juvenile delinquency programs were much more concerned with issues of neighborhood organization than they were with means of including neighborhood residents on their governing coalitions. This issue of neighborhood presence on the governing coalition was to predominate in the early years of the soon-to-come anti-poverty program. Conversely, in the seventies it appears that the "elitest" juvenile delinquency program planners, who gave a priority to neighborhood organization, were better predictors of the future. Current interest in the development of a self-determining black community and some of the notions of neighborhood organization in the juvenile delinquency program can be seen as compatible ideas. On the other hand, voting places on a local government-sponsored coalition have more in common with the notions of integration than they do with separatism, and to that extent they have lost some of their earlier importance.

The neighborhood-organization conceptions of New York City's Mobilization for Youth, while not typical of all juvenile delinquency projects, are worth restating because of their clarity and because they were the first to be tested in action.

"(1) To increase the ability of local residents to participate in and influence the social and political life of their community. This will have the further objective of providing an example for adolescents of a means of handling alienation constructively.

(2) To identify, document, and dramatize community needs.

(3) To widen channels of communication between lower-class persons and institutional personnel or decision makers, and thereby to increase both the institution's responsiveness to lower-class needs and the resident's knowledge and use of community resources.

(4) To increase community integration and the effectiveness of social controls.

(5) To improve the confidence of the leaders to deal with grievances and to defend their constituents' rights and privileges."

The Mobilization proposal further speculates about the consequences of success with the above approach:

"The uniqueness of our approach to community action is the encouragement of autonomy among lower-class participants. There is, of course, a contradiction inherent in the proposal to establish lower-class community organizations under Mobilization sponsorship. Mobilization is responsible to a wide variety of groups. Issues with which lower-class organizations deal may threaten some of these groups. Unless they are formed spontaneously under the impetus of an inflammatory issue, lower-class groups cannot be organized without the financing and support of such established (that is, middle-class) organizations as Mobilization. The fact that Mobilization constitutes a new structure partially mitigates the problem of control. So, too, does the Mobilization intent to protect the organization's independence from both outside pressure and Mobilization's own opinions about their mistakes. This is no real solution, however; it will be necessary for Mobilization to divest itself of responsibility for the project as soon as feasible. Encouraging the organizations to raise their own funds will be a step in that direction."

The reader may be forgiven his nostalgia for those not-so-long-ago days when white planners could speculate about the consequences of *their* unleashing the affected population. Perhaps nothing so well mirrors the movement of events as this reading of Mobilization's brave words of 1962, which now in *concept* seem so dated. The *practice*, of course, in most communities today still makes Mobilization for Youth years ahead of the present as well as its own time.

Because of its neighborhood organization activities there

were pressures on the Department of Health, Education, and Welfare (administrator of the delinquency program) to curb Mobilization's approach to neighborhood organization. As a result of federal reappraisal, the following key points were made in an HEW guideline for support to continuing efforts to "increase the competence of neighborhood residents." The first point was a strong affirmation of the legitimacy of neighborhood organization: "Amelioration of social problems like delinquency is not possible without attention to the development of the capacity of neighborhoods to become more potent forces in their communities . . ." But as a means of control, the guide stipulated that "projects should be asked to indicate (a) the issues, problems or other content areas in which it anticipates groups becoming involved, and (b) the levels of activity, channels and strategies which *work exclusively or mainly outside of established, existing channels.*"[7] After specifying a list of neighborhood action tactics that it could support, the HEW guideline goes on to specify, "projects must indicate which of these lawful strategies it sees as possible and usable and why. The government cannot fund projects which will use *only* the protest route."

The facts in the juvenile delinquency demonstrations did not reflect the anxiety apparently felt by federal officials when they issued these words of constraint. Few of the demonstration projects shared the more militant perspectives of Mobilization for Youth. Only in Mobilization were there continuing efforts toward the creation of *independent* neighborhood groups which sought to deal with and influence the imbalance of resources flowing into the affected neighborhood. The more usual neighborhood organization in the juvenile delinquency programs consisted either of neighborhood groups serving as an ally of the project, helping it to implement various action programs, or neighborhood units organized to work on specific, self-help problems.

[7] Italics added.

The contribution of these neighborhood organization approaches was to make clear that building communal action entities, organized around the grievances and needs of poor people, was an essential part of dealing with the problem of delinquency. This lesson was not lost on the soon-to-emerge Community Action Agencies (CAAs)—almost all saw neighborhood organization as a central program item. They took the juvenile delinquency program's slender beginnings in the area of sharing policy authority with neighborhood residents and completely redefined the structure of policy-making coalitions.

### THE COMMUNITY ACTION PROGRAM

In an article published in the British journal *The New Statesman and Nation* of August 6, 1965, the failures of citizen participation in the anti-poverty program were noted as follows: "The guts of the program, a sneaky little clause in the legislation which requires participation of the poor to the maximum extent feasible in planning and operating the various poverty battles, has never been followed in anything but form." Apart from misquoting the language of the legislation, as did virtually every other commentator, the *New Statesman*'s verdict seems strangely out of joint with OEO's actual experience.

Expectedly caustic in a *Journal of Social Issues* analysis (1965), which called the war on poverty "political pornography," Saul Alinsky correctly anticipated future developments in the Community Action Program and Model Cities Program. Alinsky wrote: "I have serious doubts about any really meaningful program to help and work with the poor until such time as the poor, through their own organized power, are able to provide legitimate representatives of their interests to sit at the programming table and have a strong voice in both the formulation and running of the program."

*Policy Participation.* The Office of Economic Opportunity's guide to the Community Action Program was issued some three months after the program began. During these three months it became clear in community after community that the composition of CAA policy boards was to be a major issue. If OEO or other federal administration personnel harbored hopes that "maximum feasible involvement" was to be satisfied by jobs in the program, they quickly learned otherwise. In many communities, aroused minority leadership, abetted by OEO as a federal agency committed to testing the boundaries of "maximum feasible involvement," made a battleground over the creation of CAA policy boards in a way that had never occurred in the delinquency demonstration program. Unlike HEW's guide to the delinquency program, the OEO guide made clear that neighborhood residents were to be part of the program's policy apparatus. The OEO guide noted: "To be broadly based, a Community Action Agency must provide ample opportunity for participation and policy making by . . . the population to be served by the Community Action Program." In a later paragraph, the guide indicated minimum standards for representation as being "at least one representative selected from each of the neighborhoods or areas in which the CAP will be concentrated."

The mere issuance of an administrative guide is no assurance that policy will be adhered to. In fact, in the anti-poverty legislation hearings of that year, Representative Adam Clayton Powell castigated one city after another for failing to seat poor people on anti-poverty councils. In retrospect, it seems that legislative language which spoke of "maximum feasible involvement," when translated into administrative policy which set a minimum of "one representative" per neighborhood, invited a period of testing and conflict. This conflict was to be partially resolved by a Congressional amendment, adopted in 1966, requiring at least one-third of a Community Action Agency's board to be representatives of the poor.

In its guidelines to construction of a CAA policy-making body, OEO introduced the idea of a "three-legged stool"—that is, a policy body with three categories of representation: (a) public and private agencies responsible for services or programs concerned with poverty; (b) elements in the community as a whole; and (c) the population to be served by the CAA. The 1966 Congressional amendment supplied legislative assurance that the population to be served would be represented by at least a full leg of that three-cornered stool. As it happened, this amendment came at a time when neighborhood representatives already controlled CAA boards in many large cities.

In a remarkably short period of time, as measured from the start of the delinquency program (1961) to the 1966 Congressional amendment to OEO's legislation, there was a radical shift in the notions of legitimacy as applied to federally funded decision-making bodies affecting the lives of poor people. Coincident with this movement ensuring a significant place on policy bodies by affected populations was an equally important movement to democratize the way in which such representatives were chosen. In 1967, this author suggested two phases of a Community Action Program where in the first phase neighborhood representatives are chosen by "downtown" figures and those who "speak for the poor" and in the second, more mature phase, board representatives are selected by the affected groups themselves. This metamorphosis was encouraged by the CAP guidebook, which said that "the selection process should be designed to encourage the use, whenever feasible, of traditional democratic approaches and techniques such as group forums and discussions, nominations, and balloting. This will minimize the possibility that a representative does not command the support or confidence of the group or area that he represents." This incipient focus on a constituency for policy board representatives was to encourage a CAA counterpart focus on neighborhood councils and neighborhood organization. This was the beginning of a representative system, later expanded in the

Model Cities Program, where neighborhood groups selected their representatives to larger policy bodies and began to hold them accountable for their voting behavior.

However, there was also a style of neighborhood action in the Community Action Program which could trace its conceptual lineage to Mobilization for Youth. This kind of neighborhood organization was much more focused on affecting the resources fed into the neighborhood by public and private agencies.

Relative conceptions of the "neighborhood" may be instructive in explaining differences between neighborhood organization in the delinquency and CAA programs. In the delinquency program, the terminology of "target" area was prevalent—a place *to which* something was done. In the CAA program, the neighborhood began to emerge as a partner, and in some of the projects, as a controlling force in the decision-making process. In some OEO programs, it was not many months before large-city CAAs gave to their neighborhood councils veto power over any CAA programs to be funded in their neighborhoods.

Much neighborhood organization in the CAA program, as in the delinquency program, was concerned with linking people to services and building a constituency for the program. But there was also activity based on the neighborhood's organizational needs, which were seen as distinct and separate from the larger community and even from the Community Action Agency itself. Interestingly, the sanction for this kind of "separatist" activity rested in OEO's *Community Action Program Guide*. In discussing appropriate activity under "resident participation," the guidebook talked about "providing staff services and other resources, including equipment and facilities, to existing local organizations in order to enable them to advise and inform the Community Action Agency and other institutions about the needs, problems, and concerns of the poor. *Where these are absent or without the confidence of the poor, staff can be made available for the purposes of de-*

*veloping local autonomous associations and organizations.*"[8]

One apparent result of the success of CAA's neighborhood organization activity was the provision of a different base for Model Cities efforts than the delinquency demonstrations had provided for the Community Action Agencies. Undoubtedly, the different mood of the black community in 1967 as compared to 1964 had a great deal to do with the readiness of certain model cities to concede a different role in decision-making to their aggrieved neighborhoods.

THE MODEL CITIES PROGRAM

Given city government sponsorship of Model Cities efforts, one might not expect to find much focus on the organization of neighborhoods for protest activities—particularly those protests aimed against established public agencies. Analyses of initially proposed Model Cities governing structures showed that there was no great emphasis on sharing authority with neighborhood leadership. Nevertheless, the best clues about what we might expect with regard to neighborhood participation do not lie in the verbal promises of proposals, but in the organizational structures that result from a city's experience in trying to develop a decision system which has legitimacy in the eyes of the people who are to be affected by the intervention. In most instances, such a decision-making system emerges through hard bargaining with the affected community, *after* the proposals are written.

In *every* case in HUD's Western Region where the Model neighborhood population was black, the governing coalition was numerically dominated by neighborhood residents. While in every case the role of policy bodies was initially conceived of as advisory, the decision system which

[8] Italics added.

evolved gave to such advisory groups a *de facto* veto over
Model Cities programs. This veto was accomplished by a
procedure which blocked the city council or mayor from
acting on funding for the Model Cities Program until that
program had been approved by the advisory group dominated by neighborhood representatives. (In two of the
Western Region's Model Cities, such advisory groups were
composed *solely of neighborhood representatives*.) As a
further augur of things to come, two of the cities gave to
the neighborhood-dominated group a technical planning
staff of its own.

An analysis of five Model Cities programs operating in
neighborhoods which were predominantly black yielded the
comparison (Figure 2) with regard to citizen participation
and potential influence on community decision-making.

Based upon the Model Cities experience, one can predict
the further diffusion and acceleration of changes in black-
dominated neighborhoods. Very probably these changes
will see neighborhood councils or congresses emerge as
quasi-governmental units for their areas in the Model Cities
Program, with jurisdiction gradually spreading to non-
Model Cities expenditures. These neighborhood groups will
be given their own staff resources with which to develop
their own program plans, and with which to refine and
counter plans drawn for their neighborhoods by other sectors of the community. The role of social broker—a friendly
third party linking the neighborhood to the bureaucracies
supplying it with resources—may no longer be viable.[9] It
appears to become less possible for third parties to seek
to stand between the aspirations of the black community

[9] We may be on the verge of entirely new "third party" roles. The
kind where courageous and well-meaning whites argued the needs of
the black community to "downtown" appears dead. But there are two
other kinds of "third party" roles which may hold promise: one where
the "third party" works as part of a coalition to tip the argument in
favor of the black community; the other, in situations of racial separation, where a "third party" (both white and black) is able to endure
the constant testing of black leadership, to serve as a bargaining link
between the leadership of the separated communities.

### Figure 2
### SIMILARITIES AND DIFFERENCES AMONG FIVE WESTERN MODEL CITIES IN 1968
(PERCENTAGES)

| Characteristic | Fresno | Oakland | Portland | Richmond | Seattle |
|---|---|---|---|---|---|
| Blacks in Model neighborhood | 55 | 80 | 45 | 69 | 81 |
| Blacks on citizens' policy board | 67 | 90[a] | 52 | 82 | 70 |
| Policy body members selected by neighborhood | 67 | 100 | 59 | 54 | 100[b] |
| Does Model Cities neighborhood have numerical control of program sub-committees? | yes | yes | yes | yes[c] | yes |
| Is there provision for independent technical assistance to neighborhood-dominated policy groups? | no | yes | no | no | yes |
| Can the city council approve programs for funding without agreement by the citizens' policy body? | no | no | no | no | no |

[a] At the time of this analysis, a permanent body had not been selected in the Oakland Model Cities neighborhood. All twelve members of the neighborhood body's executive committee and the total voting body were seen as likely to approach a 100 per cent black membership.

[b] The advisory board was nominated by various neighborhood organizations but it was necessary for the mayor to concur in these selections.

[c] Richmond's bylaws do not specify the make-up of voting membership on the program subcommittees. On a *de facto* basis, all the functional committees are numerically controlled by black residents.

and local (or national) institutions. Whether local government and an emerging black neighborhood "government" can reach an accommodation which will produce significant new resources and options for Negroes in Model Cities as well as in other programs remains to be tested. Equally important is whether any such accommodation will stimulate or check the move toward a racial separation which is publicly acknowledged and welcomed by both parties.

## PARTICIPATION IN THE LOCALITY

Based upon the experience of the late sixties, federal policy and programs have established the arena within which to understand participation. Observation in seven local programs (a Community Action Agency, Model Cities Program, Public Housing, Urban Renewal, Neighborhood Health, Community Mental Health, Legal Services) supports the conclusion that these programs have created the grounds for a remarkably rich, complex, exciting communal life for a growing number of people. There seems room for optimism with regard to the practice and the potentials of citizen participation. If the reader is personally familiar with local programs involving neighborhood participants, he may be moved to discount this optimism. Citizen representatives *do* get manipulated; some professional staff seem to conspire to create the illusion of participation while control of decisions rests in the hands of staff. One can attend board meetings where there is widespread ignorance about the issues being discussed and one can be repulsed by the pursuit of jobs by citizen policy board members. One can also be appalled by the thinness of participation and the shaky grounds on which many decisions are made. And in the case of black leadership, one can be angry with the periodic anti-white rhetoric, the stridence and the sheer nonsense of some of what passes for "militancy."

It is very easy to be "turned off" by any or all of the

above failings. It is easy to come away saying that it is much more terrible than it is wonderful. Our observation suggests that such conclusions, as easy as they are to come to, would be gross errors. One must see the quality of citizen involvement within the context of all community participation. One must see it against one congressman droning away before a largely empty chamber, while a few of his colleagues are lost in their own conversation. One must see it against all of the other experiences we have about the way in which people exercise their potential sovereignty over their lives. And measured in this way, it must be concluded that there is indeed richness and complexity to citizen participation, and that the prognosis is good if federal policy continues to abet the local developments which have been observed. And the prognosis might be even better if federal policy were more deliberate, widespread, and clear about the purposes of citizen participation.

What are some of the evidences for the above optimism? For one, there is a strong impression that when blacks hold positions of influence over a decision-making body, and when they hold important staff positions, there seems to be a concomitant willingness to work together with whites and an interest in racial accommodation if not integration. While situations have been observed where blacks refuse to differ with other blacks in the presence of a white audience, there appear to be other situations where class interest rather than racial identity prevails.

It is also impressive to note the way in which the citizen representative tends to view his participation. It is true that for many black spokesmen the notion of participation has lost its relevance. It is control of decision-making, they say, that they are after. And some white "friends" of the black community insist that control is the only relevant issue and federal policy ought to move in that direction. But the local situation seems to be more diffused; it is not at all clear that the black man on the street and the black leader really want control which would involve a continued separation from the larger community. The call for control seems to mask the desires of citizen representatives to know what their decision-making prerogatives are, to be listened to if not followed, and to have strong influence over the resources and communal decisions which affect their life chances.

Ironically, the movement toward control may be hastened by the actions of some white leadership in abdicating situations of integrated decision-making. In effect, the militancy of black leadership (which can sometimes be misread as a demand for absolute control) coupled with the timorousness of white public officials may be leading to a situation where community control, adversary relationships, and increasing racial separatism are the only possible consequences. In fact there *is* evidence in the field study of the aforementioned seven local agencies that there is movement toward situations of control although it is unclear as to whether the causes of this movement rest in black demands, white disinterest and abdication, or both. The evidence includes the following:

(a) In each observed agency, except Legal Services, the percentage of blacks on a policy-making or policy advisory board exceeded the percentage of blacks in the community to be served.

(b) In four of six projects where a policy board having community representation influenced staff hiring, the director of the project is black.

(c) Community representatives generally have greater *de facto* power in making decisions than would be expected based upon the percentage of seats they hold on a board. This trend toward greater than expected influence by community representatives is exaggerated further when community representatives are black.

(d) In no case did a coalition decision group drift toward becoming advisory, and in no case did a citizen-dominated group become diluted through coalition.

(e) Of the two groups which were advisory, the one which was almost all black seemed the best able to maximize the influence inherent in its advice-giving status.

The weight of evidence in these seven projects seems to be that we are moving toward situations of neighborhood dominance and control. But our impression of the national scene would indicate that this movement is a long way from being complete, and ironically it may not be desired by neighborhood leadership or local government. None of this is to argue that there is not a black (or a brown) community whose grievances are deep and whose special interests as a group are real. Some federal policy has been specifically concerned with the inclusion of these aggrieved special interest groups in decision-making. In fact the notions of "citizen representative," "community representative," "community involvement," "community decision maker," "neighborhood representative," are all alternate terms used by federal agencies to refer to representatives of aggrieved groups. But there remain real and very different options as to how the participation of these representatives shall be structured into community decision-making.

One option is to organize the aggrieved group as an advisory adjunct to the decision-making process. Another option is to include representatives of these groups as part of a coalition of decision makers as generally exists in the Community Action Program. Yet another option is to turn decision-making and program control over in its entirety to representatives of these aggrieved groups. At this stage in the development of citizen participation policy, and in the conflict between races, all of these seem appropriate structures for citizen involvement. It is much less clear that a structure confined solely to advice-giving (such as the federal highway program) is tenable in big-city black communities, and attention should be given to the hybrid decision structure that has been observed in the Model Cities Program. In this hybrid a neighborhood-dominated advisory group acts as advisory to a city council, but the city council in turn is barred from any program moves affecting the neighborhood without the *consent* of the neighborhood-dominated advisory group. This has been labeled the "dual green light" system, and it may hold great promise in our search for decentralized modes of decision-making which simultaneously allow for the application of central rationalities (e.g., those developed by various levels of government).

## A CONCLUDING NOTE

The most salient points from the above study are that citizen participation is there to be observed, it works, it seems to have secured important commitment by federal and local personnel, and it appears to have something very useful to contribute to the resolution of inequities in our society. And it fits the American experience beautifully; so beautifully that it can be argued that citizen participation is best viewed as a goal for policy rather than an instrument toward achieving other goals (although it will accomplish that, too).

Counterposed against the above visible benefits are the equally visible lacunae with regard to policy and practice. Citizen participation policy at the federal level is erratic, piecemeal, misunderstood, and possibly not really cared about. But this patchwork of federal attitudes and practices may have had great utility in contributing to federal and local experimentation, with regard to participation in the decade of the sixties. We know enough to move beyond the benefits of a benign anarchy in policy, to a setting forth of what it is we have learned and where we want to go with regard to federal and local policies for citizen participation. To continue the "benign anarchy" of current citizen participation policy and practice through the seventies would be a denial of the utility of these past experimental years. Even more discouraging would be the additional evidence that we do not know how to create a sequence between the development of knowledge and the development of policy.

## FOR FURTHER READING

Altshuler, Alan. *Community Control.* New York: Bobbs-Merrill, 1970.

Cahn, Edward S., and Jean C. Cahn. "The War on Poverty: A Civilian Perspective." *Yale Law Journal,* 73 (July 1964), 1317–52.

Doldbeare, Kenneth, and James W. Davis. "Little Groups of Neighbors." *Transaction,* 6 (March 1969), 34 ff.

Hallman, Howard. *Community Control.* Washington, D.C.: Washington Center for Metropolitan Studies, 1969.

Mogulof, Melvin. *Citizen Participation: The Local Perspective.* Washington, D.C.: The Urban Institute, 1970.

Moynihan, Daniel. *Maximum Feasible Misunderstanding.* New York: The Free Press, 1969.

Oakland Task Force. *An Analysis of Federal Decision Making and Impact: The Federal Government in Oakland.* San Francisco: Praeger, 1969.

Turner, John B. (ed.) *Neighborhood Organization for Community Action.* New York: National Association of Social Workers, 1968.

# CHAPTER 7

# THE WEALTH OF CITIES: SCARCITY AMIDST PLENTY

## *Phillip Weitzman*

Cities have historically been the storehouses of a nation's wealth. The great cities of ancient civilizations as well as our own have been the focus of abundant resources in terms both of material goods and of human talent. Our great urban centers are still the magnets attracting the most profitable industries and the most talented people. Yet even as the cities fulfill this task, the quality of goods and services available in urban centers deteriorates, and sources of taxable income dry up. Once this cycle is begun, it seems to accelerate. As services decline, those who would provide the income to pay for these services leave the cities to live in the suburban rings; as their money is no longer available, the quality of services goes down even further.

The only way to break this cycle, according to Phillip Weitzman, is to rearrange our methods of financing essential goods and services through a shift in some costs to the state and federal levels, while introducing new institutional forms of government to tackle metropolitan problems on a metropolitan scale. Only when the wealth of those who utilize the cities— but live elsewhere—is tapped will the problems of financing our cities be solved.

Phillip Weitzman is a professor of economics at New York University, and a specialist in urban finance; he is involved in the university's Metropolitan Leadership Program.

*A lot of the rules of our society will have to be changed before anything meaningful can be done to make right the wrongs of our most disadvantaged citizens. We should do it in the name of justice. We should also do it in our own self-interest. . . . There are economic advantages in doing what is just. But little will change without a political commitment from the larger society. It will not be enough simply to preach to the larger society that "perhaps the measure of a free, democratic society is the condition of life of its most abject citizens."*

—National Commission on Urban Problems

SOME of the greatest concentrations of real wealth and productivity ever known can be found in the metropolitan areas of the United States, particularly in the large central cities. Cities provide access to transportation and communications, a large pool of labor with all the skills necessary to support a modern industrial society, and a relatively easy journey to work. They are increasingly attractive locations for the fastest-growing and richest sectors of the nation's economy. But gradual changes in the nature of the American economy and continual internal population movements have redefined the social and economic role of the central cities.

Economic growth and affluence are ordinarily considered major blessings because they permit people to respond to new and better alternatives. And for the nation as a whole this may well be true. However, one of the major consequences of a dynamic economy is to increase the problems of governing and providing essential public services to those who live in central cities. Recently, these difficulties appear to have reached crisis levels. The number of Americans on local welfare rolls has risen dramatically to well over twelve million. Much of the burden of caring for them rests on the shoulders of the major central cities where, for example, in New York more than one out of every seven people is on welfare, in Newark where almost one out of three is on welfare, and in Washington where the figure is one out of ten. In New York

City alone during the five-year period 1966–71 the welfare budget increased 247 per cent to more than $1.7 billion per year.

Another critical area is public education. During the 1960s local school budgets doubled or even tripled. To cite a few examples, in 1961 annual public school budgets in Baltimore were $57 million, New Orleans $28.5 million, and Boston $35.4 million; in 1971 these figures rose to $184 million, $73.9 million, and $95.7 million respectively.

Local governments have been hard hit by this rise in costs and many have simply been unable to raise the necessary revenues. During late 1970 and early 1971 the nation witnessed an almost unparalleled number of reductions or serious threats of reductions in local public services. In Los Angeles the high school day was reduced from six to five instructional periods and almost fifteen hundred teachers and other employees dismissed. Teachers were laid off all over the country including Detroit, Chicago, and even some New York suburbs. School districts in Youngstown, Santa Barbara, Philadelphia, and Chicago edged to the brink of bankruptcy. City fathers reduced trash collections in Cleveland and San Diego; Baltimore ordered all departments to halt future planning; and Denver dipped into its capital construction funds to pay for current expenses. At the same time, local voters actively opposed increased local taxes, especially on property and rejected proposals for property tax increases and school bond issues at unprecedented rates.

Why, when cities are rich in productive wealth and economic power, are they rapidly becoming centers of poverty, decay, and fiscal bankruptcy?

## THE METROPOLITAN ECONOMY

Throughout modern history cities have traditionally been the centers of commerce, industry, and culture. People who produce or trade require access to their markets; they need rail, water, and air terminals and trans-shipment facilities. To support trade and manufacturing activities, they also require a concentration of service establishments such as banks, insurance companies, attorneys' offices, government bureaus, printing shops, warehouses, and showrooms. Small industries directly serving individual consumers must be near the center of population clusters to minimize their distribution costs. Similarly, educational, medical, and cultural institutions require large concentrations of population in order to attract sufficient patronage to survive. As the economy of the United States has grown, cities have become more and more the matrix of an industrialized nation. Manufacturers, bankers, scholars, professionals, and immigrants from the farm and from abroad were drawn to the cities for the expanding opportunities in profits, income, and social mobility they afforded.

More recently, however, changing technology and a growing desire for home ownership have altered the composition of economic output of metropolitan areas. This is most evident in manufacturing. Prior to the First World War most manufacturers (other than refiners or bulk processors) operated in loft buildings in high-rent districts in the downtown areas. One of the most extensive changes in manufacturing technology, however, was the introduction of continuous-material-flow systems and other automated processing methods, which made many of the existing plants and structures obsolete. Manufacturers now needed large single-floor sites to accommodate the newer and more efficient methods of production. As land assembly and acquisition costs in the downtown areas were increasingly prohibitive, entrepreneurs looked to the outlying sections of the city for large tracts of undeveloped and relatively inexpensive land. However, without the development of a large trucking industry, the non-central city manufacturers would have been denied access to urban markets and necessary transportation terminals. Without the automobile, busses, and extensive road construction the manufacturers would have found it difficult, if not impossible, to attract a labor force to staff the new plants. These factors combined to bring a net shift of manufacturing out of the downtowns (and gradually out of the central city) and enabled additional millions of people to break their ties to the city, many of them eventually moving into working class suburbs that began to spring up around the major cities.[1]

The exodus of manufacturing and population did not leave other sectors of the economy unaffected. As population shifted, local retailers, food markets, and personal service establishments (barbers, laundries, shoe repair, dry cleaning, etc.), which relied on close proximity to the population clusters, soon followed. Even more dramatic was the post-World War II development of the shopping center. Oriented toward the automobile, geared to one-stop shopping, and aimed at suburban tastes, these centers offered fierce competition to downtown shopping areas. In general, central city retail stores have been unable to meet this competition and are now gradually declining. Central city retailers are now confined to serving local residents, downtown office workers, and tourists, and to providing certain specialized products for the entire metropolitan area.

Wholesalers, while somewhat slower to respond, have also felt the centrifugal force which new transportation facilities and shifting population densities have exerted. These trends in population, manufacturing, retailing, and wholesaling are illustrated in *Table 1*.

Yet central cities are not suffering from severe economic problems; the city is simply losing those activities which it no longer handles efficiently, i.e., routine manu-

---

[1] Many southern and western cities that emerged following these technological changes were able to avoid the fate of the older industrialized centers of the East and Middle West. Instead, neither industry nor residences were ever really concentrated in a strong downtown and from the start were spread out far and wide from the nominal center of the metropolis.

TABLE 1

Suburban Ring Share of Standard Metropolitan Statistical Area[a]
Employment and Population, by Selected Years (1950 Central
City Boundaries)

| Item | 1948 | 1954 | 1958 | 1963 |
|------|------|------|------|------|
| Employment | | | | |
| Manufacturing | 33.1 | 38.6 | 42.0 | 51.8 |
| Wholesaling | 8.2 | 14.5 | 20.7 | 28.6 |
| Retailing | 24.7 | 30.6 | 37.2 | 45.4 |
| Services | 15.2 | 21.6 | 26.1 | 31.3 |
| Population | 36.0 | 43.5 | 48.2 | 54.3 |

[a] The Bureau of the Census defines a Standard Metropolitan Statistical Area as a county or group of contiguous counties with at least one city of 50,000 or "twin cities" with a combined population of at least 50,000. Contiguous counties must be metropolitan in character and socially and economically integrated with the central city. The definition varies somewhat for New England cities and towns.

*Source:* John F. Kain. "The Distribution and Movement of Jobs and Industry," in James Q. Wilson, ed., *The Metropolitan Enigma*. Anchor Books. Garden City, New York: Doubleday and Company, Inc., 1970, p. 30.

facturing, bulk wholesaling, mass retailing, and operations requiring large-scale land sites. For the most part these are not the fastest-growing sectors of the economy. The growth sectors are precisely those for which large- and medium-size cities are most appropriate umbrellas: banking, finance, insurance, communications, government, central office functions, convention facilities, and specialized medical, educational, and cultural institutions. Also remaining are those industries which feature rapid response to changing environments, such as high fashion, advertising, and publishing. Requiring continual face-to-face contacts among the decision-makers of various firms and institutions, each of these industries is able to draw upon the amenities of mass transit, restaurants, cultural opportunities, and interurban transportation that only the city can offer. Thus the downtown central business districts remain vital and dynamic elements of their metropolitan areas, although the suburbs and the outlying portions of the central cities are capturing increasing proportions of manufacturing, wholesaling, retailing, and now even some office functions.

### ECONOMIC GROWTH AND AFFLUENCE AS CAUSES OF URBAN PROBLEMS

These changes in the structure of the metropolitan economy have paralleled a trend of general economic growth and of increasing affluence for large segments of the American population. They have had profound effects upon urban life and society. In particular, a higher standard of living has reinforced the population movement to the suburbs and has burdened local governments with greater demands for public services.

Automobile ownership, a prime centrifugal force in American society, must rank among the most important causes of current urban problems. Demands for massive expenditures on traffic control, parking facilities, and highway and street construction have burdened all governmental levels, especially the municipalities. The escape to the suburbs has caused increased inner-city traffic congestion as people try to get to work in downtown areas. The widespread use of the automobile has caused not only an increase in noise and pollution but also a decline in the use of mass transit facilities, especially during the previously profitable off-peak hours. As demand and funds for mass transit began to dry up, many of the urban poor have been deprived of access to the jobs opening up in the outlying areas.

But perhaps the most serious consequence of America's economic growth has been the post-World War II waves of in-migrants to the central cities. Blacks, Spanish-speaking Americans, and Indians voluntarily migrated or were pushed into the large urban centers. They sought and expected to find the same educational and economic opportunities which accelerated the upward mobility of European and Asiatic immigrants. Instead they found serious racial and ethnic discrimination, and have been confined to low-wage unskilled jobs. Discrimination and poverty led to extremely overcrowded housing conditions and to the expansion of our central city ghettos. Truculent housing discrimination in the suburbs and inadequate mass transportation substantially hindered the ability of ghetto residents from taking advantage of the new jobs and better educational and shopping facilities in suburban areas. At the same time, the masses of relatively young urban poor greatly increased the need for schools, public housing, public health, medical services, and all the redistributive activities normally undertaken by local governments.

Thus the growing affluence, widespread automobile ownership, and federal home-ownership assistance have led whites gradually to abandon the central cities. While a few middle-class blacks and browns have been able to participate in this general suburban trend, our central cities are rapidly being converted into poor, racially tense, congested, and polluted areas whose governments are called upon to provide more and more services. The people who could afford to pay for these services, however, have left the city's jurisdiction.

THE POVERTY OF MUNICIPALITIES

Because cities are legislative creatures of the state governments, their specific powers and responsibilities are largely defined by each state. Generalizations about what local governments do can therefore be hazardous; nevertheless, a wide degree of uniformity exists in the functions and tax powers delegated to them. In most urbanized areas local governments provide schools, police and fire protection, traffic control and street maintenance, parks and recreation activities, and various social welfare services.

In addition, many localities assume responsibilities in waste disposal, public health, hospitals, urban renewal, mass transit, ports and harbors, etc. *Table 2* indicates the distribution of per capita local government expenditures both within and outside metropolitan areas.

Many studies have been undertaken recently to discover what determines differences in per capita expenditures on urban public services. Although some of the evidence is conflicting, higher local expenditures seem to vary according to per capita personal income, local property tax base, population density, amount of federal and state aid, and the city's non-resident (daytime) population. Surprisingly, total population of the local jurisdiction appears to have little effect on per capita urban government expenditures. But the implications of these findings are ominous. Population density and size of the non-resident population place severe pressure upon central cities to deliver more public services, yet they are being placed under increasingly stern revenue limitations in trying to provide these extra services.

*Table 2* shows that the primary source of local government revenues is the property tax. Traditionally, local governments relied upon the property tax as the only major means of taxation not pre-empted by the national and state governments. The federal government relies heavily on personal income taxes—one of the most broadly based and fastest-growing sources of revenue. States, on the other hand, have depended primarily on various business taxes, sales taxes, and automobile-related excises. The property tax provides 65.9 per cent of all self-generated general revenues in metropolitan areas; the other major sources of local government general revenues are general sales taxes (3.8 per cent), income taxes (3.1 per cent), and various charges levied on the beneficiaries of certain city services (15.3 per cent, e.g., public housing rents, hospital charges, parking meter revenues, museum and zoo admissions, etc.).

The heavy reliance on the local property tax is one of the root causes of municipal poverty. Because of greater

## TABLE 2

Per Capita Government Expenditures and Revenues, Within and Outside SMSAs, by Type, 1966–67.

| CATEGORY | Within SMSAs | Outside SMSAs |
|---|---|---|
| Direct General Expenditures | $330.32 | $245.11 |
| Local Schools | 143.19 | 132.30 |
| Capital Outlay | 20.49 | 18.10 |
| Other | 122.70 | 114.19 |
| Higher Education | 7.16 | 4.14 |
| Transportation | 25.21 | 27.82 |
| Public Welfare | 24.17 | 11.88 |
| Health and Hospitals | 18.30 | 13.70 |
| Police Protection | 16.73 | 6.56 |
| Fire Protection | 9.77 | 3.46 |
| Sewerage and Sanitation | 15.83 | 7.03 |
| Parks and Recreation | 8.70 | 2.41 |
| Natural Resources | 2.64 | 3.02 |
| Housing and Urban Renewal | 9.76 | 2.61 |
| Correction | 2.60 | 0.82 |
| Libraries | 2.90 | 1.40 |
| Parking Facilities | 0.90 | 0.41 |
| Administration and Control | 11.63 | 9.53 |
| General Public Buildings | 3.96 | 2.73 |
| Interest on General Debt | 12.16 | 6.46 |
| Other | 14.73 | 8.85 |
| Intergovernmental Revenue | 105.55 | 98.16 |
| From State Government | 94.83 | 92.72 |
| From Federal Government | 10.72 | 5.44 |
| General Revenue from Own Sources | 220.59 | 142.01 |
| Taxes | 171.33 | 103.06 |
| Property | 145.41 | 95.25 |
| General Sales | 8.31 | 1.80 |
| Selective Sales | 5.13 | 1.32 |
| Income | 6.75 | 0.56 |
| Motor Vehicle Licenses | 0.69 | 0.79 |
| Other | 5.03 | 3.33 |
| Current Charges | 33.74 | 28.82 |
| Miscellaneous | 15.52 | 10.14 |

*Source:* United States Bureau of the Census. *1967 Census of Governments,* Vol. 5. Washington: United States Government Printing Office, 1969, 222–23.

central city expenditures, property tax rates tend to be higher in the city than in its suburban ring. To the extent that high property tax assessments affect residential and industrial location decisions, the net effect is to encourage businesses and homeowners to leave the central cities. Furthermore, the greater the difference in property tax rates, the greater the resistance of property owners to the increased property taxation that would meet growing demands for public services. This brake on central city property taxation has the effect of starving city government and making it more difficult to provide a suitable urban environment.

Perhaps the most important effect of heavy dependence on property taxes is that the major burden of the tax is on the housing of local residents. In almost all areas of the country, property is taxed on the value of the land *plus* the value of the structures built upon it. Thus high property taxes discourage not only new housing construction but also the renovation and rehabilitation of deteriorating housing. High-density, luxury, high-rise apartment buildings then become the only profitable form of new-housing construction, while older middle- and lower-income neighborhoods in the cities deteriorate into blighted areas. Moderate income families who amass some small savings are increasingly attracted to the suburbs with their newer, more homogeneous neighborhoods and lower taxes.

Another equally unfortunate effect of the property tax system is the phenomenon of "fiscal zoning," by which large lots are required for any new residential construction. By zoning out low- and middle-income families,[2] upper-income suburban governments are able to provide superior public services at relatively low property tax rates. At the same time they force other less spacious political jurisdictions to shoulder the problems of low-income residents and to pay for the education of large numbers of children. Similarly, newer suburban municipalities are often

[2] The NAACP and other groups have recently challenged these zoning ordinances on the grounds that they violate federal and constitutional provisions on civil rights.

in a position to use their lower tax rates or concessions to attract large, "clean" industries or new housing developments to share the total tax burden. In both cases, the older, congested, and poorer central cities or suburbs are at a severe competitive disadvantage.

As a response to these detrimental effects of property taxes, many local governments have resorted to other forms of tax revenue. General sales taxes of 1 to 3 per cent have proved reasonably popular additional forms of taxation and small income or payroll taxes are now being adopted throughout the country. These two sources combined amounted to 8.8 per cent of metropolitan area local tax revenues in 1966–67, up from 7.6 per cent in 1962. Except at very low rates of taxation, these taxes can be self-defeating. For the most part, these additional levies are paid by those who live, work, or shop in the taxing locality. While it may be somewhat difficult to change the location of one's job, it is fairly easy to move or shop outside the city limits. These revenue sources are thus rather limited; cities must search for still other means to raise funds without losing the tax bases that support them.

One of the most promising devices is the "user charge." Because many of the services that local governments perform are for general purposes and not for particular individuals, funding out of general revenues is commonly accepted. Such government services include administration, police, courts, street lighting, public education, and certain services which are essentially redistributive in nature (e.g., public assistance, social services, etc.). But some local government services are not primarily redistributive, nor are the benefits completely diffused; instead individual users chiefly benefit. Many local governments already charge the direct beneficiaries all or part of the costs of providing these services, in the form of parking garage fees, water taxes, public housing rentals, swimming pool and tennis court fees, etc. Local governments face difficulty in extending this practice because people believe that public services should be provided "free" and equally to all who wish to consume them. What this amounts to, however, is a subsidy to many middle- and upper-income families to partake of these services *at the expense* of using scarce public resources for more general or more urgent uses.

It would have a number of beneficial effects if user charges were imposed on a more extensive basis to include additional aspects of sanitation and waste disposal, parks and recreation, libraries, highway usage, on and off street parking, and so on. First, it would encourage the present users of these services to economize on them. What was previously "free" would now require a payment better reflecting the cost of providing the service. Second, it would enable local governments to capture at least some of the costs imposed upon them by non-residents' use of these services. Many of the city facilities, such as zoos, marinas, museums, beaches, reference libraries, and cultural attractions, are not available in the suburbs. Third, user charges should ultimately allow a more equitable sharing of local tax burdens so that those who benefit the most will be forced to pay the costs to the greatest possible extent. If it were deemed desirable that low-income people should not be excluded from some of these benefits, then it is technically feasible to work out special provisions to provide for them. And finally, user charges could help reduce over-all tax burdens or at least release existing revenues for other, more urgent, needs.

The most rapidly growing sources of local public revenues are the state and federal governments, which account for about thirty per cent of revenue for public services in metropolitan areas. The states primarily support education, highways, and public assistance; while the federal government most heavily assists education, housing and urban renewal, waste treatment facilities, and airport construction. The effects of federal and state grants-in-aid can potentially be extremely important. They can help the cities pay for services that benefit individuals who live out-

side their immediate jurisdiction; they can alleviate disparities in local tax bases or expenditure requirements; and
they may help spread tax burdens more equitably over
the population.[3]

ALTERNATIVE APPROACHES TO SOLVING
URBAN FISCAL PROBLEMS

It should be apparent that if our large cities are to
survive economically and retain their ability to provide a
favorable environment for the personal development of
their residents, at the very minimum new sources of revenue will be required. Very possibly new institutions for
local government will be necessary.

As already indicated, cities are not entirely helpless in
working their way out of this dilemma. Many western and
southwestern cities are still legally free to annex outlying
areas; and some are expanding their tax bases by including some of the more affluent suburbs within their jurisdiction and by obtaining land suitable for further industrial and residential development. Local circumstances have
also permitted many urban areas to enjoy relatively low
property tax rates and to have other possible revenue
sources. While these untapped revenues should be used
wherever possible, there is always the danger that in the
competitive race for large tax *bases* (residents, industry,
business), high tax *rates* in one municipality become self-
defeating in time. Unless a city is providing noticeably superior services than its neighbors, higher tax rates can
be hazardous to its economic health. Higher demands for
public services and a greater concentration of poor people
make the central cities particularly vulnerable in this respect.

Another avenue that many cities themselves can explore

[3] See Chapter 12.

is land assembly for the creation of industrial parks. With judicious site assembly and attention to high-level services, older cities and suburbs may be able to exploit unique locational advantages and attract modern industry and employment. Care would have to be taken to attract those firms which have long-term growth potential and which provide a net social and economic gain to the city and region rather than additional burdens. Such a task is difficult yet feasible.

Expansion of user charges can also help to finance city services, especially to capture some of the costs of providing services to non-residents. User charges might be extended to tolls on bridges and tunnels leading into the city, museum admission fees, on- and off-street parking fees, and sanitation charges, among others. Frequently cities provide water, sewage, and other utilities to their suburbs. Sometimes cities prefer to subsidize some of their own residents by charging them less than full cost, although this may be a questionable practice. But it is inexcusable not to charge full or even more than full cost to suburban users.

Along these same lines, cities should explore the possibilities of taxing their non-residents. A number of cities have tapped this relatively unused source of revenue by imposing some kind of wage or income tax on all incomes earned in the city.

An idea that may be gaining some momentum is to relieve municipalities from financing certain services that are primarily area or nationwide in scope or importance. One such program that may soon be removed entirely from local financing is public assistance. The Nixon administration's Family Assistance Program and other similar measures would go a long way toward recognizing that relief from poverty cannot really be accomplished on the local level. There is little justification for requiring cities and states to pay for the problems resulting from nationwide population movements and long-term or cyclical unemployment. Federal responsibility for the program would also help to ensure some degree of equality of treatment for the poor rather than allow widespread disparities in benefits—a condition that may well tend to increase the in-migration of the poor into certain cities. In a similar vein, federal regulation and funds will ultimately be required to mount a comprehensive attack on air and water pollution; municipalities cannot effectively grapple with these problems because many of the offenders are situated in other local jurisdictions or states.

Another idea that is still in its infancy is to shift the financing of local public school systems to the state level. The central cities and older suburbs find it extremely difficult to finance an adequate school system through the

TABLE 3

Per Capita Personal Income, Local Taxes, and Current Public School Expenditures[a] in the Thirty-seven Largest SMSAs, Within and Outside Central Cities, 1964–65.

| Item | Within Central City (a) | Outside Central City (b) | Ratio/ (a/b) |
|---|---|---|---|
| Personal Income Per Capita | $2482 | $2552 | .97 |
| Local Taxes Per Capita | 173 | 137 | 1.26 |
| Local Taxes as a Per Cent of Personal Income | 7.0 | 5.4 | 1.31 |
| Current Public School Expenditures | | | |
| Per Capita | 82 | 113 | .73 |
| Per Pupil | 449 | 573 | .78 |

[a] Unweighted averages. If the averages were weighted according to the population of each SMSA, the disparities would generally be greater.

*Source:* National Commission on Urban Problems. *Building the American City.* Washington: United States Government Printing Office, 1968, 414.

property tax augmented by limited state and federal aid. This places the residents of these areas under further disadvantage because a relatively poor and newly urbanized population may require higher average expenditures and additional programs merely to provide an education equal in quality to suburban schooling. *Table 3* shows that even with lower per capita incomes and higher tax levels, central city school districts are spending less money per pupil than suburban areas. It is likely that both city dwellers and suburbanites will become more willing to allow the state to finance local public schools out of general revenue, leaving school boards with their present powers of administration and control. Not only would the property tax base be released for other purposes but—more importantly—a more equitable school system becomes more likely.

### INSTITUTIONAL CHANGES

Most observers would readily agree that our present high degree of political fragmentation within metropolitan areas contributes greatly to local fiscal and political problems. Highly fragmented jurisdictions force each municipal government to supply all or most local public services. They also allow for and perpetuate widespread disparities in local tax bases and rates because of the tendency for different areas to have varying concentrations of the poor, the affluent, the young, and industry. In addition, no single decision-making body has the power to deal with problems which affect the entire metropolitan area, such as mass transit, zoning, public assistance, and outdoor recreation. Political fragmentation also helps create a scarcity of professional public servants to administer local services.

Some individuals and interest groups are therefore turning toward the creation of new institutions designed to make area-wide decisions on an area-wide basis with area-wide financing. One of the more striking trends in metropolitan administration has been the proliferation of area-wide special purpose districts or authorities (SPDs). Usually the SPDs are charged with the responsibility of fulfilling one specific area-wide function, such as education, parks and recreation, sewage, harbor or airport administration, or soil conservation. Districts have the authority to borrow funds for capital construction projects and/or they are given the power to impose user charges or levy taxes (usually on property). Thus the SPDs are able to circumvent various restrictions that the states have imposed on local governments: debt limits, tax rate ceilings, civil service requirements, and confinement to a single local jurisdiction. The district authorities are thus able to attack problems on a regional basis, to ignore the everyday constraints of local politics, and to enjoy whatever cost savings may arise from a larger scale of operations.

The SPD device contains two severe limitations, however. Although some metropolitan services can be provided on a more unified and more efficient basis, there is still little or no *co-ordination* among services within one area. For example, there may be virtually no cooperation in the planning of airports, mass transit, and bridge and tunnel construction if these are the responsibilities of three entirely separate authorities. Secondly, the rapid growth in the number of SPDs in metropolitan areas to over seven thousand in 1967 (up over three thousand from 1957) has led to a further political fragmentation in urban areas. Although many of the districts are nominally responsible to an area-wide electorate the fact that increasing numbers of vacancies must be voted upon by the same voter makes it increasingly difficult for the individual voter to keep track of the activities of his representatives. The SPDs may therefore be more vulnerable to the influence of special interest groups than might otherwise be the case. Despite the advantages of the special districts, most reformers are opposed to their further proliferation because of the difficulties in control and co-ordination.

Those seeking to restructure local government have therefore turned to some form of metropolitan federation or consolidation. This idea has been presented in many forms, but the two most popular are (1) the creation of a new metropolitan government to integrate and administer area-wide services and planning and (2) the urban county, which would assume many of the functions now administered by municipalities without creating an entirely new governmental structure. The purpose behind these proposals is to provide some sort of federal political structure for an economically integrated area which would be consistent with the American tradition of local responsibility and control. Ideally, while metropolitan government would entirely or partially administer area-wide functions, purely local activities would remain the responsibility of existing municipalities.

These ideas immediately present two problems. The first is where to draw the line between local and metropolitan functions; where consolidation has been attempted, bitter disputes have erupted over the division of responsibility. Perhaps equally serious is the necessity for the county or metropolitan government to encompass the entire metropolitan area. If the political integration of the urban area is prevented by county or state boundaries, then many of the original problems may remain.

The idea of metropolitan federation or consolidation is not especially popular in the United States: out of eighteen consolidation referendums held between 1950 and 1961, the voters rejected ten. Both cities and suburbs are jealous of their own prerogatives and often oppose a major restructuring of authority. Although the spectacular success of the Metropolitan Toronto government has rekindled hopes among reformers, the emergence of black majorities in some of the older central cities has all but made consolidation a dead issue for most central cities and suburbs in the United States.

FEDERAL AND STATE REVENUE SHARING

Although local governments are not utterly destitute, in the long run new forms of revenue must be made available. Metropolitan consolidation and the SPDs may also help to ameliorate the problem. Yet the demands on local governments for more and better services are likely to expand faster than existing revenue sources. Thus most students of the problem ultimately look to higher levels of government to bail out the cities. The primary purpose of state and federal funds would be to mitigate revenue and expenditure disparities among localities. As noted above, many local jurisdictions are blessed with relatively large quantities of industry or high-income residents, while others suffer from a concentration of low-income families. Furthermore, those areas which have higher expenditure needs are most likely to find substantially increased tax efforts self-defeating. To be truly effective any additional federal or state aid would have to favor those localities with relatively higher ratios of needs to resources.

Since the 1930s the federal government has greatly expanded its aid to states and localities, particularly for education, housing and urban renewal, and public assistance. State aid to local governments has also increased markedly. Much of this conditional or matching aid has been highly desirable because either due to lack of funds or the fact that not all benefits accrue to local residents, the municipalities have been reluctant to spend money in specified areas. Furthermore, with some exceptions, the net effect of grants-in-aid programs has been equalizing among states and localities. This means that at least some of the disparities in local tax revenues have been alleviated. This system should be expanded because it gives impetus to programs otherwise lacking in appeal to local taxpayers. Examples of such programs are public assistance, sewage treatment facilities, mass transit, and all types of "demonstration" grants for experimental projects.

But conditional or matching grants, however beneficial, do not strike at the root of municipal poverty. The cities need a constantly growing source of revenue which will not damage their competitive positions with neighboring areas and which they can use for general purposes. This implies some sort of revenue-sharing device through which the federal and state governments will share their more elastic revenues with the localities. In particular, the federal government taxes personal and corporate incomes, which grow faster than the economy as a whole. If the national government were to earmark a fixed percentage of this tax base to state and local governments in such a way as to equalize the relative burdens of local taxpayers, it would be a giant step forward in reinvigorating our cities. Many variants of this idea are currently under discussion. However, some of the proposals before Congress do not guarantee that *any* of the funds would go to local governments; all would go to the states. Other proposals allocate federal revenues to states or localities on the basis of federal tax collections at the point of origin. This kind of proposal would offer little help to financially strapped central cities with their high proportions of the poor and the aged. To repeat, what is most urgent is to equalize tax burdens and to help those areas with the most pressing expenditure needs. Revenue-sharing schemes can easily be constructed toward these ends. A pilot program may soon be inaugurated on the federal level that will move the country in this direction.

## CONCLUSIONS

America is indeed a rich country. Its metropolitan areas are by far much richer than the remainder of the country; yet the central cities as well as much of their surrounding territories are in a deepening financial crisis. It must be repeatedly emphasized that America has the resources to meet its public service needs. What it lacks is the will. As the more affluent members of society have fled the central cities, they have tended to forget that their absence weakens the cities. But more importantly, as suburbanites resist the entry of blacks or other low-income groups, as they prohibit high-density housing, as they engage in "fiscal zoning," they are confining many persons to a life in the central cities. At the very least, the non-city dweller must begin to realize that he is a major contributing factor to the poverty of our central cities.

Some have suggested that the large cities should tighten their belts and attempt to live within their means. Such a policy would result in the erosion of essential services and the loss of even more jobs and middle- or upper-income families to the suburbs. But most importantly, if we do not rescue our local governments and ensure a high standard of public and social services, we will be abandoning the heritage of our cities as the place where new generations of Americans receive the skills and confidence to survive in an industrial society. Once this is appreciated, then the specifics of institutional changes or revenue sharing become mere technical matters.

## FOR FURTHER READING

Chinitz, Benjamin (ed.). *City and Suburb: The Economics of Metropolitan Growth.* Englewood Cliffs, New Jersey: Prentice-Hall, 1964.

Crecine, John P. (ed.). *Financing the Metropolis: Public Policy in Urban Economics.* Urban Affairs Annual Reviews, Vol. 4. Beverly Hills: Sage Publications, 1970.

Hoover, Edgar M., and Raymond Vernon. *Anatomy of a Metropolis.* Garden City, New York: Doubleday, 1962.

Jacobs, Jane. *The Economy of Cities.* New York: Random House, 1969.

National Commission on Urban Problems. *Building the American City.* Washington, D.C.: United States Government Printing Office, 1968.

Netzer, Dick. *Economics and Urban Problems: Diagnoses and Prescriptions.* New York: Basic Books, Inc., 1970.

Thompson, Wilbur R. *A Preface to Urban Economics.* Baltimore: Johns Hopkins Press, 1968.

Wilson, James Q. (ed.). *The Metropolitan Enigma.* Garden City, New York: Doubleday, 1970.

# CHAPTER 8

# CITIES AND THE ENVIRONMENTAL CRISIS

## *Betty D. Hawkins*

For most people, the environmental crisis conjures up images of polluted streams with dying fish, magnificent forests gutted by greedy loggers, and other similar ravages by man of nature. Yet the severest form of the crisis is to be found, not in rural areas, but in America's cities. Nowhere else is the air so poisonous, the water so polluted, the problems of waste disposal so immense. Smog, after all, is an urban phenomenon.

In a sardonic tour of the urban environmental landscape, Betty Hawkins points out that these problems are here—now—and unless we begin to grapple with them in new and imaginative manners, our cities will sink beneath piles of garbage and sludge. Moreover, she attacks those who would evade the responsibility of dealing with these problems, and calls for an increased citizen awareness and action.

Betty Hawkins has had wide experience in the field of environmental protection. She is a former staff member of the League of Women Voters of the United States, where she wrote a number of informational pamphlets on the environment. She is currently involved in the fight to protect the Hudson River basin.

WHEN every school child is at last being taught to appreciate and respect the interdependence of man and all living things on this earth, is it at all legitimate to focus environmental attention merely on the cities of the United States? In many ways, it is not. Controls and permanent solutions must indeed be rural and urban, national and international in scope. As with so many other crises, however, environmental dangers first come to a head in our highly industrialized, heavily populated cities. Like the pesticide-laden penguins found in the Arctic, the fast-deteriorating quality of urban life is a warning bell, a caution light, a barometer that indicates that something is out of whack. To use the technologically advanced United States and its urban concentrations as a laboratory, therefore, is not without validity.

We are only six per cent of the world's population, yet we consume about two fifths of the world's resources. The American family, with its increasing (though unevenly distributed) affluence, its insatiable demand for goods, gadgets, land, electric power, highways, chemically laden products and processes, jets, and recreational space, is putting at least twenty times more strain on the environment than is an average Asian family. The resultant contamination and exploitation of resources make us man's— and nature's—worst enemy. A few experts give us only thirty years of survival if we continue our arrogance against ourselves and our air, water, and land. Others talk in hardly generous terms of one hundred years. As C. P. Snow points out: "Technology, remember, is a queer thing; it brings you great gifts with one hand, and it stabs you in the back with the other."

In environmental terms, our metropolitan centers, where almost seventy-five per cent of the population is now concentrated on only three per cent of our available land, are vivid testimony to Snow's observation. Although no spot in the United States, from the top of Whiteface Mountain to the bottom of the Grand Canyon, is free from pollution, it is the urban dweller who is bombarded day and night by man-made insults. He is getting it in the lungs, the eyes, the ears, the nervous system, and the psyche, as well as "in the back." Although man is resilient, there are limits to his tolerance, unpredictable limits, psychological, physical, and especially political. Sheer frustration with an economic and social system which eagerly creates and perpetuates such assaults on man and his environment may force a change in direction sooner than some physical crisis will.

## DON'T BREATHE THE AIR

An air-pollution hazard exists which might cause a large segment of our people to experience temporarily illness or discomfort. Some increase in mortality is possible. I am therefore ordering 18 major industries and a hospital to cut back immediately on certain emissions. Citizens must cooperate and refrain from aggravating this situation.

This crisis warning on February 17, 1971, to the 130,000 residents of Chattanooga, Tennessee, drew back-page space, if any, in the nation's press. Such so-called "episodes" are considered routine. During the week of August 22–29, 1969, an area covering all or part of twenty-two states from west of the Mississippi to the Atlantic coast was subjected to an air-crisis affecting more than twenty million people. The London (1952), Donora, Pennsylvania (1948), and New York City (1966) episodes are, of course, classics.

Only a rainstorm saved the citizens of Birmingham, Alabama, from a five-day crescendo build-up of rust-colored soot. A temperature inversion had trapped and concentrated the level of pollutants from the huge steel mills and cement factories to over three times what is considered critical by federal agencies. A health warning was about all the local officials could manage, however, in face of a dilemma common to many cities. As one frustrated Birmingham official put it: "We are so damned economically dependent on the mills—all of us: the blacks, the whites, those who are making it, and those who are not—that we have to keep them open. Yet we know the mills and all of our other factories are contributing to our own ultimate death." The state's Attorney General, however, did not have to tread quite so lightly. While admitting that Alabama's present anti-pollution laws are all but worthless, he filed suit under an old "nuisance law" against thirteen Birmingham industries and demanded installation of control devices within six months or a close-down of the plants. A power struggle, with political and economic ramifications, is obviously underway, but if a plant is actually shut down, it will be practically unique in American history.

What, exactly, are the health effects of air pollution? The medical profession is by no means agreed on this question and is extremely loath to pinpoint certain pollutants as the direct cause of a specific disease. The complexity of the human body and the new variety of pollutants going into it makes this attitude understandable. Yet one has to wonder whether this tendency to insist on a body count before admitting the existence of danger is one of the reasons why more and more air- and water-pollution control programs are being removed from federal, state, and city health departments and put into separate agencies.

Medical experts do agree, however, that concentrated doses of air pollutants exacerbate a variety of existing diseases. The Maryland state medical society, for example, has issued a set of air-pollution-alert rules which persons with respiratory illnesses should memorize. In the above-mentioned Birmingham crisis, such persons were advised to vacate the city entirely. It is the sick, the aged, and the very young who are the most vulnerable, from a health standpoint, yet fetal defects, too, are believed by some researchers to be caused by pollutants let loose in our mutagenic society. Some members of our urban populations may be forced into pitiful bands of nomads, searching the countryside for some place merely to breathe and therefore survive.

If doctors need corpses as conclusive, scientific evidence, so be it. Such an approach may, in fact, help control the level of hysteria. But the citizens of Denver are not hysterical; they are downright angry. For 150 days in the year they cannot even see their mountains, so near yet shrouded in smog. In the Denver metropolitan region, auto registrations are keeping pace, at least one-to-one, with population growth. Mass transit is the only answer, admit officials, but meantime the citizens weep.

Although motor vehicles emit at least half of all air contaminants, some experts say that these emissions are not necessarily our most important problem because none of these contaminants is highly toxic, at least if mixed with air. They will dirty the landscape and bring tears to your eyes, goes the argument, but they won't kill you.[1] Removal of all or most of the tetraethyl lead in gasoline is supported by specialists, chiefly because lead particles in the exhaust interfere with the proper operation of certain types of catalytic-muffler devices which can cut down on other pollutants. The point, it seems, is to adjust one technology in order to make another function more efficiently.

How are industry and government reacting to the auto-emission crisis? On New Year's Eve, 1970, President Nixon signed into law a congressionally written bill stronger than his own proposals and much stronger than the auto-related industries wanted. It imposes a January 1, 1975 deadline by which time auto companies must make a ninety per cent reduction of hydrocarbons and carbon monoxide in auto emissions. January 1976 is the deadline for emissions of nitrogen oxide. A one-year extension of both deadlines was the compromise necessary in order to prevent defeat of the entire Clean Air Bill. The auto industry is giving grudging pledges that it will comply, though it still thinks

---

[1] Air samples taken in the Los Angeles area in 1962 and again in 1969 showed lead increases ranging from thirty-three to sixty-four per cent.

1980 would be a happier deadline date. Lobbyists against the bill made their own traffic jam in the Halls of Congress just before the vote. A partial list included representatives of the National Lead Association, American Petroleum Institute, Coal Policy Conference, American Mining Congress, Manufacturing Chemists' Association, the cement lobby, parts of the aviation industry, plus the "big four" auto-company presidents in person. That this concentration of power lost out is indeed a ray of hope, but governmental enforcement of deadlines will be the real test. Pressures, compromises, and backsliding are possible on both sides, but fear that research will soon turn up a viable substitute for the internal combustion engine may stimulate the auto industry to get moving.

Exhaust emissions are not the only problem created by motor traffic in our congested areas. Over sixty per cent of the land surface in many major cities has been meekly turned over, without plans and without restrictions, to auto-related functions such as roads, superhighways, bridges, parking garages and open lots, billboards, motels, service stations, and car washes. Ecologically, economically, and socially, this practice can spell disaster. Paved-over surfaces block needed absorption of water into the ground, forcing additional run-off and erosion, and in city after city, superhighways along riverbanks and coast lines are blocking access to the water by the very urban citizens who already lack adequate park and recreational facilities.

An alternative to more and more highway invasion into our metropolitan areas is, of course, decent and efficient public transportation. What we are being offered today, with few exceptions, is far from that. Bus and subway fares are going up; equipment and cleanliness are breaking down. Noise levels in older subways are intolerable; convenient facilities just don't exist. It is clear that some of the alternatives to highways take more imagination than money; others take a lot of both. Whether Congress is willing to buck the strongest lobby there is and divert some of the Highway Trust Fund monies to mass transit facilities is doubtful. Despite Lewis Mumford's delightful comment that "those who believe that transportation is the chief end of life should be put in orbit at a safe lunar distance from the earth," urban dwellers require and are entitled to a low-fare transit system which does not restrict their mobility, poison their lungs, or hamper job opportunities within expanding metropolitan areas.

Automobile, bus, and truck pollution may be the most constant annoyance to city dwellers, but belching smokestacks, long the symbol of prosperity, are pumping even more noxious junk into the air. Some of the emissions you can see; some you can't. The latter are often the more dangerous. Inefficient incinerators, cement plants, paper-making factories, power plants, steel mills, and oil refineries are only some of the stationary sources of air pollution.

Prodded by a newly aroused public and stiffer legislation, more and more privately owned factories are being equipped with filters, electrostatic precipitators, stack scrubbers, and other devices, to the tune of many millions of industrial dollars. But has industry as a whole made a total commitment to cleanup? The president of a major petrochemical company put it this way to a complaining stockholder at the 1971 annual meeting: "United States industry will not be made the scapegoat for the sudden urge of the American people to get a little fresh air in their lungs." The private sector, to be sure, has its own hard choices to make. Available quantities and quality of fuel, competition, technological know-how, and stockholder interests all play a role in just how good an environmental neighbor each plant is prepared to be—a concept, it must be pointed out, which has seldom troubled the corporate mind until now. As James M. Roche, chairman of General Motors Corporation, complained in a March 1971 speech in Chicago, "irresponsible" critics and even, at times, the government and the courts are subjecting free private enterprise to "a form of harassment unknown to businessmen in other times." It would appear that alert citizens are no longer content to settle for generous corporate donations to the

Heart Fund or the local Little League when they know that those same companies are angling in Washington to defeat environmental-control legislation.

Which level of government should set air-quality standards? As a matter of fact, the basic concept of setting ambient standards for separate pollutants is questioned by those who point out that the key question is not the quantity of each by itself but what happens when a pollutant mixes and mingles and combines with other known and unknown contaminants. Some conservationists have also questioned the concept of national standards, based on health considerations only, for fear that these minimum standards will become the maximum that any polluter will feel obliged to attain. They hope that states will be permitted to set stricter standards than the federal ones and that these stricter standards will hold up in court.

But standards, no matter who sets them, have yet, by themselves, to improve the emissions of one single factory. *Enforcement is the key to cleanup.* One need only recall that the Refuse Act of 1899 played little or no role in protecting our rivers and streams simply because, until 1969, it was never enforced. Local crack-down on air polluters, however, especially in one-industry cities, is particularly difficult, both politically and economically. U. S. Steel plants in Gary, Indiana, for example, employ three quarters of that city's working population. It is unfortunately not surprising that, until recently, air-pollution inspection and control of those plants has been almost as minimal as tax assessments on the corporation's property.

To get around this dilemma faced by many mayors and city councils, present federal law gives primary responsibility for enforcement to the states. Yet inspection personnel at the state level are totally inadequate, both in numbers and in training. New York State, for example, must check 90,000 major heating plants and 25,000 incinerators for compliance, plus over 100,000 industrial-emission sources, some of which must be analyzed by actual stack testing. With present stack-testing personnel—two teams of three men each—only about fifty stacks per year can be tested. "That work requires the nerves of a steeple jack and the mentality of an engineer," said a state official. "Not only can't we afford them; we can't even find them." Yet to rely solely on voluntary, or even required, emission reports from the factory managers themselves is hardly satisfactory, except perhaps in the minds of those officials who have permitted their own state pollution-control boards to be packed with representatives of the very industries to be regulated.

### MORE POWER, MORE POLLUTION

In no other area of national policy are the hard choices between an expanding economy and the need to protect the environment more sharply delineated than in the devilishly complex question of how, where, when, and at what cost we will produce electricity. Our highly industrialized society feeds like a glutton on electric power. "Brownout" has become a household word in the heavily populated northeastern states, especially in the New York metropolitan area, where Consolidated Edison—beside itself over how to cope—has suddenly flipped from high-saturation advertising to a public campaign to "Save a Watt." Its slogan would have been "Kill a Watt," said a company spokesman, had not its fellow private utilities flashed high-voltage objections.

The United States electric power industry, with revenues running at the rate of $30 billion a year, burns more than half the nation's coal, five per cent of the oil, and seventeen per cent of the natural gas. What happens in this industry happens also to our environment. Yet only one quarter of one per cent of its revenues are being spent on research to improve performance and devise new techniques for protecting the environment. The electric power industry in this country, unlike Britain, France, Russia, and Canada, does not even maintain a single major research and testing laboratory. It farms out the work to its local suppliers, whose objectivity could be debatable.

The types of fuels burned in electric generating plants play a major role in the types of resources we mine, be they oil, gas, coal, or uranium. What we burn we also reap by way of air pollutants. Use of high-sulfur coal and oil, for example (and low-sulfur-content fuels are in extremely short supply) forces over twenty million tons of sulfur dioxide a year into the air. According to Russell Train, chairman of the President's Council on Environmental Quality, "sulfur dioxide is the most serious pollutant in the atmosphere today, damaging and corroding $8 billion worth of property per year." About seventy per cent of the total sulfur dioxide being released into the atmosphere of metropolitan Chicago comes from coal-burning power plants. New York City's Environmental Protection Agency says that by 1975, almost twenty-five per cent of the city's total sulfur oxides will be coming from one single source, Consolidated Edison's expanded Astoria plant.

In the past fifty years, the United States has consumed more fossil fuels than in the whole previous history of the world. And through inefficient burning techniques, we are messing up the environment in the process. Almost two thirds of the heat in the fuels burned in conventional electric generating plants goes up the chimney or into the condensing water. What this released heat is doing to our climate and to aquatic life is not yet totally clear, but scientists throughout the world are concerned. Dilemmas like these are pressuring us to accept the fast breeder reactor, which promises unlimited supplies of fuel (plutonium) and no thermal pollution, but poses a lot of unanswered safety questions.[2] Breeder reactors, development of our oil-shale supplies, and research on gasification of coal are the heart of the Nixon administration's program announced in June

[2] "Since plutonium is the stuff from which Nagasaki-type atomic bombs are made, a black market could put the 5 kilograms of plutonium it takes to make an atomic bomb into the hands of anyone willing to pay." (*Science,* 9 April 1971, 143.)

1971, a program far short of a true national energy policy but quite satisfactory to the private utilities. The "power panic" is also offering oil- and gas-extracting companies a perfect alibi to develop immediately every new resource discovery without worrying about options for future generations.

Which fuels we burn is only one of the environmental problems connected with the electric power industry. Siting of new plants, whether fossil-fueled or nuclear, is perhaps the most sticky. Like highways and landfills and jetports, no one is especially keen on them as next-door neighbors. Yet utilities have naturally wanted to locate as near their heavy-load customers as possible to avoid expensive transmission facilities. Fossil-fueled plants, in fact, have been permitted, more or less without restrictions, along any river or lake where management saw a big market.

A new trend is noted, however, whereby power plants are locating near sources of coal rather than near their customers. Thus, new power plants are springing up in once rural or recreational areas, where the factory directors hope the pollution won't be quite so noticeable.

While the prospect of three hundred or more nuclear-powered plants in the United States within the next thirty years is being touted as the "clean" and inevitable solution to power demand, the safety factor of such plants is still strongly contested. An operational explosion, similar to a nuclear bomb, is simply not possible, according to reputable experts. It is hinted, however, that some present plants have developed low-level radiation leaks, due to faulty welding or other miscalculations, the consequences of which could be dire if not explosive. Although the effects, especially long-range genetic effects, of such leaks are not and cannot yet be documented, some scientific journals are claiming that medical X-rays may be far more harmful than the minuscule radioactivity escaping from nuclear-fueled power plants. Such reports, no matter how interpreted, are less than comforting. Another hazard involves back-up cooling systems, which AEC specialists admit do not yet function as planned. A Chicago-based group, Businessmen for the Public Interest, is actively challenging the AEC to perfect these emergency systems or close down power plants.

The accident factor is of special import when one talks of nuclear installations. Precautions, double and triple, are being taken, but so were they, according to the oil company, when two of its freighters ran into each other in San Francisco Bay. And who could believe that a naval ship, in San Diego Harbor for a washdown, would suddenly go to the bottom because the aft crew of workers went to lunch without notifying the forward crew? But if an earthquake occurred or an airplane happened to crash into a nuclear plant, it would not be just another horrible but isolated incident.

Many experts suggest that all nuclear plants be built underground, as is done in Sweden and Switzerland. Others insist that they should at least be isolated from high-density population areas. This has been standard American policy, but with the current pressure to expand production plus the difficulty of finding acceptable sites anywhere, rural or urban, the encroachment on metro areas has begun. While the Atomic Energy Commission is planning a "nuclear park" at the Hanford site on the Columbia River, where—not counting fish—the population is sparse, Consolidated Edison of New York plans at least five more nuclear units on the lower Hudson River, where the 1980 population will be enormous. Seven to ten plants are either underway or planned for the populated shores of Lake Michigan, and Southern California Edison Company talks of ten new nuclear facilities along the coast.

Both conventional and nuclear plants dump fantastic quantities of heated water back into our rivers and lakes, chiefly because management is not yet willing to install costly closed-cycle cooling systems. Disruption of the aquatic ecosystem is especially dangerous in very cold bodies of water, such as our Great Lakes. Yet that very coldness makes in-plant operations function much more efficiently.

As the Atomic Energy Commission has neither the statutory responsibility nor the interest to ask questions about potential dangers from thermal pollution, public-interest civic groups have taken the initiative. Citizen suits, for example, have forced plants near Gary, Indiana, and at South Haven, Michigan, to agree to installation of cooling facilities, even though the companies admit no guilt and no damage. They are only agreeing, so they say, in order to get on with production and get those silly citizens off their backs. But in a surprising but welcome move, the federal government, through its Environmental Protection Agency, has stepped into the dispute by proposing a strict thermal policy for the whole of Lake Michigan. All nuclear plants would be prohibited from dumping any heated water, and the twenty-four coal- or oil-burning generating plants already in operation around the lake shore would be required to add or upgrade cooling devices. Although this bold approach must be approved by the four states involved and may end up in court, it serves notice on industry that when ecological risks are involved, the government—as regards thermal pollution, at least—favors a go-slow, protective policy, if only to allow time for needed environmental studies. Eventually, thermal pollution may be taken off the crisis list, but one cannot ignore the fact that the waste heat generated by power plants has to go somewhere into our environment.

Far less optimism is permitted, however, concerning the disposal of the inevitable radioactive waste products from nuclear power plants. Like sewage treatment plants, nuclear power stations create a sludge product, a leftover, whose radioactivity can persist for thousands of years. Even the most ardent supporters of nuclear energy admit to a certain uneasiness about the potential hazards of present disposal practices. We have learned a few things since the infancy days of nuclear development when schools and homes in the Grand Junction, Colorado, area were built out of construction blocks molded from tailings and debris from uranium mines, but we by no means have definitive answers yet. The Atomic Energy Commission, in the meantime, has over eighty million gallons of high-level wastes on its hands, stored underground for the time being.

The problems involved in energy production are colossal, and a strong national energy policy is absolutely essential. We must expect painful readjustments if, in fact, environmental considerations are to be cranked into over-all policy. As William Ruckelshaus, former administrator of the Environmental Protection Agency, said in 1971: "We can no longer stand back and gaze with awe and wonder at where the forces of technology are taking us."

### DON'T DRINK THE WATER

To outline some of the complexities of environmental pollution from power plants is legitimate, but to itemize the present condition of our urban waterways is both obscene and patronizing; the facts are common knowledge, so common that they risk a banal acceptance. It is true that rivers and streams, and to some extent lakes, have an amazing ability to cleanse themselves, if given half a chance. But again we have overtaxed nature. As metropolitan areas have spread and bumped into each other and as the use of chemicals unknown just a few years ago has increased, so have the stench and the poison and the dead fish and the oxygen-consuming pollutants. One city's outfall pipes lie cheek by jowl with the next city's intake facilities. Beaches have had to be closed, fish caught in many urban rivers are inedible, epidemics crop up on occasion, and in some parts of the country, city dwellers take bets on whether their drinking water on Friday morning will be brown, foamy, or foul. A 1970 Bureau of Water Hygiene survey revealed that forty-one per cent of American water-supply systems tested were delivering water of inferior or potentially dangerous quality.

While air pollution comes chiefly from industrial sources, responsibility for the degradation of our waterways must

be shared by industry, agriculture, and the cities themselves. Many private companies are spending considerable
funds for new control equipment or in-plant process
changes in a genuine effort to comply with state and federal
standards; others, however, still cling to the old assumption
that United States waterways exist merely to carry away
industry's daily garbage. The February 1971 civil suit
brought by the Justice Department against the United
States Steel Corporation charged that the Gary, Indiana,
plant was continuing to pollute the Grand Calumet River
and Lake Michigan with discharges of oil, iron, ammonia,
phenols, cyanides, nitrogen, and solids. "A hazard to all
living organisms and to human health," the government
suit charged. A year earlier, that same company's Chicago
plants had to be taken to court; in June 1971, its facility
near Birmingham, Alabama, was on the carpet for dumping thirteen million gallons of waste per day into Opossum
Creek.

But municipal sewage from cities large and small is perhaps the most interesting facet of the water-pollution problem because the citizen, at the voting booths, is asked to
dip into his own pocketbook to clean it up. In the late
1950s and early 1960s, despite modest federal matching
funds and occasional state aid, bond issues to build sewage
treatment facilities went down right and left. The voters
of St. Joseph, Missouri, for example, voted at two different
elections (1958 and 1960) to reject construction of a
treatment plant. "We already have a sewer system," they
argued; "what more do we need, with the river right here
to carry everything away?" Meat-packing plants in the
area agreed, and continued to clog both the sewer pipes
and the river with their debris. The actual health menace
became so intolerable that the federal government began
court action, the first and only time, however, that it has
used its 1956 enforcement powers against a municipality.
Other cities along the Missouri began to think that they
might be next on the list, so a rash of bond issues was

passed. But most of the plants constructed with the new funds gave only minimal treatment to the sewage.

As more and more people woke up to what was happening to their rivers and lakes, as "sewage" became an acceptable topic for dinner table conversation, pressure built for more specific legislation and stricter standards. The concept of secondary treatment began to take hold, and treatment plant construction started in earnest. As recently as March 1971, however, the League of Women Voters of the United States testified before the Subcommittee on Air and Water Pollution, Senate Committee on Public Works, that "a public investment of $30 billion a year over the next five years is a modest estimate of what will be needed to reach secondary-treatment levels in the United States."

The sad truth is that we are barely holding our own. We are not spending enough money; we are relying on outmoded techniques. The western part of Manhattan alone is dumping two hundred million gallons of raw sewage per day into the Hudson, and treatment plants in the filthy Troy-Albany area are still not completed. From the Houston Ship Channel to the Great Lakes, the desecration continues. The city of Atlanta is dumping thirty-two million gallons of untreated wastes into the Chattahoochee River, in violation of both state and federal water-quality standards. Detroit, Cleveland, and Atlanta in 1971 were threatened with federal court action. Urbanism created the problem; urban America is still stewing in it. In early 1971, the Nixon administration suggested a federal contribution of $2 billion a year for three years to help all fifty states, yet treatment facilities for New York City alone will cost up to $1.5 billion. An equal amount will be needed if we are ever to clean up the Great Lakes.

Basically, we are still using a sixty-year-old technology, and one can only wonder whether plants now under construction will be obsolete before they become operative. Barry Commoner, director of the Center for the Biology of Natural Systems at Washington University in St. Louis, calls it "sheer insanity" to continue financing and building treatment plants that just cannot do the job. Every treatment process, current or proposed, seems to cause its own additional waste problem. Municipalities today, anxious to do their environmental duty, are totally frustrated in their search for a harmless dumping ground for the huge quantities of sewage sludge which are created as waste products from their treatment plants. In 1970, the Food and Drug Administration had to close a 120-square-mile area off the coast of Delaware and New Jersey to all shell-fishing operations, so polluted is that region from dumped sewage sludge. The city of Philadelphia had been burying its sludge in landfill sites, but with land no longer available for this purpose, city officials fear they must again turn to the sea. As a temporary solution, disposal beyond the Continental Shelf has been suggested, but that, too, raises serious doubts among oceanographers. Chicago is reported toying with the idea of pumping its sludge, which has a consistency "somewhere between that of tooth paste and maple syrup," according to one engineer, some one hundred miles to farm country, for use as fertilizer. Since most non-coastal cities incinerate their sludge, researchers are taking a serious look at the German practice of burning sludge as fuel for power plants.

When government officials suggested in 1971 that the sludge might be used to restore land that has been scarred by strip-mining operations, the Commissioner of the New Jersey Department of Environmental Protection warned that sewage sludge today "contains such a quantity and variety of industrial chemicals that it would probably kill everything in sight." Toxic industrial wastes from factories that have been allowed to share city treatment plants may become an increasing embarrassment to the decision makers. These joint industrial-municipal facilities have been strongly encouraged in the past ten years by both state and federal officials. Some metropolitan regions have even offered free use of their sewage facilities in order to attract tax-paying factories to their area. On the other side of the coin, housing developers, small industrialists, and shopping-

center promoters have won their way into the hearts of
local zoning boards by promising to finance joint facilities
in exchange for a variance on land use. Many expanding
suburbs have already been bamboozled by real estate developers who put septic tanks into totally unsuited soils
and then depart, leaving town officials and irate homeowners to cope. Burned once, mayors and alert citizens
will hopefully double-check the types of pollutants, as well
as the quantity, before opting for joint industrial-municipal
sewage facilities. When ecologically feasible, however, and
if industry really pays its full share to the city, this co-
operation can be a happy arrangement for both parties.

Older cities such as Boston, Hartford, New York, Albany,
Washington, and Chicago are plagued with yet another
type of joint facility, combined storm and sanitary sewers.
Urban runoff from certain types of composition roofs,
tarred highways, and salt-strewn roads carries all kinds of
crankcase oil, chemicals, paper, and street filth. At times
of heavy snow melt or rain, the treatment plant at the receiving end of these joint storm and sewer pipes just can't
handle the volume coming in. The in-flow is cut off, forcing
both rain water and raw sewage to bypass the plant and
careen into the nearest river or lake. Estimates for actual
separation of sewer and storm pipes run into the many
billions of dollars, and the process would involve ripping
up practically every street in every city in the country.

## CO-OPERATION AND SANITY

The municipal sewage problem is not a simple one, financially or even technologically. Politically, however, environmental crises have promoted some long overdue co-
operation among neighboring jurisdictions which previously
had been operating in isolation. Recognizing that air,
solid-waste, and water pollution do not respect political
borders and that uniform standards and/or economies of
large-scale collection and treatment may prove to be more

practical for each of them, urbanized communities are beginning to think in terms of regional solutions.

In the Seattle area, for example, where water recreation is a way of life and where suburban populations have been doubling every few years, the voters finally realized that if the offensive pollution of Lake Washington and Puget Sound were ever to be halted, the job could not be left to each of the 130 different units of local government within King County. After an unbelievably dogged citizens' campaign, including several setbacks, the voters in 1958 approved creation of the Municipality of Metropolitan Seattle, with a mandate to handle all sewage disposal for the region. Construction of four new treatment plants, one of which is the largest in the Northwest, proceeded on schedule, and by 1970 Lake Washington and Seattle's commercial waterfront were once again available to the people, free from sewage pollution. Although the citizens of Metropolitan Seattle did not go so far as to include solid waste, transit, air-quality control, or land-use planning within the functions of "Metro," the mechanism is there; the experiment in regionalism has begun.

Pressure from environmentalists in the San Francisco Bay area has forced another interesting type of regional approach. Shocked into action when they saw their precious bay resources being eaten away, acre after acre, by unrestricted dredging and filling and diking, concerned citizens lobbied the California Legislature to establish the San Francisco Bay Conservation and Development Commission. Charged with protecting the waters of the bay and reconciling shore line development with good conservation practices, the agency was made permanent in 1969, and its protective plan for the bay has been accepted.

Leaving in abeyance any evaluation of specific forms of co-operation, it is clear that recognition of real or potential environmental problems is adding a powerful stimulus toward creating structures of government more relevant to an urbanized society. If these new organizational patterns can, at the same time, incorporate better decision-making techniques, with citizen participation built in from the start, the environmental movement will have accomplished what many social scientists have advocated for years. How government responds to change—to new conditions, to people-oriented needs, to environmental imperatives—that is the challenge. So far, at least, the boldness, the imagination, the insistence on new budgetary priorities, and the courage to challenge corporate-political power and governmental structure have originated with citizen groups.

To satisfy an ever-growing market of consumers who have happily accepted and supported a throwaway economy, our production-oriented society continues to cut the forests, mine the limited resources, and dream up new types of indestructible plastics to wrap and double-wrap products that nobody needs. In the U.S.A., every man, woman, and child, on the average, creates *six pounds of solid waste per day*. How to get rid of the junk has concerned no one, with the possible exception—now that we are being swamped—of a few mayors, some congressmen, a handful of engineers, and an awful lot of citizens. Disposal questions, such as air and water pollution, are seldom cranked into cost-benefit analyses before products hit the market.

Enlightened officials, planners, environmentalists, and concerned citizens, disillusioned with ocean-dumping, burning, or burial, are looking in the seventies to re-use and recycling. Both big cities and small villages are submitting legislation to ban the non-reusable bottle, tax the non-destructible container, and require a percentage of reprocessed content in certain goods such as coat linings. Private bottling companies are conducting active campaigns to collect, recycle, and re-use containers, and others are researching new techniques for separating and salvaging trash. New York State is discussing, only halfheartedly because of a fiscal squeeze, the potential of so-called recycling parks, where solid waste from a whole region would be collected, separated, and treated for re-use. Factories right on the spot would, in turn, produce new products from the re-claimed materials.

At the federal level, Congress in 1970 passed the Re-source Recovery Act, authorizing $463 million over a three-year period to help local and state governments plan and build solid waste disposal-and-recovery systems. Meager as that authorization was, President Nixon, in his 1971 budget message, requested only $19 million for the fiscal year 1972. Divide that among the fifty states and our major metropolitan communities and its inadequacy is obvious.

Although Congress has taken this first small step, old national policies which encourage the gobbling up of our natural resources go on unchanged. It is cheaper, through various subsidy or tax arrangements, to transport virgin ores than it is to ship reprocessed scrap metal; lumber companies get depletion allowances, but paper-recycling plants get no bonus at all. At a national meeting in early 1971 on the state-of-the-art in solid waste management, attended by specialists from industry and government, several speakers admitted that in today's economy, it is cheaper to continue to use virgin materials than to gear up for recycled goods.

Whenever this passion to deplete our natural resources is questioned, some official or "interested party" is bound to salute the flag of national security. Under that banner, pressures build for new pipe lines, more exotic aircraft, offshore oil drilling, and excessive lumbering and mining of our nationally owned lands. Next in line will be the mysterious ocean floor. Military weapons on the sea bed, food for all humanity, incalculable mineral wealth, scientific deep-sea labs—all sorts of projects are being dreamed up, in the name of God and country, for that next frontier. Whether ecological warnings will be heeded remains to be seen.

Important as is the ocean floor, perhaps the most threat-ened natural resource today is the fragile coast line, with its estuaries and salt marshes. This uniquely dynamic and biologically productive zone, part river and part sea, is constantly under assault from urban pollutants, governmental projects, and developers who just cannot pass up the profits from shore-line exploitation. Port development, bridges, highways, marinas, power plants, apartment houses, dredging and filling operations, garbage dumping, and airport expansion are some of the major intruders into this fertile estuarine zone. The nation's seven largest metropolitan areas are on the ocean coasts or the Great Lakes, bringing with their increasing population all the pressures of an industrialized society. Coastal counties contain only fifteen per cent of the land area of the United States, but one third of the population and two fifths of our manufacturing plants are located there. The impact is staggering, and both federal and state governments are realizing the necessity for protective legislation. Despite strong opposition from private interests and even a few local governments, almost all of the coastal states now have some form of control on their books. However, in 1970, broad coastal management bills were defeated in both the state of Washington and in Rhode Island. The Washington proposal was successfully opposed by builders and developers; the Rhode Island bill ran into local government opposition. In New Jersey, too, state legislators from the very shore areas to be protected tried their best to scuttle a bill which finally passed in September 1970. Long-range environmental protection will always have a tough fight against the lures of short-term profit.

But some interesting and hopeful decisions have already been made. In June 1971, the Delaware Legislature passed a most unusual bill banning all heavy industry from the coast line, despite pressure from the chamber of commerce, the oil and gas industries, cargo shippers, and even the U. S. Departments of Commerce and the Treasury. In signing the bill, Governor Peterson gave credit to the numerous citizen groups "who came forward to help combat the tremendous professional lobbying brought to bear" against the legislation. "Jobs are very important to our people," he said, "but so is the over-all quality of our environment." Oregon, always protective of its public beaches and now fearful of a heavy in-migration from other states, has placed a moratorium on any coastal construction which might interfere with its estuaries. As has been mentioned, the San Francisco Bay Conservation and Development Commission has come up with a comprehensive control plan for that huge estuary. A recent National Academy of Sciences report has recommended defeat, chiefly for environmental reasons, of a proposal to extend the J. F. Kennedy Airport into New York's Jamaica Bay.

Although government-owned lands are occasionally mismanaged (or misleased in order to fill strained coffers), public acquisition of endangered shore lines is unquestionably the most reliable route to permanent protection. The costs of delayed action, financial and especially ecological, can only go up.

If we are beginning to protect our estuaries, will this new environmental awareness penetrate our attitudes and policies toward land use in general? Could we not, for example, halt the ecological folly of building on flood plains and paving over the few remaining farm lands near urban areas? Future state or federal incentives to encourage population dispersion and wise industrial location is not an unrealistic prediction, but it will call for a new, creative breed of planner, politician, and public attitude.

A land-use planner from Alaska is reported in the press to have come to this conclusion: "Managing the environment," he said, "is the most radical movement in the last two centuries. It makes private ownership almost meaningless."

The decisions and revisions called for in the seventies —be they concerned with a steady-state economy, cost/benefit formulas, pricing, public management, governmental structure, new-city concepts, social myths, or personal habits—will demand open debate of all conceivable alternatives. The one issue not open to debate, despite the inevitability of trade-offs, is fundamental ecological truth. We must learn to put the balance of nature ahead of industrial expansion whenever the two conflict. This is no "disaster" theory; it merely suggests that the decision-makers think ecologically before they act destructively. Putting ecological health ahead of economic expansion does indeed have radical implications. It could require a total reorientation of our production and consumption patterns, our biological reproductive excesses, our corporate-political power structure. But nature itself has set the parameters; man must respect them, no matter how painful the adjustment.

## FOR FURTHER READING

Bryerton, Gene. *Nuclear Dilemma.* New York: Ballantine Books, 1970.

Disch, Robert (ed.). *The Ecological Conscience: Values for Survival.* Englewood Cliffs, New Jersey: Prentice-Hall, 1970.

Dubos, Rene. *So Human an Animal.* New York: Charles Scribner's Sons, 1968.

Ehrlich, Paul R., and Anne H. Ehrlich. *Population, Resources, Environment.* San Francisco: W. H. Freeman, 1970.

Esposito, John C. *Vanishing Air.* New York: Grossman Publishers, 1970.

Helfrich, Harold W., Jr. (ed.). *Agenda for Survival: The Environmental Crisis—2.* New Haven: Yale University Press, 1971.

*Man's Impact on the Global Environment: Assessment and Recommendations for Action.* Cambridge, Massachusetts: Massachusetts Institute of Technology Press, 1970.

Meek, Roy L. and John A. Straayer (eds.). *The Politics of Neglect: The Environmental Crisis.* Boston: Houghton Mifflin, 1971.

Roos, Leslie L., Jr. (ed.). *The Politics of Ecosuicide.* New York: Holt, Rinehart & Winston, Inc., 1971.

Starr, Roger. *The Urban Choices: The City and Its Critics.* New York: Penguin Books, 1966.

Taylor, Gordon Rattray. *The Doomsday Book: Can the World Survive?* London: Thames and Hudson, Ltd., 1970.

Whyte, William H. *The Last Landscape*. Garden City, New York: Doubleday, 1968.

# CHAPTER 9

# THE CRISIS IN URBAN EDUCATION

## *Daniel U. Levine*

Historically, Americans have turned to the school systems for aid in solving numerous problems caused by social dislocations, and for the most part, the schools have responded well. Certainly the school system played the major role in Americanizing millions of immigrants and training them for absorption into a pluralistic society. Yet in the most severe crisis of the last one hundred years, the social strain created by urban problems, the schools have been slow to respond, and their responses have so far been futile.

The problem is twofold, according to Daniel U. Levine. On the one hand, schools do not address themselves to social reality, and thus have lost their authenticity with the parents and children they are supposed to serve. On the other, the general stratification of our society has placed intolerable stress on the school system. Moreover, children of all classes are affected. While the poor and the black may feel it most, there is undeniable evidence that schools are failing the children of blue-collar and middle-class families in both cities and suburbs. While specialists and interested laymen both have suggested possible solutions to this problem, the chances for solving it are bleak as long as we view schools out of the social context in which they function.

Daniel U. Levine is involved in education as teacher, researcher, and active community participant. The author of numerous articles and pamphlets, he is currently head of the Center for the Study of Metropolitan Problems in Education at the University of Missouri in Kansas City.

TEN YEARS ago any discussion about a "crisis" in urban education most likely would have begun with references to an "impending" crisis. By 1970, big-city school districts were releasing reports which showed, for example, that one fourth of the pupils in the New York City public schools were reading two or more years below grade level and forty per cent of the pupils in Philadelphia were below "functional levels" needed to handle basic texts. But problems in the schools were by no means confined to inner-city neighborhoods inhabited mostly by racial and ethnic minorities: a New York City survey indicates that reading scores in "predominantly white areas seem to be going downhill faster than [in] predominantly nonwhite areas," and alienation among students emerged as a major force in sedate middle-class neighborhoods. A study released by the House Subcommittee on General Education reported that nearly one fifth of the nation's high schools experienced "serious student protests" in 1969. The crisis has arrived, and it is insolubly linked to problems of authenticity, identity, and motivation experienced by large numbers of young people in differing parts of the metropolitan area.

## ECONOMICALLY DISADVANTAGED INMATES OF THE INNER CITY

Behaviorist psychologists have been laboring for years to show that man, like other animals, generally will tend to repeat behaviors that are reinforcing and to cease behaviors that are non-reinforcing. Behavior patterns are thus strategies for obtaining rewards and avoiding punishments.

Something curious happens, however, when an animal's responses to threats and other stimuli in its environment bear no consistent relationship to whether it is rewarded or punished for how it responds. For example, dogs which are placed in a conditioning apparatus and are given electric shocks regardless of what action they take soon learn that their responses indeed make no difference in determining what happens to them. They have learned that they are powerless to control their environment and are at the mercy of hostile external forces which determine their fate.

Humans, too, can be taught that living is primarily frustration, that hostile, external forces are working to ensure their defeat, and that lackadaisical behavior at least has the virtue of temporarily relieving frustration by providing them with something to do. Such a response pattern, in fact, is exactly what is being taught to hundreds of thousands of economically disadvantaged youngsters confined by socio-economic stratification and racial segregation to the inner-core parts of the metropolitan area.

For a substantial proportion of youngsters in the inner city, a frustration-avoidance pattern is achieved by placing a child in a social and physical environment in which:

— curriculum materials used in the school deal with unfamiliar or uninteresting subject matter; educational tasks require skills they have not previously mastered or even had an opportunity to master; thus, no matter how much you are trying to help a child succeed, he will fail continually and will regard school not only as a dreadful bore but also as a threat to his self-esteem.

— the great majority of the people whom he sees in his neighborhood have achieved at best only a very modest amount of economic success though many of them work very hard and some have a good deal of formal education. He sees that people like himself and his family are destined to fail no matter how hard they try to make good, and thus that it doesn't really matter whether or not he succeeds in the school or other parts of the "straight" world. He now has all the excuse he may need to opt out of a difficult competition for which he knows he may be inadequately prepared in the first place.

— opportunities to engage in activities much more exciting and prestigious than those likely to be found even in the most stimulating classroom are near at hand and easy to join. A large and influential peer group is present, with opportunities to engage in gambling, illicit sex, hard narcotics, and other "adult" activities, making it difficult and in some cases impossible for parents to maintain control of their children against the competition of the streets.

In short, if you set out to develop behavior characterized by hopelessness and frustration, your goal would be achieved by placing young people in an inner-city environment in a large metropolitan area, and it is not surprising that many of the people confined to this environment exemplify attitudes and behaviors characteristic of the role of prisoner.

### ILLEGITIMACY OF THE SCHOOL IN THE INNER CITY

Referring to the school as being not "legitimate" to many economically disadvantaged students does not mean that the school necessarily is viewed as having no right to function in an inner-city neighborhood, nor does it mean that education is perceived as an undesirable activity or a useless commodity. As a matter of fact, inner-city families—especially black families—generally place very high value on obtaining an education and strongly believe that educational attainment is the best route to social mobility. What it does mean is that the inner-city school typically does not function as an integral part of the neighborhood in which it is located and is not attuned to the problems and characteristics of the children whom it serves.

Schools frequently are foreign elements in the lives of inner-city students and in the affairs of inner-city neighborhoods. The language used in the school is usually standard English, but many inner-city students speak nonstandard dialects or languages other than English at home, and do not understand or utilize abstract concepts in the standard dialect. Curriculum materials still tend to deal primarily with concepts and phenomena which are outside the immediate experience of the inner-city child; thus they violate one of the best established principles of psychological research—namely that material is likely to be better learned if it is meaningful and practically important to the learner than if it is foreign and insignificant to him. In addition, to function successfully in existing schools generally requires a good deal of independent activity on the part of the learner, but inner-city students frequently have not learned how to work this way in the classroom.

These examples of lack of fit between the school and inner-city realities are obvious and well known, but surprisingly little has been done to modify curriculum and instruction in the inner-city school. Objective surveys as well as the reports of countless observers indicate that for the most part the curriculum in inner-city schools and the instructional methods used to teach it are not fundamentally different than they were ten, twenty, or thirty years ago. In most cases, changes to reduce the illegitimacy of the school in the inner city have been superficial and piecemeal.

One reason is that effective change on a wide front costs money, and big-city school districts do not have the financial resources to underwrite massive reform. Another reason is that hunger, poor housing, and other environmental conditions which hamper learning still exact a heavy toll in the lives of residents of the inner city. An equally important consideration, however, is that reform proposals more often than not have been based on a one-sided frame of reference. School officials frequently have limited themselves to asking how the child can be helped to adjust to the school, not *how the school can be changed to help the child*. School critics often have been wedded to one or another simplistic prescription calling only for change in the institution: if teachers would expect more of the child, if the school would recognize and respect the human worth of the child, the academic deficits of disadvantaged students would be largely overcome. Neither of these one-sided positions is likely to prove helpful. That is, if disadvantaged children are to succeed in our schools, the schools themselves will have to undergo comprehensive change.

Few schools in the United States have been very effective in the sense of motivating and guiding pupils to learn a fraction of what most are capable of learning. Students who have come to school well prepared for existing programs and highly motivated to succeed in them have tended to learn a good deal, and students to whom the school has seemed foreign and artificial have learned very little. Social class and family background correlate highly with motivation and preparation to succeed in existing school programs. Unless it is presumed that youngsters from poorer families are born with fewer of the intellectual and attitudinal resources needed for success in the schools, the only possible conclusion that can be drawn is that the schools simply have not been able to affect substantially the social and educational advantages and disadvantages that accrue to individuals as a result of their social class and family background.

Approached from this perspective, the problem of educating disadvantaged students reduces itself to that of overcoming the obstacles which have made the public schools as a whole—not just the inner-city schools—generally impotent. Instructional practices and organization must, therefore, be radically improved to achieve goals that educators have futilely reiterated for at least fifty years. The challenge in the inner-city school is to live up to ideals that till now have received plenty of verbal affirmation in American education but precious little real implementation.

Among the more important items on any agenda designed to implement this goal are reorganization of curriculum and instruction, to allow a greater focusing on the actual needs of the individual learner; the adaptation of modern technological tools to facilitate learning and to use more effectively the teacher's time and abilities; a restructuring of the school and its administration, to connect the teachers and supervisors with their clients, the students and the community.

Beyond making schools more effective regardless of the social class of their students, inner-city schools must place special emphasis on activities which might counteract the isolation and powerlessness of its clients and the illegitimacy and "foreignness" of the schools themselves. Here again the remedies have been repeated time and again, but have failed to be adopted, and thus bear reiterating: increasing the independence and self-control of disadvantaged students, so they can cope not only in the classroom but in the real world outside; effecting greater involvement and/or control by the community, to reinforce the basic tenet that the schools exist to serve the community, and not vice versa; minimization of the "failure syndrome," by replacing the criteria of the bureaucrats with those attuned to the needs and experiences of the children. In addition, inner-city students need to have a greater self-definition, a more positive image of themselves and their antecedents, to counteract the crippling psychological blows they receive in their daily lives.

The importance of insisting that any plan for improving inner-city education must be comprehensive and systematic is difficult to overemphasize. Despite large expenditures, compensatory education programs generally have had little or no discernible effect on academic achievement, but they seldom have been given a fair testing. In most cases, for example, teacher retraining programs have provided only a fraction of the amount of training required to bring about a substantial change in classroom methodology. Where substantial retraining programs have been conducted, training often has concentrated *either* on improving teachers' understanding of disadvantaged students *or* on developing skills useful for teaching in the inner city;

neither approach by itself can be expected to result in much improvement in the performance of disadvantaged students. Where adequate training has been provided for some teachers, its effects usually have been dissipated in a few classrooms without changing the norms and expectations held by a majority of students and teachers. In the few cases where a unified faculty effort has been made, little has been done to involve parents in an effort to unify the school and the home. Such piecemeal attempts at reform offer little hope for making the school a more legitimate and influential institution in the lives of children who are castoffs within metropolitan society.

For a substantial and possibly growing minority of inner-city youngsters, however, alienation from the school already is so great that even the best-conceived and most comprehensive plans for institutional reform will make little difference. For students who have long since psychologically dropped out of school after repeated failure or who are so hostile toward the institution that its expectations hold virtually no meaning for them, what is called for is not so much institutional reform as new institutional settings; that is, the only way the goals of the institution can be achieved is by transforming the institution to reduce or eliminate the chasm.

## MIDDLE-CLASS BREAKOUTS OF THE SUBURBS

Not too long ago a treatise on the crisis in urban education could be limited almost entirely to a consideration of the problems of disadvantaged students in the inner city. Today the situation of youngsters in relatively homogeneous upper-middle-class communities in outlying parts of the city and its suburbs manifestly has become almost equally critical.

Many reasons might be given to account for the increasingly visible revolt which has been taking place among upper-middle-class students in suburban communities. Even though too little empirical evidence is available to identify the underlying causes with any degree of finality, there is little doubt but that the alienation of youth in suburbia—and hence in suburban schools—centers on the same general issues of authenticity, identity, and motivation which are responsible for the crisis in inner-city education, and, in fact, create almost mirror images of dissatisfaction and protest.

Whatever else one may think about the middle-class suburb, it often fails to provide much sense of reality for the young people who grow up in it. By definition, the suburb is only a small slice of modern urban society, a slice designed to achieve placidity, security, and domesticity—exactly the qualities which young people must learn to transcend as part of their struggle to make their way in the larger society. If it is youthful oversimplification to capsulize these communities as "plastic" and "one-dimensional," at least these terms aptly communicate the aura of unreality and inauthenticity which suburban institutions apparently are generating among middle-class youth.

Another factor tending to detach young people from established institutions such as the school is the effect that relative affluence[1] has on perceptions of social reality. Since most middle-class youngsters no longer have to take part in a desperate struggle to earn the necessities of life, schooling is less likely to be valued primarily as a means to acquire material possessions. For this reason, the school must become meaningful in its own right rather than assuming, as it has till now, that an economy of scarcity will invest it with unquestioned importance.

[1] As used here, the term affluence does not suggest the absence of major financial difficulties and concerns among middle-class families but rather refers to what Orr and Nichelson have termed a "state of mind," which "has to do with relaxation from primal economic fears and with the belief that a number of satisfying options are financially possible . . . The middle-class youth may choose to drop out and assume an impoverished style of living, but the mark of his affluence is his ability to drop back in at will."

Whereas the problems faced by inner-city youngsters are associated first and foremost with unequal and insufficient opportunities, the difficulties experienced by middle-class youngsters are tied to a surfeit of available opportunities. Since a limitless range of opportunities seems possible in this type of society, with its instantaneous exposure to a bewildering variety of life styles and cultural patterns, it has become more difficult for youth to work out a stable and personally rewarding identity. At the same time, the empiricism which flourished in Western culture during the past five hundred years developed an openness to experience which makes it conceivable—indeed, for some, obligatory—to try out numerous roles and identities. For a person to function successfully within an institution such as a school, he must know who he is and why he is there.

An obvious reason upper-middle-class students question the credibility of major social institutions is that they are better informed and more knowledgeable about the immense gap between social ideals and social realities in the United States than any large group of middle-stratum young people has been in the past. To a degree, awareness of this gap reflects the relatively high level of education and cultural awareness attained in the middle class, but it also reflects the development of national and international mass communications. Upper-middle-class youth constitute the first sizable sub-culture in the United States to realize that science and technology by themselves not only do not guarantee but in some ways block social progress and the fulfillment of human needs. Youth faces a dilemma similar to that which confronted Western society hundreds of years ago when the Church lost its central influence, except now the dilemma is more excruciating because the forces of modernity which discredited religious views no longer provide a plausible alternative to replace what was discarded.

One frequently noted cause of dissatisfaction has been the emergence of career patterns that require many years of attendance in high school, college, and graduate school. Some observers believe that prolonging adolescence through a decade or more of educational training makes neither economic nor psychological sense of any kind; others point out that definite social functions are served by keeping unskilled young people out of a technological economy. When schooling becomes a highly competitive struggle to prepare oneself for still more rigorous competition in abstruse future tasks at which only a few are likely to excel, educational institutions are apt to be questioned and rejected by participants whose commitments to their goals and traditions are less than total.

Many middle-class youth who tend to value independence do not always adhere to philosophies favoring individuality. Social scientists have painstakingly demonstrated over the last decade that middle-class parents explicitly set out to raise children who can handle the initiative and independence required to make the sophisticated decisions which are the essence of upper-middle-class professions. Yet, the very same forces which require that young people be socialized to think and act independently also tend to place them in institutions in which they are expected to be conforming and dependent. "Automatized and computerized industry," historian Staughton Lynd has pointed out, "requires more and more young men and women who have white-collar skills but behave with the docility expected of blue-collar workers."

So, too, the educational dilemma is posed by the tension created when schools try to treat students simultaneously as individuals and as clients of a complex bureaucracy. On the one hand it is apparent that learning is always ultimately individual and that the educational process depends on providing experiences appropriate to each individual. On the other hand it is also apparent that schools utilize standardized procedures to educate large numbers of students. Technological change requires students to master advanced and abstract bodies of knowledge (which requires successful individualization of instruction) while simultaneously creating larger and more bureaucratic educational institutions which treat clients impersonally and interchangeably (thus causing students to question the plausibility and hence the legitimacy of the institution). The inherent contradictions between these two opposing trends are responsible in no small part for the alienation now becoming increasingly acute in middle-class schools.

## IMPLICATIONS FOR URBAN SECONDARY SCHOOLS

There is, obviously, some similarity in attitudes which are produced by schools among economically disadvantaged students in the inner city and economically privileged students in the suburbs. The alienation of middle-class students obviously has somewhat different roots from that of the disadvantaged student in the inner city, but the two school systems resemble each other in producing students for whom the traditional high school is largely inauthentic and meaningless. For both groups, alienation from traditional high school programs has been turning into open rebellion on the part of a substantial proportion of students. For neither group is there much prospect that the traditional high school will be perceived as providing valid and worthwhile educational experience. For both groups, high schools must become very different institutions than most are today if they are to be anything more than custodial facilities in which students are confined until old enough to withdraw or graduate. Fundamental changes must occur or there is little hope that schools will serve a useful purpose in the lives of alienated students.

Here again, a check list for achieving this goal includes many familiar items. Schools must be debureaucratized in order to educate those who now question their authenticity, and the operational structure must reflect a real concern for community needs. Schools must be opened up, must become pluralistic, not only in the student body make-up, but in the types of educational experiences which the schools provide. To do so, the schools will have to reach out into the community and utilize the resources of non-academic people. Our cities are literally treasure houses of cultural, commercial, and artistic skills, and imaginative educators have conclusively demonstrated how effectively these resources can be utilized by the schools. Finally, the schools must allow students a greater voice in what they learn and how they learn it. The schools until now have created artificial learning experiences, based more on abstract than on real encounters. By allowing students a greater voice in their own education, schools can give youngsters a chance to come to grips with reality. Voluntarism does not mean abdication of teacher responsibility, but merely that students gain more if they have some say in their education.[2]


## SCHOOLS OF THE FUTURE

There is nothing startling about the foregoing outline of general possibilities for alleviating the festering and explosive crisis that exists in so many urban high schools. Most of these imperatives have been advocated so often by one or another  group of educational or social reformers as well as by students themselves that they would be *ad nauseum* platitudes if much of consequence had been done to modify urban education in accordance with their logic. Unfortunately, nothing of the sort has occurred in the great majority of urban high schools. Here and there a school may have become slightly less bureaucratic or marginally more voluntary than it was before. A few schools have made gestures toward freeing learning from the tight confines of the classroom, and occasionally efforts have been made to provide a more pluralistic context for educa-

[2] A recent experiment with student-directed curricula in Los Angeles has proven particularly successful in resolving some of these problems, as well as securing greater parental involvement.

tion. But, in general, urban high schools are constituted and operated very much as they were forty years ago when few of their students contested the legitimacy of their goals and programs.

What will urban high schools which strike out in new directions responsive to the urban education crisis of the 1970s tend to look like? Rather than following one or two standard "models," they probably will draw inspiration from a variety of sources, each school devising its own eclectic combination of programs and concepts. For example, aspects of the "School Without Walls" projects already underway in Philadelphia and Chicago might be incorporated into the regular program of the urban high school, particularly their arrangements for independent study of student-selected courses taught by craftsmen, businessmen, and other lay citizens and for cross-age grouping of several hundred students guided by teams of certified teachers and a host of neighborhood and pre-professional volunteers. For alienated inner-city youth, wider use could be made of the "street academy" approach in which a few instructors work with a small number of students in informal programs that reject pre-determined curricula but retain an emphasis on mastery of basic skills. Whether conducted as adjunct "outposts" located at a distance from existing schools or established as "in-school" academies and "free" schools within a high school proper, these approaches can provide a way to reduce the bureaucratic and custodial character of the traditional high school.

In most schools and for most students it may be sufficient to modify current practice in order to accommodate a greater range of choice in the urban high school and make it less isolated from the outside world. For example, a few high schools have begun to set aside half of every day or one day a week or one week a month for optional studies which students pursue singly or in small groups outside as well as inside the school. One particularly promising possibility utilizing such a schedule is to provide community service opportunities or even institute community service requirements for all adolescents and young adults. A few visionary educators and laymen, for example, have dreamed of the benefits that might be realized if all secondary-age students participated in organized efforts to improve the physical environment of the city or to operate day-care centers for the children of working mothers. Besides offering magnificent opportunities to combine learning and service, programs of this nature might also help reverse what today has become in many respects an unhealthy, prolonged exclusion of youth from adult society. Within the next few years, hopefully, federal officials as well as local community leaders will give serious consideration to such possibilities.

A related alternative for economically disadvantaged students is to offer more work-study opportunities leading directly to jobs in business or industry. In programs of this nature a student works half time in a paid position designed to help him learn a trade or occupation and to lead directly into the firm after graduation. Optimally, curriculum and instruction during his half day in the school also are substantially changed to tie in with his interests and experiences on the job. Of course, so-called "cooperative" education of this type has been offered for decades in many urban high schools, but usually only for a small number of students who were relatively unalienated from the school in the first place. Now, as in the case of one Boston high school, mini-schools offering work-study programs for two or three hundred alienated inner-city youths are being established or planned in several cities. In other cities, such as Detroit and Philadelphia, large local industries are being asked to "adopt" a particular high school with which to co-operate in expanding work-study opportunities and in providing services such as "personalized" career counseling.

Beyond this point, suggestions for responding to the crisis in urban secondary schools become blurred and murky. Mindful of the causes of alienation among large numbers of urban youth, one plausible conclusion is that a major part of the high school curriculum should enable students to explore a variety of possible life styles and synthesize a stable and satisfying identity from among them, should consist of humanistic learning experiences which simultaneously respect and enhance the individuality and autonomy of every student, and should help young people learn to lead fulfilling lives in a society increasingly concerned with the quality of everyday experience. The only trouble is that there are no specific and tested examples of how to accomplish these goals through formal education, and it is not even certain that they can be achieved through the schools at all.[3]

### ISSUES IN URBAN EDUCATION REFORM

Generalizing on a topic as complex as urban education tends to imply that an author has more confidence in his diagnosis and prescriptions than the uncertainty of the subject possibly could warrant. For this reason, it is well to conclude by specifying some of the most important unresolved and, at this time, unresolvable issues involving the future of urban education.

First, there is a real question whether disadvantaged students can succeed in inner-city schools no matter how much money is made available to improve their programs. Since the psychology of being segregated in a poverty environment is itself profoundly linked with the failure of the school and other social institutions in the inner city, it is not surprising that compensatory education has

---

[3] It is true that a few scattered attempts are being made to develop and disseminate curriculum concentrating on identity building, humanization, and aesthetic skills for daily life. The average high school, however, is functionally if not ideologically unconcerned with many of the most salient considerations in the lives of urban youth. Recognizing that enormous amounts of economic and social resources are consumed by public school systems in the United States, the situation in our high schools properly can be viewed as a bizarre example of a social institution gone awry.

not as yet resulted in substantial gains in the achievement of disadvantaged students in the big cities. Perhaps if funds for inner-city education were doubled or tripled and, more important, were spent to bring about fundamental changes in curriculum and instruction, academic retardation in inner-city schools might be significantly reduced or eliminated. But until it is demonstrated over a period of some years that most youngsters can have a decent childhood and receive an adequate education in an inner-city environment, to place much faith in even the best-conceived program of compensatory education would be reckless and naïve.

Second, no one knows for sure whether urban schools can be reformed quickly and thoroughly enough to avoid a "systems break" in existing arrangements for educating the young. Public school systems, for one thing, have been unabashedly organized along bureaucratic lines, and as such they exemplify the rigidities commonly found in large bureaucratic organizations. A few social scientists and educators are trying to find out how school systems and individual schools might be changed in accordance with new concepts of bureaucracy appropriate for a post-industrial society, but that such changes can be introduced, much less implemented, within existing systems is far from certain. All things considered, reform in the schools conceivably may come so slowly that advocates of free schools, no schools, private schools, and other alternatives to the existing system ultimately may carry the day.

Closely related to the issue of whether existing public schools are too rigid to be profoundly transformed is the question of whether reform can be institutionalized on a large enough scale to make a basic change in a good-sized school system. Even when intelligent reform is carried out in a few schools, problems will be encountered in attempting to expand promising new programs to serve a significant number of students in a large school system. It may not prove too difficult, for example, to establish a good School Without Walls program in a large urban community. But it is not at all certain that such a school can be expanded from a few hundred students (their present size) to a few thousand without fairly quickly exhausting the number of truly productive community learning settings which in practice are available to its students.

Third, even if widespread change can be brought about in middle-status schools in the wealthy suburbs and in inner-city schools, it is difficult to predict how much can or will be done to improve schools attended primarily by students from lower-middle-class and working-class families. While most parents in these families certainly want their children to have a "better" education, they still tend to believe that this can be achieved by intensifying the relatively ineffective instructional methods of the past rather than by fundamentally changing the school. Compared with the slums, where educational performance is so low that many students and parents have begun to insist on more effective schools, Middle America still tends to follow the example set by the generals who argued that since bombing in Vietnam was not very effective the thing to do was to drop two or three times more bombs. Partly for this reason, there is little demand for real change in lower-middle-class and working-class schools.

Fourth, it is possible that the cause of urban educational reform may suffer more from the efforts of its presumed friends than from the attacks of its avowed enemies. Some sponsors of educational reform have a rather simple-minded view of what is involved in providing better educational opportunities for urban youth. In experimental high school programs emphasizing independent study, for example, teachers and students frequently have been placed in entirely new educational settings demanding a degree of flexibility, creativity, and individual responsibility they have not been adequately prepared to handle. New programs which emphasize student choice in determining what and how to learn often have floundered because the sponsors of such programs and even the teachers employed in them apparently have believed that all you have to do is give students "freedom" to learn and learning will be assured. Eventually, if the program lasts long enough, personnel connected with such programs realize that teaching in this setting requires even more planning and skilled instruction than does the traditional school. One of the gravest threats to educational reform comes from those who try to implement reforms according to the simplistic principle that good intentions are all that is needed to bring about change.

A FINAL WORD

It is easy to lose sight of the underlying theme that much of the crisis in urban education can be traced to metropolitan stratification. The increasing segregation of social and racial groups within metropolitan society is damaging not just to the obvious victims—the poor and the racial and ethnic minorities—but sooner or later to all other groups in the population as well. When some youngsters are confined to the unwholesome physical and social environment of the inner city, when others are raised in an antiseptic, boring environment, and when masses of lower-middle-class and working-class white youngsters receive an inadequate education while deflecting their status fears and dissatisfactions on an underclass below them, no one can gain. In the long run, it is difficult to see how a minimal social and political consensus can be maintained if social relationships and geographic residential arrangements remain so highly stratified.

There is no inherent reason why a student must receive all his schooling all year long in a single classroom or school building. There is no inherent reason why every youngster cannot participate in pluralistic educational experiences for at least two or three months a year in special Metropolitan Learning Centers. Better yet, parts of such programs might well emphasize the use of community resources in learning, identity-building, interethnic studies, and other emerging educational imperatives virtually ignored in existing curricula. Who can doubt that Americans have the ingenuity to provide a pluralistic education for the young even where metropolitan stratification and segregation make it difficult to begin? Whether we have the awareness and commitment to do so is, of course, a wholly different matter.

The results of social stratification have become easily discernible in all our social affairs, fueling polarizations which our political institutions so far have been unable to compromise or moderate. In our educational systems, stratification works to ensure the triumph of tribalism over pluralism, yet how can a modern industrial social structure function successfully on a tribal base? If they do not know each other personally, how can economically or socially disadvantaged youngsters and middle-status youngsters perceive each other as individual persons rather than stereotypes? How can high-status youngsters think of the sons and daughters of blue-collar workers without disdain if a status-conscious society keeps them physically separated? How can youngsters of all these differing social backgrounds learn to work in broad-based coalitions for mutually beneficial social progress?

One can say that teachers, parents, and ministers should instruct the young to reject the intergroup prejudices and stereotypes which are likely to be present in any pluralistic society. Unfortunately, the job cannot be accomplished so easily. People have bases, whether reasonable or unreasonable, for their beliefs, and one of the best-established findings of social psychology is that verbal exhortation seldom has much effect on intergroup hostilities and mythologies. Sustained face-to-face contact in a setting that requires differing people to work toward a common goal, on the other hand, at least opens up possibilities for building positive attitudes, though it does not necessarily guarantee them.

## FOR FURTHER READING

Ball, Richard A. "A Poverty Case: The Analgesic Subculture of the Southern Appalachians." *American Sociological Review*, 33 (December 1968), 885–95.

Coleman, James S., et al. *Equality of Educational Opportunity*. Washington, D.C.: Government Printing Office, 1966.

Greene, Mary Frances, and Orletta Ryan. *The Schoolchildren: Growing Up in the Slums*. New York: Random House, 1965.

Hannery, Ulf. "Roots of Black Manhood." *Transaction*, 6 (October 1969); 13–21.

Havighurst, Robert J., and Daniel U. Levine. *Education in Metropolitan Areas*. Boston: Allyn and Bacon, 1971.

Herndon, James. *The Way It Spozed to Be*. New York: Simon & Schuster, 1968.

Klapp, Orrin E. *Collective Search for Identity*. New York: Holt, Rinehart & Winston, 1969.

Kohn, Melvin L. *Class and Conformity: A Study in Values*. Homewood, Illinois: Dorsey, 1969.

Orr, John B., and F. Patrick Nichelson. *The Radical Suburb*. Philadelphia: Westminster, 1970.

Passow, A. Harry (ed.). *Reaching the Disadvantaged Learner*. New York: Teachers College Press, 1970.

*Phi Delta Kappan*, 50 (February 1971). Issue on reform of urban education.

Reimer, Everett, and Ivan Illich. *Alternatives in Education*. Cuernavaca, Mexico: Centro Intercultural de Documentacion, 1970.

Sennet, Richard. *The Uses of Diversity*. New York: Alfred A. Knopf, 1970.

Silberman, Charles E. *Crisis in the Classroom*. New York: Random House, 1970.

Suttles, Gerald D. *The Social Order of the Slum: Ethnicity and Territory in the Inner City*. Chicago: University of Chicago Press, 1968.

# CHAPTER 10

# URBAN PLANNING: OLD REALITIES AND NEW DIRECTIONS

## Shirley S. Passow

Despite sections of great beauty, most American cities are the result of unplanned growth. Vast areas have been given over to single purpose uses, and what should be a harmonious whole is a disjointed conglomeration of ill-fitting pieces. As urban social problems have increased, this lack of planning has exacerbated already difficult situations. Perhaps too late Americans have begun to explore the possibilities of rational planned development.

A number of historic and political conditions, however, mitigate against full use of planning skills. Shirley Passow notes that political power-plays as well as aversion to too great a central authority have forestalled the adoption of planning on a large scale. While billions of dollars have gone into developing suburban sprawl and building thousands of miles of highways, a relative pittance has been appropriated for planning and land-use evaluation. Now, when it may be our last chance to adopt comprehensive planning, the realities of a war economy may preclude our taking this step.

Shirley S. Passow has had careers both in teaching and in city planning, and is currently a staff member of the New York City Department of City Planning; she has also written on land planning in Sweden.

*As never before, the ordinary unfettered operation of the supply and demand system threatens to weed out all but the most profitable uses of land. Time after time, our cultural and architectural heritage has yielded to new office buildings, as landmark structures are torn down. In city after city, low-income tenants are displaced, as land with old but structurally sound housing is put to a more economically profitable use.*

—DONALD ELLIOTT,
New York City Planning Commission

URBAN planning, a system for predicting and guiding the orderly growth of cities, is thriving outwardly, funded substantially, adopted occasionally—but for the most part bypassed in the American decision process. Haunted by crises, eager for solutions, and bent on profit, Americans may be unsuited to the discipline of rational planning. Yet, as the urban centers decayed and their citizens clamored for rescue, the federal government in 1969 appropriated $290 million for comprehensive urban-planning projects. In a budget of nearly $200 billion, this amounts to roughly .01 per cent, the merest feint toward a system of rational planning.

If planning is to serve the public interest in our cities, it must somehow merge with and modify three dynamic but hostile forces: private enterprise, the paramount theme in American society; political expedience and its offshoot, crisis-response; and citizen conflict over jurisdiction, priorities, and power.

URBAN TURMOIL, TRIGGER OF PLANNING

In 1970, the American population passed the 204-million mark. Demographers were projecting 300 million by the year 2000, at a birth rate exceeding the nation's capacity to plan and to produce the life-support systems for maintaining a decent environment. To accommodate 100 million more Americans would require the reconstruction of as many buildings as had been erected since the founding of the nation. Some planners urged a network of one hundred New Towns, nationally funded and developed on public domain lands. When Secretary George Romney's Department of Housing and Urban Development drafted a bill along these lines, the Administration quietly buried it in June 1970. Although inflation was scored for the action, it could be argued that a nation whose budget approached $200 billion and whose gross national product was $1 trillion could have financed a New Towns policy and all the infra-structure needed to prepare the land for private developers. In December 1970 Congress did pass a modified New Towns program as part of the omnibus housing bill.

Of all the symptoms of the urban crisis, housing leads the list. Sub-standard housing was estimated in 1968 at some eleven million units. Though the census data are notoriously incomplete, especially for poor citizens, this figure suggested that about forty-five million persons were living in decayed housing units. Homelessness has reached the flash point in all the big cities, igniting the squatter take-over movement of 1970 which converted abandoned or boarded-up tenements, often lacking electricity and water, into instant shelter. Professor Chester Rapkin of Columbia University, speaking in 1970 at a meeting of the City Planning Commission of New York City (of which he was a member) etched the catastrophe in outline:

We are moving into the worst housing shortage this country has ever known, and it will be felt most acutely in the low-rent portions of the housing supply. First, many Public Housing authorities are on the verge of bankruptcy. Second, abandonment of housing is proceeding at a rapid rate. As buildings come up for refinancing, owners are unable to borrow at present peak interest rates, cease collecting rents, stop their services, tenants move out; vandals, addicts and squatters arrive. Within a matter of weeks, many a good building disintegrates. Third, as background to this, the escalation of building and labor costs, combined with the highest bank rates in history, has made it impossible to build under the low, rigid federal subsidy limits.

Government itself is largely responsible for the housing plight of the poor, despite a series of housing laws designed to expand the supply of low-income units. Between 1949, when the Housing Act created Urban Renewal and targeted a decent home for every American, and 1967, government action alone (primarily through the highway construction and Urban Renewal programs) destroyed half a million more homes than it built for the poor. According to the National Commission on Urban Problems, some 1,054,000 units were torn down and only 520,000 units of public housing were built in those eighteen years. Moreover, murmurings that Urban Renewal meant Negro Removal spread through the years, helping to corrode relations between the poor and the wider community.

Symptoms of the urban crisis abound. Crime increased by two hundred per cent during the 1960s. As fear and drug traffic made the cities and later the suburbs insecure, the accusations of police brutality were succeeded by partisan activism, handgun violence by private citizens, and fatal shootings of police. Municipal services declined rapidly, first in the ghettoes and then in widening areas. Enraged citizens protested deterioration in the public schools, in air and water purity, in hospital care, and in mass transit facilities. A new political self-consciousness clustered around the rallying cry of Black Power, or its ethnic imitations. The political gains of the sixties failed to meliorate the racial animosities which repeatedly broke the community's peace.

Inevitably, the dissolution of community, however superficial it may have been, crumbled the foundation of planning, since consensus on goals is a prerequisite for any kind of planning. On its base, priorities are set and budgets constructed. To understand the planning function in the United States today, three questions must be answered:

1. What is planning, theoretically and realistically, and who are the planners?

2. How has our historical experience shaped Americans' attitudes toward planning?

3. What new directions should public-interest planning take, to enhance its effectiveness?

## WHAT PLANNING IS—OR TRIES TO BE

Simplistically, planning has been defined as who gets what, when, where, and how. Comprehensive urban planning respects the interrelatedness of all community elements and seeks the equitable distribution of community resources. Its focus is the major activity systems which encompass access to transportation, housing, jobs, schools, health care, shops, parks, and public utilities. Government's planning powers are centered on the development and regulation of land use. Its tools for planning are chiefly the comprehensive or master plan for long-range growth, special area plans, zoning codes, site-plan review, and eminent domain or condemnation powers. In one sense, these seemingly broad-sweep techniques are half measures: they are the best government can do in a society where private ownership and development of land take precedence over public ownership. However, the most effective and rational examples of public-interest planning are to be seen only in countries which practice public land ownership: Sweden, England, Holland, Denmark, and others. Because of the resistance to public land ownership, Americans must seek to influence goals, designs, types, and intensity of uses through the techniques listed above, and through continuing negotiation with developers and community groups. The ultimate decisions on planning are expressed through the finality of the capital budget, a document usually controlled by forces beyond the planners' grasp.

Technically, the urban-planning ritual contains these

steps: diagnosis of existing conditions; anticipation of large-scale growth; projection and analysis of its magnitude; evolution of goals; recommendations for alternative actions, strategies, or "probabilistic schemes" for change. These alternate options or plans mature by stages within tentative time schedules, backed by financial commitments from public, private, or combined sources. To ensure flexibility and reality, dynamic planning should incorporate a feedback mechanism to handle the flow of criticism and response; when it operates properly, it can unite planners, community, and government.

Of all the techniques of the discipline, the comprehensive plan is the most valuable for integrating the major elements of the city: people, land-use patterns, communications, and other community facilities. The plan seeks to develop a program of capital growth geared to the changing needs of population over the foreseeable future. Essentially physical for decades, master plans are now moving toward social policy planning as the impetus for physical development. Possibly the best example of a physical plan was Philadelphia's 1960 master plan and its implementation in the *Capital Program 1966–1971*. Published in 1965, the latter document reported progress and charted a six-year budget clearly related to the 1960 master plan. When Philadelphia's planners put a price tag of $4 billion on their 1960 proposals, they could write calmly that the plan is a "blueprint of a new kind of city, its beginnings already in evidence, which is within the financial and physical means of Philadelphia's people to bring to full realization in the remaining decades of this century."

Nine years later, a less confident New York City published its lavishly illustrated, 450,000-word comprehensive *Plan for New York City*. Critics promptly attacked the absence of traditional planning devices, such as projected land-use maps, capital program schedules, specific goals linked to general policies and individual projects, and long-term trend lines indicating population or facilities increments. Angry blacks denounced the initial volume (there are six in all) as "the Masters' Plan" when Chairman Elliott presented it to the Regional Plan Association conference in November 1969. However, one influential critic, Ada Louise Huxtable of the New York *Times,* defended the city's "courage" for producing a social plan and noted that Chicago and Los Angeles were working on similar treatment of their own comprehensive proposals.

Philosophically, city planning is losing its absorption in urban design. This stance was natural enough for a profession once dominated by engineers, architects, and land surveyors, charged from antiquity with creating living places out of virgin land. In an urbanized society, however, the focus shifts to people's economic, social, and political needs as determinants of the physical megastructure, the city. This view of planning gathers a cross section of expertise: planners, lawyers, sociologists, and economists, along with architects and engineers for the physical design aspects. Thus, descendants of the master builders who initiated urban planning with the Athenian Acropolis and the Roman Forum, and who still run most of Europe's planning departments, are moving over to admit the new professional colleagues.

## ZONING CODES

The belief that environment shapes human behavior motivated the architects and engineers who designed ancient and medieval towns that tourists enjoy to this day. Baron Haussmann's Paris, a Victorian triumph, continues to delight residents and visitors. Camillo Sitte and Reinhard Baumeister made nineteenth-century Vienna a model for planning, through their aesthetic and engineering contributions. Street layout, sewerage, and zoning districts were Baumeister's province; Sitte popularized the interpretation of such concepts as medieval town scale, the centrality of cathedrals, the uses of plazas and open space generally. Among contemporaries influenced by such elements as the "surprise factor" in winding medieval streets is Lawrence Halprin of San Francisco and New York, designer of the Auditorium Forecourt Fountain in Portland, Oregon, and the Nicollet Mall, which transformed Minneapolis' downtown shopping district.

Rarely have the visual delights of physical planning been allowed to outweigh the demands of economic feasibility in this country. Private developers view land as a commodity which must be made to yield a profit. When government realized that property owners would exercise their right to build whatever they chose on their parcels—including meat-slaughtering plants or chemical processors in residential neighborhoods—government turned to regulation through zoning codes. Once adopted by the local legislature, zoning controls the uses, densities, building heights and setbacks, sky exposure planes, parking requirements, and open space proportions permitted in each category of district. Generally, the districts are defined as residential, commercial, or industrial, though some cities are experimenting with compatible mixed-use districts. New York City drafted the nation's first zoning resolution in 1916, and operated under its sections until the major amendment of 1961 and its subsequent text changes.

Two landmark events in the 1920s established the legality of zoning. First was the publication by the U. S. Department of Commerce of the State Standard Zoning Enabling Act (1923), a model for municipal and state legislation. Second was the only zoning case the United States Supreme Court has agreed to hear, *Village of Euclid, Ohio,* v. *Ambler Realty Company* (1926). Extending the nuisance factor recognized in English common law, the Court upheld a municipality's right to regulate land use through zoning under its police powers. The Court declared that government could limit a property owner's rights, without going so far as to constitute a taking of property, when exercise of those rights substantially affected the public health, safety, morals, convenience, or general welfare.

Recent critics of zoning argue that the instrument is

being misused for parochial purposes. Richard Babcock has castigated it as "the device for protecting the homogeneous, single-family suburb from the city," thereby blocking a regional land-use plan. The National Committee against Discrimination in Housing has sponsored a major study to document its belief that zoning is a bar to low- or moderate-income housing for families who need to follow industry out of the core cities into the hinterlands. Paul Ylvisaker, then Commissioner of Community Affairs in New Jersey, failed in 1968 to win legislative support for a bill which would have empowered the state to review local zoning ordinances. Recognition that local zoning codes should be subject to higher review is a growing trend, but its implementation will probably depend as much upon litigation as on education.

## THE NEW TOWN MOVEMENT

New Towns have always offered central governments and their architect-planners the best opportunities for creating good environments. Early in America's history, William Penn, a lawyer seeking freedom for his fellow Quakers, designed and developed Philadelphia (1682) on land chartered by Charles II of Britain. At the request of George Washington, Major Pierre L'Enfant designed Washington, D.C. Detroit owes its grid street system to surveyors, who could hardly predict the horrendous circulation pressures of the modern city. In the 1930s, Secretary of the Interior Harold Ickes initiated an ambitious scheme for several greenbelt towns; but except for one in Maryland, he failed to win congressional funding for the projects. Contemporary efforts at building some one hundred New Towns are all under private auspices, including such firms as Boise-Cascade, Gulf Oil Company, American City Corporation, and General Electric Company.

The two operational New Towns (all the rest are in design) are Reston, Virginia, and Columbia, Maryland. A half hour's drive from Washington, D.C., Reston, an eleven-square-mile town with a projected population of seventy thousand, is considered one of the finest examples of urban design in the country. However, negotiations for an access road to a near-by expressway were delayed and this may have hampered initial property sales. More serious was the fact that construction costs exceeded the fiscal capacity of Robert Simon's original development corporation. Gulf Oil took Reston over in 1967 in an effort to save a $15-million investment. On the other hand, fiscal solvency was a basic reason for the success of Columbia, the fifteen-thousand-acre city adjacent to the busy Washington-Baltimore corridor. Its founder, James Rouse of American City Corporation, received commitments of permanent financing from an insurance company consortium. His contribution to New Town planning was the recruitment of a work group of experts on human behavior to supplement the physical design team. The assignment for the sociologists, psychologists, economists, educators, recreationalists, and health and communications specialists was to undertake research for a work program encompassing community life services, urban land use and structure, real estate economics, and over-all planning for a community whose eventual population would be one hundred thousand. A similar scheme is being adapted by the Rouse firm in Hartford, Connecticut, where the Greater Hartford Corporation retained the developer in 1969 to evolve a long-range plan for the city-region. It will be interesting to see what patterns of co-operation emerge between dynamic private developers such as Rouse and various government bodies.

While American planner-developers put economic feasibility first, American planning theorists stress ecology and aesthetics. The early twentieth-century critics of cities who became pioneers of planning—including Lewis Mumford, Clarence Stein, Albert Mayer, and Henry Wright—took their lead from design-oriented Europeans who preached urban planning as an escape from city horrors. Most influential, perhaps, was Ebenezer Howard of London, a writer whose vision of Garden Cities won world-wide followers. His blueprints for co-ordinated communities with linkages among homes, jobs, schools, parks, and transit terminals were designed to free workingmen from the oppressive criminality of Victorian cities. Another seminal planner was Patrick Geddes of Scotland, who conceived the unitary or integrative approach to planning. Geddes' view of the interdependency of all elements in the city organism included the idea that changes in any component effected changes throughout the system. Today's systems analysts travel within this ideology, which they have labeled with an ancient Greek term, synergism. Applied to town planning, synergism says that the whole is greater than its parts, that systems generate systems, that change in any unit affects all other segments of the totality. The simple concept is almost impossible of realization, since planners rarely control all elements of the change process within cities.

Mumford and his cohorts did develop certain lasting principles. First, the planet's ecology must be respected and cherished; mankind and cities are at once a threat to and the prime beneficiaries of nature. From Clarence Stein and Henry Wright came the prototype communities of Radburn, now part of Fair Lawn, New Jersey, and Sunnyside Gardens, Long Island. These realized the neighborhood unit ideas of Clarence Perry of the Regional Plan Association, which envisioned common green space instead of miniature individual gardens; separation of pedestrian paths from street traffic; schools and shops within a set convenient radius of small homes; a hierarchy of roads to serve different types and volumes of traffic; and population limitations. Beyond the neighborhood and the city were the regional planners, who clarified the larger macrocosmic effects of goods production, distribution, housing, and job location. They were warning against suburban sprawl long before the federal government's ill-advised highway program shredded communities and made commuting a daily plague.

American technology now has restructured these concepts through systems analysis applied to massive data. Techniques include economic base studies and economic matrices that use input-output analyses to crystallize regional production and consumption or any other type of complex activity; PPBS, or the planning-program-budgeting system; mathematical models for projecting transportation trends and linkages; computerization for an infinite number of informational programs. While this approach tends to stress planning for economic growth, to the injury of housing and other social demands, the significant factor of modern planning is its unanimity on holistic or synergistic approaches to problems.

## THE DILEMMA OF BEING A PLANNER

Specialized university training in urban planning is now the entry route for most new planners. Some of these still bring an architectural or engineering background to the field, but large numbers of others have received undergraduate preparation in the liberal arts, sociology, law, economics, mathematics, or history. Women, blacks, and Puerto Ricans are increasing their numbers, though they still represent fewer than fifteen per cent of practitioners. Many people see planning today as a vestibule to political power, an appealing notion to those who still believe in bettering and not wrecking society.

Controversies over the "relevance" of planning, the roles of advocate versus establishment planner, the relation of planners to political leaders and to allied professions, the extent of involvement in social responsibility as compared to strict adherence to technical skills—all these matters reflect the identity crisis within the profession. As "generalist co-ordinators," how should planners fit into the decision-making structure?

More highly trained than earlier technicians; armed with more punch cards, field surveys, aerial photographs, and hardware than Ebenezer Howard ever imagined, American city planners make up a profession under siege. Pressures, internal and external, have drained them of the calm assurance indispensable for seers. Shall they memorize the rules and procedures for technical competence in the university, apply these on the job, color land-use and housing maps, calculate population changes and project job or school needs, produce area studies and master plans, submit these to their employers and sit back, hoping for approval? Or must they do more: deal with "clients," the neighborhoods and towns whose fates they may be altering? Deal with politicians, whose words may praise or bury any plan? Fight for their plans in public? The old-style technicians, public and private, exhibit fewer insecurities than the younger generation, even when a meticulous plan is shelved. Their job ended when the plan was delivered to the proper authorities. With professional goals so fluid, it is no wonder that planning is still groping for the right meld of physical, social, and technical learnings. Ironically, at the same time that synergism has become a byword in planning theory, the complexities of urban life are forcing most planners into narrow specializations.

In an essay on the place of planning within the decision hierarchy, Henry Cohen declared that outside forces largely determined that placement. Rarely, certain charismatic planners—for example, Edmund Bacon, who is credited for the renaissance which flowed from Philadelphia's 1960 master plan, and Edward J. Logue, formerly of Boston and now Chairman and Chief Executive of the Urban Development Corporation (UDC) of New York State—will catalyze major changes. But usually, planning technique will not tip the scales for decisions. "Far more controlling," said Cohen, "are the social, economic, and political forces which shape the structure and role of government. . . . The weight given different ideas, values, and aspirations is more likely to determine at any given time how strongly the planner fits into the decision-making system."

To judge from budget allocations and salary levels, the

planning function is increasingly appreciated, if not yet decisive in government operations. A 1967 survey of local governments showed that municipal bodies had spent about $300 million for all planning, zoning, and building regulation activities. The American Society of Planning Officials (ASPO) reported that city planning agency expenditures had increased 14.7 per cent between fiscal 1968 and 1969, while metropolitan and regional agencies revealed a 24.1 per cent rise in planning budgets that same year. Top-level professional planners in urban areas in 1970 commanded salaries ranging from a high of $33,000 in Los Angeles to a low of $11,000 in Orlando, Florida. Private planners averaged higher incomes than public, though the dependence of consultants on government contracts tended to cancel their advantage. Before the 1970 recession forced layoffs and pay cuts, median salaries ranged from $8,580 to $22,144 nation-wide.

Efforts to raise professional standards included examinations for full acceptance by professional societies, as well as co-operation with Civil Service in defining criteria for experience and education. Planners began to resolve the frictions with allied professions, as a team approach to problem-solving became more common. Internal pressures, however, were proving considerably less threatening to planning as a system for protecting the just society, than were the three hazards cited at the outset: political expedience colored by crisis; citizen disputes over power; and the social price of private enterprise.

POLITICAL EXPEDIENCE AND CRISIS

Elected heads of government advance or kill planning. Archives and bookshelves conceal many admirable plans for New Towns, outdoor recreation preserves, housing estates, mass transit systems, inner-city expressways, and industrial complexes. Their common denominator is veto by one or more political leaders who judged them ill-timed, either for lack of money or voter appeal. Professional planners recognize that they succeed only to the degree that they are able to persuade the elected policy makers not only that their plans are viable but that they will enhance the political leaders' image in some way. The 1970 gubernatorial campaign in New York State offered a plain example. With delicate timing, artists' renderings and architects' models of the proposed $200-million New Town on Welfare Island in the East River, New York City, went on display in September at the Metropolitan Museum of Art. Architecture critic Ada Louise Huxtable commented in the New York *Times:*

Just one year after the master plan for Welfare Island was unveiled with some political fanfare at the Metropolitan Museum, the design development of the first stage of the plan is being presented at the same institution, suitably in advance of Election Day. It is the showpiece and star performance of the New York State Urban Development Corporation, which was created by the State Legislature to expedite housing and urban renewal. As such it can't do Governor Rockefeller any harm. But this is more than a political event; it is a planning event of the first magnitude.

Gone is the era when reformers campaigned for and established autonomous civic commissions of high-minded citizen planners. When Hartford, Connecticut, authorized the nation's first planning commission (1907), it set a fashion. But the weakness of the form soon showed. It is not apolitical appointees but elected officials who advance or reject plans, by voting the funds for implementation. This is as it should be, since the political leaders and not the technicians are accountable to the voting public. However, and this is the tragedy, plans disintegrate when crisis explodes. The long process of studying a plan, its feasibility, costs-benefits, and priority, can be short-circuited by any of the violent episodes that shatter urban peace almost daily. Political leaders who have spent months considering a plan will spring to action at notice of a prison riot, fire in an obsolete tenement, a strike of hospital aides, a shoot-out between police and the new breed of urban guerillas. This is government by knee-jerk: not merely the opposite of planning, but the bitter fruit of failure to plan.

The crisis mentality condemns American society to endemic crisis. The political response to problems treats planning as a tool for advancing power, the only real objective of politics. Thus, the allocation of programs will be guided by such matters as rewards for political allies, largesse for influential or swing groups of the electorate, consolation or token prizes for angry communities, and, of course, the fiscal limitations. But absent from the crisis-politics stance are the intrinsic purposes of planning as a blueprint for rational growth.

The second obstacle to effective local planning is the clash of numerous small groups which generates community hostility. Since 1954, federal legislation has mandated safeguards for citizen policy-making, both through law and administrative fiat.[1] The Workable Program of the Housing Act of 1954, prerequisite for obtaining federal funds for Urban Renewal, includes citizen representation among its seven points. Other major programs, from the 1964 law creating the Office of Economic Opportunity to HUD guidelines that favor tenant participation in management of public housing projects, all support the concept of citizen participation in planning. Inevitably, the failure to attain the promised housing and good environments, often due to government procrastination but also traceable to the quarrels and ineptness of the citizen councils, fueled wide bitterness and disillusion. Under the Model Cities guidelines, citizen committees were given the unreasonable assignment of producing a comprehensive neighborhood plan within one year. They suffered from internecine jealousies, the inevitable result of dangling largesse before too many competitors. Controversy delayed plans for years, not only in ghetto areas but in middle-class and wealthy communities where plans split the voters deeply.

[1] See Chapter 6.

One planner's dream is many a community's nightmare. New housing and schools sound splendid until locations pinpoint an already established neighborhood. Few communities willingly pay the price for new facilities when their own homes or traditions must be sacrificed. As the bulldozer cleared sites of their previous occupants and structures, angry citizens turned to a new kind of spokesman, the advocate planner (so named by Paul Davidoff). Motivated by a humanist view of planning, which sought to establish the priority of human values above commercial profits or tax ratables, the advocate planners sought to strengthen the poor and their rights within the system. Thus, they aided citizens to articulate planning goals, to apply for government subsidies and permanent financing for housing projects, to conduct rent strikes or squatter move-ins as a protest against government's housing failure, to identify sites for needed public housing. While their record is a mixed one, the advocates have contributed to widening awareness among citizens of planning's potential for upgrading their own neighborhoods.

But to recognize planning is not equivalent to managing it properly. Citizen battles over Model Cities funds in Harlem stymied progress on all but four of forty-six approved projects in 1970. In Oakland, California, a prolonged battle between the city and the West Oakland Planning Committee accelerated in 1968 when the WOPC demanded $92,000 out of the city's anticipated HUD grant of nearly $500,000. The money was won and applied to a planning program based on "self-determined goals" and implemented by a planning staff hired by WOPC. However, when the citizens committee threatened to delay two prime undertakings for revitalizing Oakland, construction of the Bay Area Rapid Transit and redevelopment of the central business district, the city's political machine fought back and proved it was still in charge.

Not all citizen committees are poor or ghetto residents. In wealthy Westchester County, New York, the Sleepy Hollow Valley Committee spent four years and $80,000 fighting a proposed 2.8-mile road to link two major arteries, Routes 9 and 9A. They joined with three other groups to attack the alignment, but while the litigation was still on a court calendar, the road was opened in November 1970.

The chief flaw in citizen campaigns so far is that they can often obstruct, but seldom advance, planning. New forms of negotiation are needed to link citizens productively with public-interest planning. Public hearings are satisfactory theater, but they throw scant light on the tough problems. Rage, confrontation, manipulation, all miss the point if that point is the solving of problems. A new style of community collective bargaining may be the direction toward planning that works.

### THE PUBLIC-PRIVATE CONFLICT

There is one arena in which collective negotiation would be a sure loser: the turf on which private profits and public-interest benefits face each other. The two recurring collision points are clashing views of land use and industry's waste products as pollutants.[2] Because private industry tends to be immune against all persuasion save the bottom line on the balance sheet, government regulation, enforcement, and penalties are the preferred tactics in these cases.

On occasion, government units can be decisive in meeting problems caused by industrial waste or other processes. The Suffolk County Legislature in Long Island, New York, passed an ordinance forbidding the sale of most detergents as of March 1, 1971. In the first legislative action of its kind in the country, Suffolk was responding to warnings from the county Board of Health and the Water Authority that the underground water supply was being threat-

---

[2] See Chapter 8.

ened by the seepage of detergents into the soil. Crisis was imminent because this recent development area lacked a planned sewerage system and relied on septic tanks for waste disposal. Industry blamed the lack of sewerage for the declining purity of the water supply, arguing that detergents were being made the scapegoat, but the legislature held firm. While it is true that suburban development should include utilities and modern waste removal systems, the step to halt pollution of the water system was progressive.

To New Yorkers, their own giant utility, Consolidated Edison Company, is a chief offender against clean air. Its smokestacks blacken the skies; its failure to plan for expanding population needs has been blamed for power failures which reduced voltage available to serve subway riders, air conditioners, and commuter railroads. Walter Sullivan, science editor of the New York *Times,* called the utility's poor performance a planning breakdown. The company had resisted budgeting for such technological improvements as supercooled transmission lines, which, he said, "would be very costly to install, but would make possible the movement of vast amounts of power with almost no losses . . . At present, however, the need to show a profit inhibits companies from experimenting with such costly transmission techniques."

How can public-interest groups fight to protect our natural resources? One strategy, favored by author James Ridgeway, is exposure of misdeeds as a prelude to political action. He documents charges that all but 25,000 of the nation's 280,000 manufacturers discharge wastes into overloaded municipal sewers, for which they pay low fees. He warns that industry's spokesmen will try to force the public to foot the bill for pollution control through taxes or higher prices for products. Another strategy is strict government regulation of land use and open space, measures favored by such environmental planners as Ian McHarg of Pennsylvania. McHarg sounds like a furious

Jeremiah as he recites the litany of Americans' abuse of nature and denounces those who act as if America "had formulated a national policy for the eradication of natural beauty and integrated this into policies for highways, housing, industry, transportation and agriculture . . . God's Own Junkyard—the chosen symbol of our time and society."

After pollution, the development of land as a profit venture is the main anti-public effect of private enterprise. The nation's deep faith in private property stems from the English common law dictum that an individual can do whatever he likes with his property, assuming he does not injure his neighbor. As William Pitt the Elder cautioned:

The poorest man may in his cottage bid defiance to all the force of the crown. It may be frail; its roof may shake . . . but the King of England can not enter; all his forces dare not cross the threshold of the ruined tenement.

The sanctity of private property, admittedly diluted, is reaffirmed daily in law and custom. One of the stoutest testimonials rang out in the House of Representatives, during the 1966 debate preceding passage there of Title IV, Civil Rights Bill. (The Senate later filibustered it to death.) Said Congressman Flynt of Georgia:

Human rights cannot exist without property rights, and a healthy respect for both. Any attempt to destroy or weaken the right of private ownership of property is an attempt to destroy a system of private capital, and to substitute a totalitarian form of government in its place, whether it is called socialism, state socialism or communism.

By definition, property is a bundle of legal rights, created and sustained by the corpus of American law. Nonetheless, over the years government has asserted its ultimate power to limit property rights in many ways. After taxation, the most ancient and far-reaching is Eminent Domain, a judicial procedure which authorizes government to acquire private property to serve a public purpose. Two constitutional amendments limit this power. The Fifth Amendment states, "Nor shall private property be taken for public use without just compensation." The Fourteenth Amendment extended the due process and "equal protection of the laws" to property, and specifically prohibited the states from interfering with economic freedom. When public planning relies on Eminent Domain or condemnation, the process is costly and time-consuming; agencies, therefore, prefer to negotiate agreements.

Most development is initiated and performed by private entrepreneurs. They assemble land, either openly or discreetly through negotiation, or by bidding on publicly assembled real estate. To a developer, the prime criteria for a good investment site are potential yield, "highest and best use," land values, and tax benefits. Since the social damage of land assembly is incidental to the economic feasibility, redevelopment of dense urban areas has often meant that thousands of households have been dislodged, favorite old stores have been bought out, landmarks have crumpled, and hundreds of small shopkeepers have been driven out.

What seems anti-social to some today seemed different during America's adolescence. Then, the risk-taker was a hero and a nation-builder. He was the adventurer willing to plumb the wilderness, to throw rail lines across the continent, to homestead on the frontier, to face danger in search of gold, oil, trade routes. And as he succeeded, his opportunities and America's wealth seemed endless and beckoning to millions of other risk-takers. The pioneers believed there was no end to pure air and water, timberlands, sub-surface fortunes, wild life. Waste seemed a symbol of infinite riches, and the pattern of exploitation hardened.[3]

Free land was the great wish of pioneers and immigrants.

[3] See Chapter 2.

For government, it was the cheapest gift they could bestow. In the hundred years of settlement, the United States transferred over one billion acres of public domain lands to individuals and states, charging pennies per acre or nothing at all. Gradually, the European custom of common lands, often donated by the crown, faded into the ethos of exclusive private holdings. Today, the federal lands cover some 800,000,000 acres, about one third the land area of the forty-eight mainland states and Alaska. Most of the land is in the West, where the people and the metropolitan agglomerations are not.

Government's failure to reserve land for future community expansion, coupled with the tendency to sell municipal real estate to raise cash quickly, has had disastrous consequences. Planners today must attempt to find accessible space to accommodate the seventy-five per cent of Americans crowded into that two per cent of the land area which is urban. Inevitably, redevelopment has forced dislocation of current occupants and sometimes the disruption of their lives because there was no land available for the new homes, shops, or other amenities to resettle them. The bitterness engendered is hard to measure. The record of recent years is grim indeed:

—When Oakland, California, cleared sites for the Acorn Redevelopment housing project and for the city's mass transit system, thousands of ghetto residents lost their homes.

—The Greater Bridgeport, Connecticut, Housing Council estimated that rebuilding the central business district cost twelve hundred low-income households their homes between 1965 and 1970. Fewer than one hundred low-rent units were restored to the housing supply.

—As costs escalated late in the sixties for the Albany Mall in New York State's capital, low-income housing was dropped from the complex of state offices, private offices, and retail shops. Demolition erased three thousand dwelling units; no replacements were built.

—Site clearance for Lincoln Center, New York City's gleaming culture node, displaced seventeen thousand people over several years. Most of these were poor or elderly or both. Rising land values in the adjacent blocks priced many other people out of the area permanently, as luxury apartments for eleven thousand people and prestige office buildings replaced older, less expensive housing.

Was the increase in ratables worth the destruction of community? Do the visible triumphs of Urban Renewal compensate for the bitter feelings of neighborhoods betrayed by their own governments? One answer may be suggested by the opening words of the Douglas Commission report: "The anger of the slums is that of people disinherited from our society."

Against this background, the achievements of Urban Renewal are encouraging but flawed. An inventory of successes will offer San Francisco's 108-acre Western Addition Area 1, with 671 units of moderate-income housing; San Antonio's civic center, built around a nucleus of permanent structures saved from the Texas city's 1968 Hemisfair; Cleveland's Cuyahoga Community College, serving 5,000 students at its downtown location—a county-financed institution with counterparts in Chicago, Bowling Green, Kentucky, and Waco, Texas, financed under the education provisions of Urban Renewal. Rochester, New York, is the home of Fight, Inc., a black corporation which is using Urban Renewal moneys to construct 149 housing units and a 200,000-square-foot shopping plaza. The list of accomplishments is much longer, but it must be measured by the original goals set for this nation in the 1949 Housing Act:

The Congress hereby declares that the general welfare and security of the Nation and the health and living standards of its people require housing production and related community development . . . and the realization as soon as feasible of the goal of a decent home and a suitable living environment for every American family.

Unfortunately, another goal adopted at the same time came to overshadow the above. Congress declared that government should assist private enterprise to build as large a part of the needed housing as possible, since "such production is necessary to enable the housing industry to make its full contribution toward an economy of maximum employment, production, and purchasing power." A healthy housing industry meant a profit-making one, which meant that homes for middle-income households soon outnumbered those for low-income residents. By 1967, the private housing industry had produced some 10 million dwelling units for middle-income households as against a total of nearly 800,000 units of public housing—not quite the figure targeted for 1954 in the 1949 housing law.

Many planners, including Catherine Bauer Wurster, Charles Abrams, and Nathan Glazer, warned that the housing goal of Urban Renewal had been subverted to subsidize the private housing sector. Glazer condemned the program as

a way to ensure significant private profits and ultimate private ownership of land the public had spent a great deal of money and effort to acquire . . . In Manhattan, for example, the redevelopment of urban renewal property has cost the public $1 million an acre—the difference between what was paid the owners for the land in order to clear it and what the developers paid to have the opportunity to redevelop it.

The criticism was well taken. Private owners and not the public treasury benefit from the enormous rise in land values. The Douglas Commission reported that between 1956 and 1966, the market value of privately owned land (much of it rural land converted to urban uses) rose from $269 billion to $523 billion, approximately double. By selling, instead of leasing, land to private developers, city governments weakened their planning capabilities in two ways: they surrendered control over large land tracts that could have served growing populations in ways the community determined; and they lost the full value of increments in land value, as well as the right to renegotiate rents and leases at set periods. Without space and adequate revenues, big cities found themselves helpless to plan the costly capital programs their increasing populations required. It was the private investors and developers who determined the nature, location, timing, and scale of construction. Government could react to and regulate the private developers, but it was ineffectual in influencing planned development.

As choice land in dense urban centers became expensive, investors sought new ways of maximizing their capital. Office buildings, which earned the highest rents, began to displace luxury housing and even department stores. Fifth Avenue, symbol of affluent merchandising, fell victim to the trend. When a famous old store, Best & Company, was acquired by a family trust of Aristotle Onassis and Arlen Properties late in 1970, a premonition swept the business community. Alarmed customers received letters from the remaining department stores, assuring them of their intended durability. Nonetheless, the economic law of highest-and-best uses continued to direct land use.

New York City planners ponder their options. To preserve the viability of the central business district, should they amend the zoning code to ban further office buildings on Fifth Avenue? Should they require developers to incorporate ground-level retail shops in all office buildings? Should they offer floor-area bonuses to builders who include junior department stores in their new structures? In short, what could city planning do to prolong the vitality of major shopping streets, without driving private developers out of a city in search of higher returns? The question struck a nerve in cities with a hunger for tax revenues. Meanwhile, the developers moved swiftly to get their projects up and to begin recouping their investments. Government fell back on zoning and negotiation, tactics useful to restrain, delay, mitigate, or litigate, but not to implement large-scale planning with any assurance.

NEW POWERS FOR PUBLIC-INTEREST PLANNING

If public-interest planning is to thrive in America, it demands a different seedbed. Planning must take as its point of origin a judgment on the fairness with which society is allocating wealth and service to all. Society would need to ensure to its technical aides, the public-interest planners, five conditions for success:

1. A share in determining priorities and decisions, along with community residents, political leaders, and administrators.

2. Close working relations between political leaders and professional planners.

3. Improved techniques of land acquisition and regulation.

4. Public-benefit corporations for large-scale development.

5. Revenue sharing, with cities receiving portions adequate to their people's needs.

Can our society attain the most elusive of democratic ideals, the voluntary sharing of power? Small elites traditionally keep power, revealing it through such planning decisions as old slums and new schools. Now, through the OEO and Model Cities instruments, as well as through established channels, wider circles of citizens are leaving their impact on public planning. Efforts to involve citizens take many forms, all of which are being grouped under decentralization schemes for better planning and delivery of services at the neighborhood, metropolitan, and regional levels.

The comprehensive Metropolitan Service District Act passed in 1969 by the Oregon Legislature enabled area residents to vote to set up chartered districts with certain functions and financing authority. Responding to similar local pressures, the Colorado Legislature offered a proposal on its 1970 ballot for the formation of metropolitan authorities, the restructuring of county government, and the opportunity for inter-city co-operation.

Virginia devised guidelines for electing and operating service district commissions, in connection with 1968 legislation on regional planning. Late in the 1960s Dallas conducted a self-study as preparation for drafting its master plan. The city government set up a network of citizen committees to review needs and express goals for Dallas. Unfortunately, the economic recession of 1970 curtailed planned construction of civic facilities, community health programs, and acquisition of land. Other cities have funded district planning boards with limited powers of review and recommendation on capital projects, serving as advisory to key elected officials.

These arrangements are timid steps toward making room for citizens in the early stages of decision-making. With that prospect in view, some means of equipping citizens to formulate goals and priorities needs to be shaped. An over-all framework adaptable to local programming might be based on a statement such as Daniel P. Moynihan's article, "Toward a National Urban Policy," which identified ten touchstones covering such areas as these:

Poverty and social isolation in the central city are the crucial problems.

Local government must be strengthened and reorganized to deal with the metropolitan magnitude of problems.

Local governments require fiscal solvency to tackle local problems.

Long-range plans must be made in response to population migration and growth.

Sustained research and planning are essential to provide information on urban problems.

Few planners would quarrel with these familiar axioms. But many planners recognize that the nation's priorities today stress military hardware and support of war-allied programs and personnel, to the detriment of domestic needs and national security. Professional societies, led by the American Institute of Planners and the American Society of Planning Officials, have begun campaigns to awaken the public to the extent to which the federal budget is diverting tax revenues away from population requirements and into mass destruction. Douglas B. Lee, Jr., and John W. Dyckman found that the Defense Department programs, covering costs of past wars and debt service, had consumed eighty per cent of the 1969 budget, leaving only twenty per cent of the budget for all other domestic and non-military items. Between 1967 and 1970, the average bill for the Vietnam war was $26 billion a year. This breaks down into half a billion dollars every week—more than double all the federal funds allocated to urban-planning programs in 1969. Taxpayers fed the war machine $71 million every day: enough funds to produce 2,500 dwelling units, even in today's inflationary housing market. Every hour the Vietnam war cost $3 million, which was the cost of building an elementary school in big cities before inflation doubled that cost.

Citizens who believe the nation should pursue other programs than war need to join with public-interest planners in defining their objectives. Consensus will be difficult but results will justify the effort to involve residents, planners, administrators, and elected officials in their common cause. Until this model of cross-sectional co-operation evolves, planners will operate in a climate in which the top political decision makers juggle many factors—least among them, it sometimes seems, being the intrinsic merits—before adopting or rejecting development plans.

Private exploitation of land has become too great a hazard for urban societies to allow, except under community regulation. As John Bollens and Henry Schmandt point out:

In the face of mounting urban pressures, local officials and residents alike have become increasingly cognizant of the social and economic threats implicit in a system which leaves land use expansion and development almost entirely to the decisions of the market and the ingenuity of its participants. The awakened fear of permitting communities to grow like Topsy has given legitimacy and respectability to the planning function and to the professionals who perform it.

Zoning, the traditional instrument for twentieth-century land-use planning, is now more flexible and versatile than originally. But, after half a century of zoning, critics are beginning to question its value as a planning tool. Those who have studied public ownership of land argue that zoning is a weak compromise, when public-interest planning could obtain the following advantages from government-owned real estate:

1. Increments in land value would flow directly to the public treasury. The gains would be greater than through annual property assessments for tax purposes. By leasing to private developers, government would derive income without losing control.

2. Planning could proceed confidently, since land would be available for development when government wanted it. Co-ordination of transportation and activity centers would become possible.

Unfortunately, the prejudices against public land ownership are still strong, especially when financial pressures force cities into raising immediate revenues. Land sales are a tempting prospect, despite the long-term disadvantages of transferring municipal properties to private owners. Thus, zoning controls persist. One improvement proposed by the American Law Institute is a Model Land Development Code whose elements would be administered by a comprehensive land-planning agency. This body would process applications for development, evaluate them by accepted planning guidelines, process them and issue permits upon compliance with city requirements.

While such an agency might expedite local development and reduce red tape, it could not accomplish large-scale development beyond a city's boundaries. More promising is the public-benefit corporation, such as the Urban Development Corporation set up by the New York State Legislature in 1968 with power to plan, build, and finance. The record of UDC's first two years is promising: construction is underway on a downtown commercial project in Albany, estimated to cost $40 million, as well as on eleven residential projects throughout the state, whose projected costs of $82.2 million were to yield twenty-seven hundred dwelling units. Further, UDC had signed agreements with twenty-four cities and three counties committing the state to build forty-three thousand housing units; nearly nineteen thousand of these were to be in three planned new communities, Amherst (near Buffalo), Lysander (near Syracuse), and Welfare Island, in the East River across from the United Nations.

The whirlwind pace of this innovative corporation suggests that other states should consider establishing similar bodies, or finding another Ed Logue to expedite planning. Compared to the snail's pace of most other public planning, UDC is unique—but so are its powers: land condemnation; authority to issue bonds (a matter delayed for some time by the Internal Revenue Service); ability to ignore local zoning restrictions, but the diplomacy to respect these in practice; power to negotiate with developers, contractors, and local communities; and the flexibility to tackle single-block schemes as well as towns.

The super-agency may prove the model for local planning, as it cuts through the maze of bureaucracy and works co-operatively with private developers and community groups. Time is needed for the proof.[4]

Finally, revenue sharing is the medicine the sick cities need. Many cities receive from Washington as little as ten per cent of the tax revenues their residents provide. While local tax collections have risen by 499 per cent since World

---

[4] However, the 1973 legislature severely limited UDC's powers to operate outside the central city, after one of its projects for middle-income housing upset wealthy residents of Westchester County. In return, UDC's borrowing power was doubled.

War II, the National League of Cities reports that city
operating costs have soared by nearly 550 per cent. Welfare loads, mounting unemployment, and inflationary
pushes on every aspect of operating budgets have combined to force cities into drastic economies. Mass layoffs,
cessation of welfare, hot-lunch, and day-care programs,
and a freeze on capital expansion were reported late in
1970 by Dallas, Baltimore, Los Angeles, Denver, Kansas
City, New York, and Pittsburgh. Cities with good political
connections to Washington suffered less from the federal
budget cuts than did those administrations who were out
of favor. But the hardships this political equation places
on citizens demand that the nation work out a system of
fair revenue sharing.

States, too, could reduce the money struggles of urban
centers. However, since rural legislators dominate most of
these bodies, they tend to be immune to the mayors' pleas
for aid. Measures to permit fiscal autonomy for the cities
would be useful, but the legislatures would need to author-
ize these. For example, a municipal housing finance agency
has been proposed as a local copy of the federal unit.
Again, power to tax, if entrusted to cities, would be limited
by the political realities as well as budget needs. Finally,
the municipal pension funds are an untapped treasury for
many cities; these ought to be reviewed as investment resources for housing construction and other public works
planning.

Public funding is by far the greatest stimulant of planning. When the 1954 Housing Act subsidized comprehensive planning under Section 701, towns all over America
(with populations under 50,000), states, and regional planning agencies suddenly got busy hiring consultants to produce master plans and other proposals. The first year, a
single grant of $16,000 inaugurated the 701 program; by
1969, cumulative grants under 701 had totaled $236.4 mil-
lion for 5,254 plans. More planning funds have actually
been appropriated under the 1962 amendment to the National Highways Act than under 701, but these are not

itemized separately from the construction funds. Many communities have failed to exploit the planning potential of the Highways law, which permits acquisition of adjacent land for public development.

So important is federal subsidy for planning that a current aphorism within the profession observes, "Planning is whatever there are grants-in-aid of."

Comprehensive urban planning is still the Polonius of American society: overflowing with wise advice that few heed, destined too often for a premature end. Its status continues to rise, nevertheless, as the public understands its potential as an urban problem-solver. In a society that respects profit-making, planning can balance the demands of private entrepreneurs against the imperatives of public interest. In a nation prone to crisis fever and political ambition, planning offers a model for rational distribution of resources to guide growth. In a culture that worships personal success, planning proposes equity in deciding goals, priorities, and programs. America has much to gain from public-interest planning: most of all, the key to a just society.

## FOR FURTHER READING

Chapin, F. Stuart, Jr. *Urban Land Use Planning*. Urbana, Illinois: University of Illinois Press, 1965.

Fitch, Lyle C. and Associates. *Urban Transportation and Public Policy*. San Francisco: Chandler Publishing Company, 1964.

Frieden, Bernard J. and Robert Morris (ed.). *Urban Planning and Social Policy*. New York: Basic Books, Inc., 1968.

Goodman, William I. (ed.). *Principles and Practice of Urban Planning*. Washington, D.C.: International City Managers Association, 1968. 4th ed.

Meyerson, Martin. *The Conscience of the City*. New York: G. Braziller, 1970.

——, and Edward C. Banfield. *Politics, Planning and the Public Interest*. New York: The Free Press, 1964.

National Commission on Urban Problems. *Building the American City*. Washington, D.C.: United States Government Printing Office, 1968.

Ridgeway, James. *The Politics of Ecology*. New York: E. P. Dutton.

# CHAPTER 11

# URBAN CRIME AND THE COURTS

## *Martin B. Margulies*

Probably no other issue has so gripped the American political scene as that of "law and order," with its overt implications of anti-urbanism and anti-black prejudice. If one were to believe the media and the hysterical rantings of some politicians, the streets of American cities are no longer safe for any decent man or woman to walk on. As the facts show, the incidence of reported crime is undoubtedly rising, and much of it does take place in the cities, especially in the poorer areas. Yet, as Martin Margulies points out, we too often neglect to mention that the majority of the victims come from the same poor minority groups as do the criminals.

As to the charges that recent Supreme Court decisions have "coddled" criminals, he points out that all the Warren Court has done is to guarantee, at least in theory, that all citizens, rich or poor, black or white, will have equal protection under the law. And until we as a country are willing to grant that protection to everyone, and minority groups come to believe in the equity of the judicial system, there will be no solution to the problem of crime in the streets.

Martin B. Margulies has extensive training both in history and the law, and for several years taught criminal law at the University of North Dakota. He is currently engaged in private practice in New York, and writes for a popular news weekly.

*Decency, security and liberty alike demand that government officials shall be subjected to the same rules of conduct that are commands to the citizen. In a government of laws, existence of the government will be imperiled if it fails to observe the law scrupulously. Our Government is the potent, the omnipresent teacher. For good or for ill, it teaches the whole people by its example. Crime is contagious. If the Government becomes a lawbreaker, it breeds contempt for law; it invites every man to become a law unto himself; it invites anarchy. To declare that in the administration of the criminal law the end justifies the means . . . would bring terrible retribution. Against that pernicious doctrine this Court should resolutely set its face.*

—MR. JUSTICE BRANDEIS, dissenting
in *Olmstead* v. *United States* (1928).

HISTORIANS sixty years from now may look upon Earl Warren as the foremost crime fighter of his era. This statement may astonish many; the Warren Court, after all, has been accused of encouraging lawlessness by giving aid and comfort to criminals. Indeed, some Americans have singled out the Court as the principal cause of the crime wave which is supposedly gripping the nation's cities. How, then, can one support an assertion that Earl Warren and his associates have stood more firmly for "law and order" than their critics?

## THE MEANING OF CRIME

The best way to begin is by scrutinizing two of the words in the opening paragraph. One of these words is "supposedly." Why was it necessary to speak of the crime wave which is *supposedly* gripping the nation's cities? Can anyone, glancing through an evening newspaper or watching a television news program, doubt that such a crime wave exists?

One can. To be sure, the urban crime rate has been

rising steadily. This does not mean, however, that more crimes are being *committed*. It merely means that more crimes are being *reported*. The higher incidence of reported crime could represent nothing more significant than the fact that today even the poor frequently own telephones, or that police-community relations in ghetto areas are at least somewhat better than they were ten years ago. For the victims as well as the perpetrators of violent crimes are found most often among the poor, especially among the black poor, and in many instances these victims have been reluctant to take their woes to the police.

Another reason why more crimes are reported is that criminal activity has increased in white, middle-class neighborhoods. This may reflect increased resentment against whites on the part of young blacks, or it may be because blacks are roaming farther afield in their desperate search for money to support drug habits. Whatever the reason, "crime in the streets" is no longer a Saturday-night brawl in colored town—where it could safely be ignored as belonging to another world. When a prosperous white American is victimized by a burglary or a mugging, he generally reports it. And when enough prosperous white Americans are similarly victimized, their newspapers—published by other prosperous white Americans—announce a crime wave.

The second word which needs to be analyzed is *crime,* which means many things. When a black teen-ager hits a white woman over the head and takes her pocketbook, that is surely a crime. But when a white police officer uses excessive force in arresting the black teen-ager, that is also a crime, although the policeman is unlikely to be condemned by middle-class public opinion, much less charged by a middle-class prosecutor or convicted by a middle-class jury. And when a white businessman conspires with his automobile mechanic to defraud his insurance company out of its $100 deductible, that is a crime, too. However, the white businessman does not think of himself as a criminal, or call down the wrath of the authorities upon other offenders like himself.

What the average American means by crime is not crime in general, but the particular sorts of crime which are likely to be committed by poor people, who happen often to be black. They commit such crimes not because they are innately more vicious than the white embezzler who does no physical harm to his victim, but because these are the only kinds of criminal activity open to them. The criminal world, like the "straight" world, is riddled with class distinctions: men and women on welfare do not violate the anti-trust laws, any more than Wall Street bankers hold up grocery shops.

That the white middle-class American associates crime with the holdup rather than the anti-trust violation does not signify that he is a racist. It merely reflects the fact that a holdup grips his imagination more vividly than the impersonal manipulation of the market by some distant financiers. Probably, too, he can empathize more readily with the financier than with the holdup man, having juggled some figures himself when he filed his income tax return the previous April. The expletive "racist" comes too easily to the lips nowadays, perhaps because it affords so temptingly simple an explanation of many urban ills. Granted, large numbers of Americans are racist, but racism, in the sense of overt bigotry, is only the tip of the iceberg. Liberals, too, are terrified by the prospect of a holdup, yet confront with relative equanimity the possibility that the cashier at their local bank is dipping into the till.

The result is a double standard which, although not inspired in all cases by actual prejudice, nevertheless works against blacks. When the middle-class citizen calls for a crackdown on crime, he frequently means a crackdown on *black* criminals. When he demands that his local police be "independent"—independent, that is, of court-imposed restrictions—he is advocating (perhaps unknowingly) widespread harassment of the black community. And when his courts and his legislatures, filled with other middle-class Americans like himself, carry out his wishes, they reinforce an attitude already prevalent among blacks in this country: that our laws and law-enforcement officers are instruments of white repression, and as such are not deserving of allegiance.

Ironically, open disaffection emerged only during the last two decades, precisely when blacks for the first time were making worthwhile social, economic, and educational gains. The reason is readily perceived. In the past, there were comparatively few literate blacks to voice their people's grievances. Among the others, discontent was inarticulate and largely internalized: the drunken knife fight and the senseless wife-beating were the most visible expressions of frustration. Strides toward equality during the 1950s and 1960s awakened the masses of blacks, formerly quiescent, to the enormity of the differences which still remain.

Few would deny that these early strides were long overdue, and in any case their desirability is beyond meaningful debate: the process has been irreversibly set in motion. For the middle-class white who feels physically threatened by the more violent manifestations of black anger, the only question of any practical significance is what to do next. There are just two choices: to continue in the path of the Warren Court, or to roll back the procedural safeguards which the Court has fashioned—ostensibly to protect all citizens, but actually, as we shall see, to protect *black* citizens (as well as Mexicans, Puerto Ricans, and other minorities), since most Americans have long taken such protection for granted.

### THE POOR AND THE LAW

In determining which of the two choices is more desirable, the most fruitful way to begin is by examining more closely the urban black's attitude toward the police and the courts: its origins, and its effect upon criminal behavior.

Fear of violent crime is the common denominator of most men and women in large cities, transcending all distinctions based on race and economic class. Indeed, poor blacks are victimized more often than well-to-do whites, because their persons and homes are more vulnerable. There is, however, another kind of fear, which is felt only by the dispossessed: the black, the poor, the radical, the young, as well as other unfortunates (such as homosexuals), who stand out in some way from their fellow human beings, and have no powerful friends to help them. This is the fear of arbitrary arrest and imprisonment. For those who fear only violent crime, the cop on the beat is a reassuring presence. But to those who also fear arbitrary arrest and imprisonment, policemen, as well as judges, prosecutors, and even the public defender—in short, the entire legal apparatus—are sinister enemies, to be mistrusted and shunned.

The average white citizen has little reason to be afraid of the police. Therefore, he finds it difficult even to comprehend, much less share, the fears felt by others. (All the more remarkable, then, are the insight and compassion of Earl Warren and his associates, all of whom—except for Thurgood Marshall, who joined the Court in 1967—were white.) If indeed, by some chance, he himself should be victimized by police misconduct, he is frequently so astonished that he rationalizes what has happened to him. Consider, for instance, the recent experience of two conservative Staten Island legislators, out with their wives for a boating excursion on the Hudson. They were picked up by a New Jersey river patrol for violating some safety regulations, and taken to a station house, where they were roughly handled. They were even forbidden to phone their lawyers. When at last they were released, they admitted that they had lost faith in New Jersey's police, but not, they hastened to add, in the New York City police, who would never behave in similar fashion. Such ingenuousness, which seems incredible, becomes understandable when one recognizes that neither man could bring himself to believe otherwise, any more than he could renounce the basic tenets of his religion. Some truths are too unpalatable, and too destructive of our most cherished values, to be faced.

But for many urban blacks, fear of the law is not only real but well founded in fact. For, at every stage of the criminal process, from the initial contact with the policeman until the expiration of the sentence, the cards are stacked against the black defendant. To him, the words "Equal Justice Under Law," engraved above the entrance to the Supreme Court Building in Washington, remain an empty promise.

In the first place, a black is more likely than a white to be stopped for questioning. One need not posit widespread racial prejudice among police to understand why. That such prejudice exists is beyond dispute: police, after all, are drawn principally from those very elements of white society which feel most threatened, socially and economically, by the demands of black militants. Even if there were no prejudiced officers, however, problems would arise from unpleasant realities over which the police have no control. In today's disordered world, the presence of a shabbily dressed black in a prosperous white neighborhood *is* ground for suspicion; the sight of several blacks clustered on a dark street corner *is* cause for alarm. There is no getting around the fact that blacks are responsible for a disproportionate share of the commonplace offenses against persons and property. As long as this is so, blacks who are innocent of any wrongdoing whatsoever are bound nevertheless to attract the attention of conscientious patrolmen.

Once the policeman's interest is aroused, the black is more likely than the white to be arrested. He does not carry the credit cards which attest to his standing in the community. He may have difficulty explaining himself to the officer: differences in idiom and dialect often erect an insurmountable language barrier between middle-class Americans and inhabitants of the ghetto.

Next, he is more likely to issue a confession, *whether or not he has committed a crime*. The police station environment is even more alien to him than it is to the white man. He is often ignorant and frightened and lacks the verbal skills to hold his own against experienced interrogators. He will sometimes tell the police whatever he thinks they want to hear, hoping to curry favor with them and thereby obtain an earlier release.

In addition, the black is more likely than the white to be physically mistreated. The third degree, though perhaps less common than in the past, is not an aberrational occurrence. To say so is not to indict the police for being more sadistic or bigoted than the rest of us: again, to seize upon so simple and obvious an explanation would be to ignore the real problem. This is that police view themselves not as *law enforcers*, sworn to protect the accused as well as his alleged victim, but as *combatants* in a war against criminals. The policeman's definition of "criminal" is as selective as anyone else's: he does not mean the colleague who is too free with his night stick, but the street hoodlum who threatens the social class to which he belongs (or with which he chooses to identify). Such criminals are, of course, largely black; and in consequence, all blacks become suspect. Suspicion, when focused upon a particular individual, is considered tantamount to guilt: the policeman, like any front-line soldier, sees nothing wrong in employing any means necessary to give an enemy his deserts. Rationalizations abound: "He's guilty anyway, so why worry about short cuts?" or, "That's the only language these so-and-sos understand."

In addition to the pain, fear, and humiliation which a beating engenders, the victim will in consequence face more serious charges than before. This is because the policeman who brings in a bloodied suspect must justify his use of violence or face disciplinary action himself: his defense is to file "cover charges" ranging from harassment to assaulting an officer or resisting arrest, depending on how badly the suspect was manhandled. The more brutal the beating, the more serious the cover charge—which must then be supported in court by perjury.[1] Therefore, the defendant finds himself enmeshed in an escalating series of felonies, often arising out of an arrest involving a misdemeanor or violation, with scant means of redress; he is poor and friendless, and makes an unprepossessing witness, especially if he has a prior criminal record. Since most legal issues arising out of third degrees involve admissibility of evidence, his complaint will be heard not by a jury but by a judge, whose own ethnic and economic background is likely to be the same as the officer's, who may once have been a prosecutor, and who may know the policeman from other cases in which the latter has appeared as a witness.

In court, a black is more likely than a white to be convicted. If he can't raise bail, and has no steady job, he will probably be imprisoned before and during trial. This seriously diminishes his capacity to select counsel and assist in his defense. It also means that he will be led in from his cell by the bailiff instead of striding into the courtroom a free man. Who can weigh the impact of this spectacle upon the jury?

His lawyer will be a public defender, provided without charge by the state. With the best of will, these attorneys are too badly overworked to give each case the attention and preparation it requires, and have neither the time nor the money needed for extensive investigations. Their service to their clients frequently consists of "plea-copping": arranging with the district attorney to let the accused plead guilty to a lesser charge. If the accused is indeed guilty, plea-copping may nevertheless deprive him of the full bene-

---

[1] Another common deception derives from the fact that officers sometimes "trade off" courtroom appearances. This means that the policeman who takes the stand and identifies himself as the arresting officer may have had nothing to do with the case. Instead, he has been briefed beforehand by the officer who made the arrest and who, for one reason or another, doesn't want to go to court that day.

fits of counsel: a wealthy defendant, with a private attorney, might escape altogether on a technicality. And if
the accused is innocent, "plea-copping" is a powerful instrument of duress—not only for the state's attorney, but
in the hands of his own lawyer, who often assumes that
his clients are guilty, and wishes to spend as little time on
each case as possible.[2]

Moreover, public defenders and district attorneys who
work with one another day in, day out sometimes develop
cozy relationships which are not conducive to the waging
of a spirited defense. These relationships have been known
to lead to arrangements whereby the defense lawyer agrees
to plead guilty in Case A in return for a promise of leniency
in Case B. Such an agreement would supply the defendant
in Case A with a basis for a successful appeal, provided,
of course, that he somehow contrived to discover it.

If the defendant pleads not guilty and goes to trial, he
makes an unconvincing witness, especially before the pen-
sioners, predominantly white and middle class, who volun-
teer for jury duty. Many cases turn on credibility contests
between the defendant and the arresting officer, in which
the defendant—black, inarticulate, poorly dressed—is at a
distinct disadvantage next to the man with the badge, who
is probably an old hand at testifying. If he waives his right
to jury trial and entrusts his case to a judge, he is no better
off: judges, it has already been pointed out, are subject to
the same biases as juries. Not only do judges, especially
among the lower courts, attach great weight to the testimony of policemen, but many are shockingly ignorant of
even the most basic constitutional law. Their attitude was
best summarized, perhaps, by a Boston magistrate who,
when confronted with a challenge to the constitutionality
of a search, replied: "The day I throw out a warrant that
uncovers 100 decks of heroin is the day they'll throw a net
over my head." A colleague of his in the same city resolved

[2] Recently, the Supreme Court upheld the constitutionality of plea-
copping.

a conflict in testimony with the words, "Well, I don't know who to believe. Just to be safe I'll find you guilty"—notwithstanding the ancient requirement that guilt be established beyond a reasonable doubt.

If the black defendant should somehow win an acquittal in spite of all these obstacles, he has nevertheless served time in jail while awaiting trial: sometimes, in New York City, for more than a year. If, on the other hand, he is convicted—either after trial, or on a plea of guilty—he is more likely to be remanded to prison than a white man, and for a longer term. Length of sentence—or, indeed, whether one is incarcerated at all—often turns on the number of past convictions. Assume, for example, a white embezzler and a black purse snatcher. The purse snatcher may have a string of prior convictions for various petty offenses. The embezzler's defalcations may have taken place over a period of years and involved many separate acts, but the chances are that he has never been convicted of anything before. Moreover, the embezzler's lawyer will argue that his client has already been punished sufficiently by the loss of his job and his standing in the community: the black may have had neither job nor community standing to lose.

Finally: once sentenced, the black convict will spend more time in prison before being paroled. Parole reflects, in large measure, the Parole Board's appraisal of the prisoner's chances for rehabilitation, based on such factors as his job prospects and roots (friends and family) in the outside world.

As proof that this is not wild conjecture, consider conditions in Boston documented in a recent study by the Lawyer's Committee for Civil Rights Under Law. In the lower criminal courts of metropolitan Boston, a defendant's chances for being released on recognizance (without bail) pending trial are slightly better than even if he is white, and only thirty-eight per cent if he is black. Of defendants defined as "non-poor" (with weekly incomes of one hundred dollars or more), fifty-three per cent were freed on recognizance, compared to forty-seven per cent of the "poor" (seventy-five dollars a week or less). Of the "non-poor" defendants, only nineteen per cent were committed for failure to make bail. The comparable figure for the poor was twenty-five per cent. Better than four out of five defendants able to hire private attorneys were set free on recognizance or bond. In contrast, nearly half of those with court-appointed counsel were imprisoned.

The consequences of pretrial commitment become apparent from another table in the same study. Of the defendants who were set free on bail or recognizance and pled not guilty, forty-four per cent were convicted and nineteen per cent served jail sentences. For defendants imprisoned before trial, the figures were fifty-two and thirty-two per cent, respectively.

The inequities brought to light by the study persist at other levels of the criminal process as well. The poor are more likely to plead guilty (fifteen to twelve per cent), less than half as likely to be acquitted (twenty-seven to fifty-five per cent), and twice as likely to serve prison sentences (fifteen to six per cent of those charged, and twenty-five to thirteen per cent of those convicted or pleading guilty). Although no precise figures are given, the editors make it clear that many of the poor are black. It is worth commenting, moreover, that a hundred-dollar weekly income in Boston scarcely places the wage earner in the middle-income bracket. If the poverty ceiling had been higher, it is safe to conclude that the disparities would have been even more pronounced.

Thus, an indigent black is more likely than a middle-class white to be stopped, interrogated, arrested, convicted, and sentenced to prison for a long period. That an innocent man could be convicted because he is poor and black is sufficiently shocking not to require comment. It will be harder to generate widespread concern over the fact that a guilty black is likelier to get his just deserts than an equally guilty white. Yet one's concern need not be for the particular defendant, but for the future of a legal system in which an accused's prospects in court vary according to the color of his skin and the size of his checking account.

Crime, in all its manifestations, is an expression of disrespect for law. What can the Supreme Court do to teach people to respect the law, and therefore to obey it?

It can do very little to correct the economic and social conditions which are among the principal causes of *violent* crimes. (It is necessary to emphasize the word violent, since the high incidence of white-collar offenses suggests that criminal impulses are present in many of us.)

It cannot prevent the middle class, which is more numerous and more politically powerful than the poor, from feeling threatened by violent crime, and from wanting to lash out against it.

It cannot do very much about the fact that the middle class is predominantly white: that upward mobility from the ranks of the black urban poor, while greater than in the past, is still limited, and is likely to remain so for some time to come. Here, its hands are not completely tied: its civil rights decisions are calculated to ensure that, if profound economic divisions continue to exist in this country, at least they will not be based indefinitely on differences in race. But much of the remedy rests with the national and local legislatures, not with the Court.

One thing the Court can do, however, is control the processes whereby accused persons are apprehended, tried, convicted, and sentenced. Through its power to expound the Constitution, it can reach into a police station in Dubuque, a courtroom in Raleigh, a jailhouse in San Jose.

It can exercise this power in one of two ways. It can attempt to strengthen the hands of local police, by removing procedural obstacles to arrests and the accumulation of evidence, thereby increasing the proportion of convictions to known crimes. Or, it can continue to fashion procedural safeguards to protect individuals from the arbitrary acts of law enforcement officials, even if this means that in some cases guilty persons will be released on so-called technicalities.

These two ways of exercising power—for the purpose of increasing the number of arrests and convictions, and for the purpose of protecting the accused—are thought by many to serve conflicting and contradictory ends. They do not.

Both have as their ultimate aim a reduction in the rate of violent crime. This aim is less apparent in the case of the second method, because the technique is less spectacular, and because it works simultaneously toward another objective: the protection of suspects and defendants. But as a crime-fighting mechanism it will, in a stratified and deeply divided society, prove more effective in the long run than the other.

## DETERRENCE

The first approach—giving wide latitude to local police in their search for criminals, and meting out stiff sentences to convicted offenders—is defended by many on the ground that it will discourage the commission of criminal acts. Proponents of deterrence, as it is called, argue that the best way to prevent crime is to threaten the offender with swift, certain, and severe retribution, so proportioned to the gains which he anticipates from the offense that the game will not be worth the candle. This approach, interestingly enough, originated with people who would now be called liberals, since its efficacy turns on the validity of the most basic of liberal premises: that human beings are rational enough to act in their own best interests.

Those who advocate deterrence (or, as opponents label it, repression) are, one suspects, the same people who think they can quell the youth rebellion with sturdy straps or Vietnam with bombs. It is reassuringly simple, no doubt, to attribute the domestic ills of American society to criminal bogeymen, who can be exorcised with a flick of a policeman's billy club. The trouble with this view, as comforting as it may be, is that it has no relation to reality. Anyone who thinks that the streets will be safer once judges start to mete out stiff sentences is entertaining the most dangerous of self-delusions.

The "get-tough" approach will not work for two reasons. First, the underlying premise of deterrence, that potential criminals weigh gains against losses carefully and rationally, is faulty. No threat of future punishment will discourage the teen-aged mugger who needs money to support his heroin habit. Moreover, ghetto conditions inculcate profound feelings of worthlessness and self-hatred,[3] which are often internalized, as well as acted out against innocent strangers. These tendencies cause the black criminal to develop strong, if subconscious, self-destructive tendencies. The prospect of punishment will not deter such a person: he *wants* to be captured and put away.

Interestingly enough, one area in which deterrence is likely to be effective is in the prevention of white-collar crimes, committed by businessmen who balance the advantages and risks of a conspiracy to fix prices as coolly as they invest in securities. But no one, least of all in the Justice Department, is calling these days for a crackdown on shady businessmen.

Toughness may have functioned effectively in an era of lesser expectations, when blacks accepted their role, not happily, but with passivity and resignation. Its effectiveness was limited: while it did not prevent crime and violence, it did succeed in confining these largely to the ghetto, and, for white America, that was good enough. Those days have vanished. Blacks will no longer submit tamely to the rule of the night stick. The degree of force required to clear the streets of criminals would be such that the ghettos would have to be administered as if they were occupied

[3] See Chapter 4.

territories. A crackdown on a lesser scale would be greeted, not with the submissiveness of thirty or forty years ago, but with anger and violence, causing the authorities to resort to greater violence in reply. The result would be either a police state or utter chaos, either of which would destroy this country more surely and utterly than any "crime wave."

This is not to argue that our jails should be opened and our prisoners set free. Prisons do serve to keep a small number of criminals off the streets. But imprisonment is a stop-gap, or "Band-Aid," measure, which alleviates a few of the symptoms, but does nothing to strike at the root of the problem.

Respect, in short, cannot be beaten into people. But there are other, more effective ways in which it can be taught.

One who would command respect from others must be willing in turn to respect them. In the case of blacks, as well as members of other disadvantaged minorities, this means that the law must treat them in the same manner that it treats more prosperous citizens. Respect for a criminal system comes largely from knowing that one will be dealt with fairly if one is suspected of a crime: that one's prospects for acquittal will not turn on arbitrary factors unrelated to guilt or innocence. Only when one is convinced of the evenhandedness of the system will one identify with it and bow willingly to its commands.

### RIGHTS OF THE ACCUSED

Critics of the Warren Court have charged the former Chief Justice and his liberal associates with exalting the rights of the criminal above the rights of society or of the victim, thereby hypothesizing a dichotomy which does not exist. (Revealingly, these critics often speak of the rights of the "criminal" rather than the rights of the "accused," although a defendant has by definition not yet been convicted, and is therefore presumptively innocent.) The fact is that, in the long run, the interests of society, the victim, and the criminal defendant are the same. The best way to protect society from its fears of violence is to instill respect for law among those elements most prone to committing street offenses: namely, the economically deprived. The Warren Court has sought to accomplish this objective by extending to the poor the same procedural safeguards which the well heeled and well educated have always enjoyed.

The *Miranda* decision, most controversial of all the Court's holdings in the area of criminal procedure, best exemplified what the Court was trying to do. For *Miranda*, in spite of all the howls of protest raised in police stations and Rotary clubrooms, *created no new substantive rights*. What the Court did was to seize upon rights which have generally accrued to well-to-do Americans in practice, though not necessarily codified in black-letter law, and make them available to *all* persons who run afoul of the police.

True, the middle-class citizen may not always have known of his right to remain silent in the face of police interrogation, or of what legal consequences could follow if he chose to speak. *But he had access to a lawyer who could tell him these things.* He also had money, self-confidence, and friends who could help him, and was therefore less susceptible to station-house bullying.

All that *Miranda* did was to require police to warn suspects that they may remain silent, that anything they say can be used against them in court, that they are entitled to legal assistance, and that a lawyer will be appointed, without charge, if they cannot afford to hire their own. (*Miranda* also held that suspects who chose initially to speak could change their minds and break off the interrogation at any time. But the Court, through a curious gap in the holding, omitted to compel police to give notice of this right.) In short, the purse snatcher as well as the defalcating bank president is henceforward to enjoy legal advice at an early stage of the proceedings. Those who are appalled by the prospect that a few purse snatchers will therefore return to the streets prematurely might dwell upon the numbers of bank presidents who have probably escaped prison because of various technicalities, exploited by highly paid and skilled counsel.[4]

It is galling, to be sure, to see a vicious criminal turned loose because of some policeman's failure to give the necessary admonitions. But before one fulminates against the Warren Court, he should ask himself three questions.

*First:* Could the police misconduct have been discouraged in other, less drastic ways, such as punishing the police officer himself? Experience suggests not. Prosecutors (and even judges) frequently develop the same combatant's mentality which was earlier attributed to the police; they think of patrolmen as being on the same side as themselves, and are reluctant to prosecute comrades-in-arms for excesses of zeal. Departmental disciplinary mechanisms are often ineffective for the same reason. And even if the sluggish processes of justice can be set in motion, either through administrative hearings or courtroom trials, the complainant seldom prevails. Not only must he pit his word against the word of the police officer, but the burden of proof now rests with him. This burden is weighty at best, and, if he has been convicted of the offense out of which the dispute arose (or of any prior offense), it becomes insupportable. Moreover, if the case goes to court, the policeman is entitled to a jury trial. Since the jury lists are drawn from the voting rolls, and therefore include only those individuals who have fixed roots in the community, jurors are more likely to identify with the officer than with a defendant who is black and poor.

---

[4] The Supreme Court, with two Nixon-appointed justices, has recently made a serious incursion upon *Miranda*. The Court held that, while a confession or admission in violation of *Miranda* may still not be used to establish a defendant's guilt, it may be used to attack his credibility as a witness if he testifies in his own defense. The result will be to keep many defendants off the witness stand, increasing the likelihood of conviction.

Civil suits, in which the victim sues his assailant for money damages, without invoking the aid of the prosecutor, are also futile. Probably the officer does not have enough money to satisfy a judgment against him. Besides, the ways in which plaintiffs' lawyers exploit indigent clients in personal injury suits are notorious. One of the reasons why impoverished clients are often mistrustful of their own court-appointed defenders could be that their prior experiences with lawyers have been limited to these personal injury sharks, who accept cases on "contingent fees" (a stated percentage of the winnings) and who, when the expert witnesses and other expenses are paid, leave little left over for the client.

In addition, the defendant who files a complaint or civil suit will find it difficult to bargain successfully with the prosecutor for a reduction or dismissal of the charge against him. A complaint is treated by police and prosecutor alike as a challenge to the integrity of the system, to be answered by painting the defendant in the blackest possible colors. In New York City, for instance, withdrawal of any complaint is part of the customary *quid pro quo* in the plea bargaining process. As a result, a felony conviction may be a measure not of the defendant's guilt, but of his temerity in defending himself and pointing the finger at his accuser.

*Second:* Did the policeman's error place the accused at a disadvantage which would not have existed but for his poverty and lack of education? If so, imprisonment of the offender may, in the long run, defeat its own purposes. Any sensible parent knows that a child submits more willingly to punishment, and profits from it more, if he feels he was dealt with fairly. The same is true of criminals. The chances for rehabilitation, already small enough, are diminished even further when the convict believes he was victimized because of his race and socioeconomic background, to say nothing of the resentment and contempt for law which is thereby created throughout the community of the underprivileged.

*Third:* How can we best prevent the commission of similar criminal offenses in the future? It is absurd to speak, as many of Warren's critics have done, of the rights of the victim. The victim is already beyond help through the criminal processes, except insofar as these processes may gratify his retributive instincts: a worthwhile objective in itself, perhaps, but surely secondary to the reduction of crime. What should concern us, rather, is the well-being of *potential* victims. Granted, it is arguable that libertarian court decisions encourage criminal activity in the short run by reducing the likelihood, and therefore the fear, of punishment, provided one believes what we have already disputed: that criminals calculate the chances of avoiding capture and conviction. What must concern us, however, is the well-being not only of those who may become victims next month, but of those who may be victimized ten and twenty years from now. And their interests will not be served by a policy of repression.

## THEORY AND PRACTICE

In discussing the long-range impact of the Warren Court's decisions, many people have tacitly assumed that the Court's powers over the criminal process are as great in practice as they are in theory. Unfortunately, they are not. What the Court says is one thing: what local officials do may be quite another. This dichotomy may dash the hopes of those who hope that the Court's holdings will extend the safeguards of the legal system to all classes of American society.

Well over a century ago, President Andrew Jackson said of an unpopular Supreme Court ruling: "[Chief Justice] John Marshall has made his decision; now let him enforce it." Today, as then, Supreme Court holdings are not self-executing. Their implementation depends upon the wisdom and good will of thousands of men and women across the country, many of whom are hostile to everything that Earl Warren and his associates tried to do.

This is so for a variety of reasons. For one, the scope of judicial holdings is usually quite narrow. Courts deliberately refrain from passing on questions not raised by the facts before them. Since no two sets of facts are ever precisely identical, it is easy for an unsympathetic local magistrate to seize upon some distinction in a new fact-situation as a basis for deciding that a Supreme Court ruling is not applicable. And, when the Court does seek to answer questions, the answers are often unclear. Judges are notoriously poor stylists, and their opinions are Delphic in their ambiguities. The interpretation of these ambiguities is left, in the first instance, to local officials: to police court magistrates (political appointees who may last have studied constitutional law in law school) and the police themselves. Their power to subvert Supreme Court holdings, through ignorance or malice, is enormous.

Assume that a lower court decision is unfavorable to the defense. It may be years before the case ever reaches the Supreme Court. The defendant may weary, or give up because of lack of funds. If he persists, the Supreme Court may simply refuse to hear the case, without passing upon its merits, if it deems the issues insufficiently interesting or important, or politically too hot to handle. The result of such a refusal is to let the lower court ruling stand.

The time, expense, and uncertainty involved in extensive litigation have provided the police with excellent means of harassment. One who is required to submit to an illegal search, for instance, would be well advised to comply if he has nothing to hide. If he refuses, he may find himself charged with some offense or other, and the dismissal of the charge by a federal court three years afterward will be small compensation for the anguish he has endured in the meantime. (This is why so many search and seizure rulings are issued in behalf of guilty persons: they are the only ones with enough at stake to resist the unwarranted invasion of their property and privacy.) Radical groups of the "storefront" variety, established to foment dissent in the military, or assist the poor, have discovered just how effective such harassment can be. Their offices are closed down for violations of the health code, and they themselves are charged with maintaining a nuisance, often under laws which have not been enforced for years. By the time the Supreme Court or some lower federal court is ready to vindicate them, their defense costs have driven them into bankruptcy and out of business.

The good intentions of the Warren Court have foundered on other obstacles as well. The poor have access to a public defender, but not to any lawyer they choose. If the quality of service is the same, why do the rich insist upon selecting their own attorneys? (They do so with good reason: that Boston study discloses that defendants who retain their own lawyers have more than twice as good a chance of being acquitted as those with court-appointed counsel.) The credibility contests between police and defendants have, in many instances, merely been transferred to a different level. Instead of arguing over whether a confession was coerced, prosecutor and defense counsel debate whether the *Miranda* warnings were given. If the defendant signed a waiver, stating that he was advised of his rights and chose to speak anyway, the issue becomes whether the waiver was signed knowingly and voluntarily.

One of the hopes voiced by the Supreme Court was that its decisions would lead to better training for the police. Until recently, for example, the federal Constitution permitted illegally seized evidence to be used in state courts, the sole remedy being the dubious one of disciplinary or civil proceedings against the offending officer. As long as this was so, police in major cities received only perfunctory training in the law of search and seizure. Then, in 1961, the Court announced that such evidence must henceforward be excluded. Police manuals and training courses thereafter gave extensive attention to search and seizure rules—but the results were quite different from what the Court had envisioned. In 1970, a New York City judge

commented acidly on the number of defendants in narcotics cases who had accidentally allowed illegal drugs to
fall from their pockets while a police officer happened to
be standing nearby. Such "accidental" slips have become
so common in New York jurisprudence that they are
jocularly called "dropsy" cases. What has really occurred,
of course, is that officers have seized the contraband un-
lawfully, and invented the dropsy story to prevent the evidence from being thrown out of court. All that the Supreme
Court appears to have accomplished, in this area anyway,
has been to make more sophisticated liars out of the police.

A study of police practices in New Haven one summer
after *Miranda* leads to some depressing conclusions. The
New Haven police were diligent; the warnings were generally given. But they had little impact on the rate of con-
fessions. It is doubtful, in many instances, whether the
mechanical repetition of the *Miranda* formula was even
understood by many of the suspects. Fear, ignorance, and
the desire to placate the authorities usually prompted the
accused to talk.

The findings of this study are often cited with approval
by proponents of *Miranda,* to rebut the contention that
the decision has hamstrung the police. Yet if the findings
are valid on a national scale, they also demonstrate that
*Miranda* has failed in its principal purpose: to enable the
poor to confront the authorities on more equal terms than
before.

Perhaps it is absurdly optimistic, given the frailties of
human nature, to suppose that the Warren Court's approach
can solve the crime problem any better than repression
has done. The businessman, for example, is neither alienated from our system nor oppressed by it, yet he still
cheats on his income tax and insurance returns. The motor-
ist who bribes a traffic patrolman, the patrolman who ac-
cepts the bribe, are not alienated either, but their acts
are as criminal as a purse-snatching by an embittered
young black. It may be silly even to hope that people will

respect the law once it begins to treat them fairly. Why should one expect blacks to behave any better than middle-class whites?

There is this much to be said, however, for an approach which embodies such a hope; it has not yet been given a chance to prove itself, while repression has demonstrably failed. Also, it is more consistent than repression with American constitutional traditions. "Strict constructionists" should remember that the fear of official lawlessness, widespread throughout the ghetto, was shared by the founding fathers.

## FOR FURTHER READING

Blumberg, Abraham S. *Criminal Justice*. Chicago: Quadrangle Books, 1967.

Campbell, James S., Joseph R. Sahid, and David P. Stang. *Law and Order Reconsidered* (Report of Task Force to National Commission on the Causes and Prevention of Violence). Washington, D.C.: United States Government Printing Office, 1969.

Clark, Ramsey. *Crime in America*. New York: Simon & Schuster, 1970.

Lewis, Anthony. *Gideon's Trumpet*. New York: Random House, 1964.

Morris, Norvil, and Gordon Hawkins. *The Honest Politicians Guide and Crime Control*. Chicago: University of Chicago Press, 1970.

President's Commission on Law Enforcement and Administration of Justice. *The Challenge of Crime in a Free Society*. Washington, D.C.: United States Government Printing Office, 1967.

*Report of the National Advisory Commission on Civil Disorders*. New York: Bantam Books, 1968.

# CHAPTER 12

# THE FEDERAL IMPACT ON THE CITIES

## *Anona Teska*

Although cities have begun to call upon the federal government for direct aid only in the past few years, federal programs have directly and indirectly affected the American city for the last four decades. A number of programs have been specifically designed to combat particular urban ills, but many federal acts supposedly designed for other sectors have had severe and lasting impact on urban America.

Anona Teska traces the most important of these in her essay, looking not only at the Congress but at the Executive and Judicial branches of the government as well. Her conclusion is that unless we secure a strong leader committed to supporting the cities, there is little hope that the government will make an all-out effort to save them. Unfortunately, recent presidential policy seems to go in just the opposite direction.

Mrs. Teska is currently on the staff of the League of Women Voters of the United States, where she has been engaged in research and writing in areas of equality of opportunity in education, employment, and housing, and recently in general state and urban problems. She is past president of the Oklahoma State League, and has taught in schools ranging from one-room rural schoolhouses on up through college.

*We must ease the tension between central city and suburb, between rich and poor, especially between black and white. Too few have recognized how these basic democratic issues are related to local government structure and finance, to zoning policies, land and housing costs, or to national housing policies. . . . We are a wealthy Nation, so it is not really a question of whether we can do such things as we recommend. It is simply a matter of whether we still have faith in freedom, in equality, in justice, enough to make sacrifices in their cause.*

—Report of the National Commission on Urban Problems

OURS is a tremendously complex society, not only because of the diversity of its racial and ethnic population and its great size but also because of the wide variation in distribution of its great wealth among its citizens. To assess the effects of federal policies on core cities, we must consider a number of factors against the backdrop of our own national experience, goals, and practices, and of world events.

What is the city? the people in it? its economy? its physical appearance? its government? Federal policy affects all of these in a number of ways—congressional and executive actions designed specifically for helping cities; side effects of general or specific legislation not designed particularly for cities; Supreme Court decisions; and performance of the bureaucracy, since how a program works depends on the actions of those who administer it as well as on the law and the appropriations.

Public attitude, too, plays a part. No matter what the federal policy or the size of the appropriation, a program is not likely to succeed without general public support. The prohibition amendment was ratified by all state legislatures except two, yet thirteen years later it was repealed and pronounced a failure. This example does not prove that leadership cannot influence public attitudes. But for carrying out federal policy, most citizens must co-operate or, at the very least, not obstruct its purpose.

Especially in recent years, some federal policies have been designed to help cities specifically and to help state governments develop more aid for urban areas. Some, designed for other needs, have had significant and sometimes deleterious effects on cities.

## SIDE EFFECTS OF FEDERAL LAWS ON CENTRAL CITIES

During the depression of the 1930s Congress enacted many laws intended to stimulate the economy, including the National Housing Act of 1934 and the creation of the Federal Housing Administration (FHA). Its intent was to revive the construction industry through federal insurance of loans made by private banking and lending institutions for new construction or for repairing and modernizing existing residential properties. Another objective was to encourage home ownership and improvement in housing standards.

As an impetus to building of privately owned homes, this program has been extremely successful. By October 1972, FHA had insured loans for nearly 11½ million one- to four-family homes, and for about three times as many home-improvement loans. An act in 1944 to help servicemen and subsequent amendments, by December 30, 1972, added over 8 million federally guaranteed home loans, plus over 300,000 direct home loans (in rural areas). Both FHA and VA now also guarantee loans on mobile homes.

FHA and the Veterans Administration programs did stimulate the economy, but primarily in the suburbs. While middle- and low-income families had generally wanted more space—a yard and a garden—and immigrants had wanted to leave the ghetto, most of them did not have the money for the sizable down payments on properties they wanted to buy. Lending institutions were unwilling to accept a mortgage security for more than twenty or thirty per cent of the cost of the home. Families did move out of the ghettos, nevertheless, but usually to less expensive, near-by neighborhoods. The FHA and VA programs and the rapid acquisition of automobiles to get to work from outside the city stimulated the mushrooming of the suburbs.

The federally guaranteed loan programs also encouraged segregated housing. In a firm belief that the poor were bad credit risks and that the presence of Negroes tended to lower real estate values, FHA for a long time generally regarded loans to such groups as economically unsound. In fact, even after 1948 (when the Supreme Court declared restrictive agreements not to sell to Negroes unconstitutional), the FHA actually encouraged and enforced such covenants.

Another side effect of FHA and VA programs influenced taxes. Alvin L. Schorr, former director of the Income Maintenance Project in the Department of Health, Education, and Welfare (HEW), said that in 1962 the federal government expended an estimated $820 million to subsidize housing for poor people. In the same year, it subsidized housing for middle-income and affluent families, through income tax deductions for real estate taxes and mortgage interest payments, a sum of $2.9 billion which the federal government did not receive. Mr. Schorr put it another way: the $820 million to subsidize housing for the poor went to about 20 per cent of the population. For those with incomes in 1962 of over $9,000 a year, the top 20 per cent, the subsidy was $1.7 billion. The family in the top 20 per cent received about twice as much federal subsidy, on the average, as one in the bottom 20 per cent. Moreover, while they did stimulate building and home ownership in some sections of the city, FHA and VA loan guarantees siphoned off into the suburbs the more affluent and higher-tax-paying citizens.

To help the farmer, the federal government inaugurated several programs to offset an oversupply of agricultural products resulting from mechanization and improvements in crop production. It set up programs of guaranteed minimum prices for specified products and acreage controls to remove some farm lands from cultivation.

The effect of these federal programs plus mechanization and specialization in crops on larger acreages was to decrease the number of farm workers needed. The farm population, both black and white, dropped perceptibly. From 1960 to 1970, it dropped thirty-five per cent; the white farm population decreased twenty-nine per cent, the black, fifty-one per cent. People leaving the farms were poor and unskilled except in agriculture, and most of them went to the cities where they comprised a high-cost population, needing many services but able to compete for only unskilled low-paying jobs. Thus, inadvertently, a national farm policy helped contribute to increased problems and costs for the cities.

Increased use of the automobile, especially among middle- and upper-income citizens, and the growth of the suburban population coincided with federal highway legislation. Federal funds subsidized the interstate highway system, paying the costs first at the rate of fifty per cent, then sixty per cent, and later ninety per cent. As road construction expanded, the suburbs grew. The small percentage of costs required from state revenues for federal highway programs poses problems for state legislatures. The gain from acquiring the roads and from the boost to the state's economy from road building makes these programs very attractive. A requirement of only ten per cent from state funds seems like a great bargain—and it is. But are these roads bargains if they are not really needed, if there are crying unfulfilled needs that could be alleviated by the state's "ten per cent"? Might the money do more for the state if spent on urban problems? Can legislatures always set priorities for spending equitably and reasonably in the heady atmosphere created by the prospect of getting federal money at a ratio of nine to one?

At what point, when, and how should mass transit facilities be expanded to stem the encroaching concrete deserts, the increasing air pollution, the multiplying traffic jams? It was not until 1964 that Congress enacted a small federal grant program for urban mass transportation. The

President asked for $650 million for urban highways for fiscal 1974 and $494 million for urban mass transit systems. Congress passed and the President signed in 1970 a measure authorizing appropriations for urban mass transit up to $3.1 billion for a 6-year period, but the President proposed authorizations for fiscal 1974 of $605 million. The one-year presidential budget request for fiscal 1974 for space research and technology was $3.1 billion.

Road-building programs have also displaced families, usually the poor, since freeways through cities generally cut through deteriorating or low-income housing areas. Usually little attention has been given to needs of the displaced. Many move into near-by, already-overcrowded areas, adding to their deterioration and density. Only recently have better efforts been made to help the displaced.

These examples of federal policies for improving the general economy have had serious side effects on the condition of the cities. While it is not always possible to predict side effects, the federal government must certainly assess programs carefully in terms of their impact on cities if the metropolis is to be saved.

## PROGRAMS DESIGNED FOR AID TO URBAN AREAS AND/OR THE POOR

One program that arose out of the depression was the building of housing for the poor. From 1934 to 1937, through the Public Works Administration, the federal government itself built 22,000 houses in 50 projects. Then in 1937 the United States Housing Authority was set up to make loans to local public housing authorities for up to 90 per cent of development costs, thus removing the federal government from direct construction and management of public housing. Five years later the USHA and an agency responsible for building housing for low-income wage earners employed in defense industries were combined into the National Housing Agency. By 1943 there were 160,000 public housing units. As of October 31, 1972, there were slightly over 1,000,000 such housing units under management, one third of which are in cities over 500,000 in population.

Whatever the criticisms may be about public housing, it provides shelter for a large number of families with low incomes. Although in some places the properties are not maintained well and code violations are numerous, rent levels are well below those charged in the private market. However, more than half of units built in recent years have been for the elderly. The greatest housing need, for low-income large families, has not been met.

Federal policy is not entirely to blame for not meeting the need. Local governments are subject to heavy community pressures; both in the suburbs and in some sections of even the most hard-pressed cities, many people do not want public housing projects near where they live. They protest vociferously, sometimes directly and sometimes under the guise of "finding locations more suitable." Otherwise "liberal" people, who might support non-discriminatory practices in voting, in employment, in equal access to restaurants and public facilities (even schools), may voice strong protests about having public housing in their neighborhoods. The poor eligible to live in these units are likely to include members of minority groups—Negroes, Puerto Ricans, Mexican-Americans. Their neighbors-to-be fear deterioration of property values, rise in crime rates, and the presence "next door" of poor housekeeping.

For a long time, trade associations of house builders and realtors were vehemently opposed to public housing, sometimes viciously. City governments, too, were reluctant to accept it. Government-owned, public housing was exempt from property taxes and community service costs for tenants were high, although such projects do pay ten per cent of shelter rent to local governments in lieu of taxes, and children from public housing have been counted in determining a school's eligibility for funds available for disadvantaged children from Title I of the Elementary and Secondary Education Act (ESEA).

Communities were and are more amenable to housing for the elderly. Older people seem safer as neighbors; they do not have children to enter in public schools, which generally are largely supported by local taxes, so their service costs to the community are less. It is estimated that nearly half of all public housing units are occupied by the elderly. It is only fair to say that the need for housing for older people is great.

In addition to reluctance of cities to provide housing for large families, the federal government's cost limit per unit makes it easier to provide housing for small families. Furthermore, in its annual report HUD understandably likes to show construction of the largest number of units possible within the appropriation limits. It can build units for the elderly and small families at lower per unit costs than for large families requiring more rooms.

Federal housing policy, however, has not provided the kinds of services public housing families need. Not enough attention has been given to providing meeting rooms, recreational facilities, day-care centers, and social services in the projects. The congressional directive that public housing be inexpensive in design and construction has led to inadequate concern for such things as providing that garbage cans be mounted to prevent tipping by children or dogs; that there be plantings and benches, play areas for children, and accessible toilet facilities on ground floors of high-rise buildings.

The results have been that often no feeling of pride or community or hope has developed among the tenants, many of whom have personal as well as economic problems. The National Commission on Urban Problems reports that about one third of the urban poor and more than one half of public housing families are black. Caught in patterns of discrimination in employment, housing, and education, blacks find escaping from poverty more hopeless than whites.[1] Furthermore, the most enterprising and successful public housing tenants, black or white, must leave when their incomes are above the maximum limits. Thus potential and actual leaders, who might help to develop a feeling of community, are often siphoned off.

In recent years, cognizant of the many problems not solved by public housing, Congress has tried to shift ownership and operation of housing for low- and moderate-income families to private interests. In 1961, Congress provided for longer mortgage periods (forty years), interest subsidies to provide for the difference between market interest rates and a maximum low rate, and a waiver of the usual FHA mortgage insurance premium for private interests willing to build housing for low-income families. Rent reductions of about twenty-five per cent are possible under these more generous loan terms.

In practice, this and other programs which supplanted it have helped those whose incomes are too high for admission to public housing but too low to compete for good housing on the private market. Around the nation, the maximum income levels set for admission vary; nearly half are higher than the national median family income. Therefore these programs do not help provide housing for the really poor. As in public housing, there is the problem of excluding "undesirables": broken families, delinquents, those with criminal records, or problem tenants. While it is certainly not conducive to a wholesome environment to fill a project entirely with people who have such problems, neither is it equitable to exclude them from government-aided housing. The proper balance is admittedly hard to determine or to achieve.

Congress has also enacted legislation for a rent supplement program to subsidize the difference between twenty-five per cent of a family's income and the market price of privately owned housing. This subsidy is paid directly to the landlord, and cannot exceed seventy per cent or be

[1] See Chapter 4.

less than ten per cent of the market rent. One advantage is that families so helped are not publicly identified as "poor"; they live in apartment houses among tenants paying the full market price for rent. If their incomes rise sufficiently so that the subsidy ceases, they may stay on and pay the full rent. However, the program, like some other housing programs, does not disperse poor families to the suburbs because of the stipulation that the consent of a community is required before a rent supplement program can be undertaken.

Other programs include rent certificates (housing leased from private owners for the poor) and special subsidies for the poor to enable them to own their own homes. Supplying below-market-interest rates to families displaced by slum clearance or other governmental action, including highway building, has generally been designed to help those with incomes too low to compete in the private market and too high to be admitted to public housing. Effective January 5, 1973, the President ordered a suspension of all housing subsidy programs pending a re-evaluation. These suspended programs include all those described in the preceding paragraphs, and new public housing starts.

Title I of the Housing Act of 1949, "Slum Clearance and Community Development and Redevelopment," is now generally known as Urban Renewal. The changes in the title and the practices under the program tend to indicate the distortion of the original purposes: to speed up clearance of badly blighted areas, help finance acquisition of land for construction of low-income housing, and give private business an opportunity to redevelop these areas. It was not a public housing project nor was it the intent that low-income housing built in the Urban Renewal area necessarily be public housing.

In practice, too many local and federal officials emphasized secondary objectives: broadening local tax bases through increasing the value of the redeveloped area; and building for public, civic, educational, industrial, business, and higher-income housing purposes. The original primary objective of providing an equal number of decent homes for those displaced has been neglected.

Since Urban Renewal was a government program, purchase of property in blighted areas could be accomplished under the right of Eminent Domain. Public agencies could therefore buy slum property and resell it at a lower price to a developer. The federal and local governments would bear the cost of the write-down in price. The difference between costs—acquisition and demolition, site improvement (curbs, drains, schools, playgrounds, parks, etc.) and other attendant costs—and the price realized from sale to developers was to be paid by the federal government's assuming two thirds and the city's contributing one third of the difference. For cities under fifty thousand in population, the federal government eventually contributed three quarters. (This change reflected a kind of discrimination against larger cities in allocation of funds.)

Because cities were financially hard-pressed and neither federal nor state governments were providing much aid, it is perhaps understandable that the purposes of Urban Renewal were sometimes lost in the shuffle. City officials saw a way to help the city improve its tax base and boost its economy. They could replace low-tax-income slum properties with high-tax-income office buildings, high-rise luxury apartments, and businesses without greatly increasing the cost of services. Urban Renewal did help the city in these ways, but the problem of where the poor who had lived in the renewal area were to go was not adequately solved. Their dwelling units were demolished, to be replaced by relatively few low- and moderate-income units. Most of the new units in Urban Renewal areas have been for upper-middle and affluent families.

In 1956, Congress did on its own take the initiative to help displaced families and businesses. It provided for a maximum of $100 for moving of families and property losses and $1,000 for businesses. Later these amounts were raised to $200 and $3,000 (up to $25,000 for moving of businesses). There is now also a payment not to exceed

$5,000 to reimburse a displaced owner-occupant of a residence toward the difference between the average replacement house and the acquisition price of his former home. In early 1967, HUD changed its regulations to assure more low-cost housing in renewal areas. The Housing Act of 1968 required that at least 50 per cent of all housing units built in Urban Renewal projects must be for low- and moderate-income families, at least 20 per cent for low income.

Funds authorized by the federal government from 1949 to June 30, 1971, for Urban Renewal activities totaled over $10 billion. In addition, many billions of dollars of private and urban government funds have been expended and pledged. The physical appearance of hundreds of American cities has been improved, from Market Street and Independence Hall in Philadelphia to the south side of Chicago. The increases in property tax base provide more tax revenues for cities. Some well-to-do families, especially those without children and the elderly, have come back to the city or been encouraged to stay, and extension of university campuses, hospitals, and industrial parks has accelerated.

However, to complete an Urban Renewal project takes an excessive amount of time; *The Report of the National Commission on Urban Problems* states that a "considerable proportion of the total number of projects took more than 4⅓ years even to put into contract form." In fact, from start to finish most take from six to nine years, some as long as fifteen years. In both Urban Renewal and road-building projects, improving housing or finding adequate housing for the displaced poor and minority people has been inadequate. The present and future social and economic costs of the policies that generate Urban Renewal and highway improvement are immeasurable. President Nixon in his budget message for fiscal 1974 proposed a very small appropriation (less than ten per cent of amounts spent in 1972 and estimated for 1973) to assist in closing out the Urban Renewal programs.

The Model Cities Act of 1966 attempted an integrated approach to problems of deteriorating areas: to improve housing, jobs, educational facilities, health conditions, recreational and cultural opportunities, and transportation from home to job. Cities of all sizes are eligible if they provide five-year estimates of needs and projected year-by-year costs, and meet grant requirements. The program requires co-ordinated efforts of a number of federal, state, and local agencies, and the co-operation and participation of citizens in the neighborhoods within cities that were the target areas.[2] By June 30, 1971, 150 projects had received federal planning and supplementary grants totaling over $1 billion. Many of them were in cities under 100,000 in population.

The Nixon administration considerably revamped this program by reducing the role of citizen participation, giving more control of the program to local mayors, enforcing a unified interpretation of procedures at regional and local levels, and eliminating red tape. The strengthening of the mayors' role in Model Cities plus uncertainty about its future has served to line up support among the Model Cities mayors (now totaling 150), some of whom had earlier been skeptical or lukewarm.

Nixon proposed in the 1974 budget to terminate this program as of June 30, 1973, and to incur no grant obligations during fiscal 1974. In its place, he asked for special revenue sharing for Urban Community Development for an estimated $2.3 billion in fiscal 1975. During fiscal 1974, HUD would be expected to administer its 1973 funds (about $7.4 billion of outstanding obligated balances[3]) in such a way that cities could maintain the capabilities of

---

[2] See Chapter 6.

[3] According to a HUD News Release, January 29, 1973, this $7.4 billion outstanding balance includes: $806.7 million—Model Cities, $122.9 million—Neighborhood Facilities, $5.685 billion for Urban Renewal, $17.5 million for Rehabilitation Loans, $288 million for Open Space, $390.0 million for Water and Sewers, and $94.2 million for Public Facility Loans.

local units of government for programs such as Urban Renewal and Model Cities during 1974 and then could continue them with the proposed special Urban Community Development Revenue Sharing, if they desired.

Title I of ESEA, which authorizes federal funding for children from low-income families as a supplement to local and state funds, has focused national attention on the need for special aid for these children. However, results of the expenditures are difficult to measure. There is little agreement on just what kind of training is most useful, what the goals should be, or how effects of expenditures can be measured. As in many other areas, we judge, train, and evaluate on the basis of white, middle-class values. However, Title I experience has begun a re-evaluation of our goal assumptions, a search for ways to involve parents and citizens in neighborhoods, and an attempt to define and pin down accountability.

Title I funds are now channeled through the state governments, which allocate money to appropriate school districts on the basis of a number of factors—e.g., concentrations of children from Aid to Families with Dependent Children (AFDC), or families with incomes $2,000 or under. Over 16,000 school districts currently receive Title I funds, but children in the AFDC category are more concentrated in the core cities. In New York, for example, all of the more than 750 school districts received funds, and city school systems all over the country have undoubtedly benefited.

President Nixon has proposed that funding for educationally deprived children be cut from $1.5 billion (estimated for fiscal 1973) to $411 million, and that $1.937 billion in education special revenue-sharing funds be appropriated, for broad purpose grants, including elementary, secondary, and higher education and adult and continuing education programs.

While the purposes of federal legislation in control of water pollution were designed in the national interest (to help cut down pollution of rivers and lakes), one effect was to provide money to cities for building sewage treatment plants. The terms of the original appropriations and later amendments to the act do, however, reveal a kind of congressional discrimination against larger cities.

The Federal Water Pollution Act of 1948 provided for grants to cities for building of sewage treatment facilities. Half of the federal funds were to go to cities under 125,000 in population. The federal contribution to a single plant was to be 30 per cent of the cost or $250,000, whichever was less. Since treatment plants for the larger cities were much more costly than for smaller cities, federal grants rarely amounted to 30 per cent for larger cities; regardless of costs, they would receive the smaller amount, $250,000.

The 1961 amendments to the act raised the maximum figure to $600,000, retaining the 30 per cent stipulation; joint projects involving several communities could receive grants of 30 per cent of total cost or $2.4 million, whichever was less, thus encouraging co-operation among communities. In 1965, amounts provided to individual cities were raised to 30 per cent or $1.2 million, whichever was less. The amendments of 1972 provide for 75 per cent of the cost of waste treatment plant construction.

The increases in these grant funds allowed to larger cities and the apparent discrimination against them implied in the earlier legislation point up an important fact of life about both congressional and popular attitudes toward big cities.

CONGRESSIONAL REFLECTION OF POPULAR ATTITUDES

At the time of the convening of the ninety-third Congress in January 1973, in the 100-member United States Senate, 12 senators (12 per cent) came from cities of over 500,000 population. According to the 1970 census, there are 25 such cities. Excluding Washington, D.C., because it has no representation in the Senate, the population of the 24 largest cities was over 30 million people, 15 per cent of the population. These cities are in 18 states, and if each of these states elected 2 senators from cities over 500,000, there could be 36 senators from large cities. Sixteen senators came from communities under 5,000 in population, and 22 (nearly one fourth) from cities and communities under 10,000. However, both senators from 6 states came from the largest city in their state.

There is no evidence to show that statesmanship or a concern for national interest is related to the size of community from which a congressman comes. Nor do these figures indicate that the Senate is more parochial in approach to urban problems than the House, whose apportionment is population-based. However, with other indices, these figures might indicate a popular attitude toward big cities different from the pride in the early Greek city-states of both the people who lived in them and those outside the gates who identified with them.

A great many people feel that the city, especially a big one, is wicked and corrupt, and well able to look after itself. Such attitudes exist not only outside cities but also within them. These feelings may stem from a nostalgic attachment to immigrant forebears from small European communities or farms, from concern about relatives still living in rural areas, or from a belief the cities are politically and economically powerful. In addition, the increasing mobility of today's citizens provides little opportunity to put down roots and identify with a community. Further, because of an over-all lack of consistent, good land-use policies or long-range planning, cities in their physical appearances often offer little to inspire pride.[4]

There are, of course, cities that generate a feeling of excitement. People may be proud to say, for example, that they live in Boston or Philadelphia for reasons of the histories of these cities; or in San Francisco because of its climate, color, charm, and pride in its heroic re-

[4] See Chapter 10.

building after the earthquake of 1906; in New Orleans because of its traditions and uniqueness. Yet these cities, like big cities generally, declined in population from 1960 to 1970.

Members of Congress are likely to be as disinclined to identify with cities as their electors. Both the federal government and the citizens have lacked a real national commitment to measures needed to improve the cities, to do what they cannot financially do for themselves, or to develop an urban policy. Yet when pollution of lakes and streams and even the ocean continues, all of us suffer, no matter where we live. And no matter what our social or economic status or how well we may try to insulate outselves, we all suffer from discriminatory practices and inequities inflicted on fellow Americans. In the national interest, sensitive and sensible planning must come from the federal government.

## PRESIDENTIAL LEADERSHIP

Leadership from the executive branch of the federal government is a must if there are to be successful solutions to urban problems. Many of the programs we now have for cities or for minorities came about through presidential initiatives. Some critics say that presidents have promised too much and delivered too little. High expectations for swift change and improvement have been dashed by unfulfilled promises, with consequences of disillusionment and frustration with the "system." But nearly every proposal for reform has had to survive attack from its opponents. To get enough votes for congressional passage, the final legislation is often a compromise, something considerably less than the original proposal.

Sometimes a combination of circumstances creates a special opportunity for leadership. At the time of the assassination of President Kennedy, many of his domestic programs were in deep trouble in Congress. President Johnson poured tremendous energy into gathering wide backing for the Civil Rights Act of 1964, the most far-reaching such legislation since Reconstruction days. Its passage in Congress was preceded by the first successful cloture vote in the Senate in history against a civil rights bill filibuster. It gave the federal government broad new powers to combat discrimination in employment, public accommodations, voting, and schools. Fulfillment of the promise of this legislation has been slow, but at least it was possible to get it passed.

The combination of public shock and the leadership of President Johnson, who as majority leader in the Senate had demonstrated special talents in producing legislation, resulted in a most productive second session of the Eighty-eighth Congress of 1964. The Economic Opportunity Act (EOA) of that year, for example, authorized a three-year program to attack domestic poverty. The Office of Economic Opportunity (OEO) it created was to supervise ten programs, among them the Job Corps for training young people, a community work-training program for employment of young people, and the Community Action Programs (CAP). Other legislation expanded the food-stamp program, funded old and new low-cost housing programs, modernized existing hospitals in urban areas, and provided for desegregation of their facilities in the five-year extension of the Hill-Burton Act.

Whatever valid or unfounded criticisms or gaps between promise and fulfillment there may be about the anti-poverty programs inaugurated under President Johnson's leadership, they jolted the public into awareness of the magnitude of poverty in this country and of the pervasiveness of discrimination. The urban poor, particularly, had their sights raised. Whatever backing and filling has ensued to diminish their expectations, something irreversible happened to the American conscience. Private citizens, businesses, organizations, many of them for the first time, saw the crisis in the cities, saw the poor and the blacks, the Mexican-Americans and the Indians. They met with them, talked with them, participated with them in a host of new arrangements.

More than any other single person, the President has unique opportunities to influence public opinion and engender support for his policies. He is the best-known public figure, has access to all the people through television and radio channels, is the leader of his party. He is also subject to tremendous pressures not only because of the awesome responsibilities of his office and the decisions he must make about foreign and domestic affairs but also because of the need for both congressional and public support. His own and his party's future as well as his nation's are at stake in the domestic judgments he must make.

Presidential commitment to short-term and long-range goals for improving the urban condition, and leadership for implementing them are necessities. So are state and local governmental input and citizen contributions in decisions that affect them. The President can both lead and listen. But the broad objectives must be clear. Unless he sees the problems of megalopolis as the most pressing of domestic problems, he cannot build support.

## THE JUDICIARY

The noted historian, Henry Steele Commager, commenting on the role of the Supreme Court in making federal policy, once wrote:

Upon them [the justices] the Framers [of the Constitution] and History laid responsibility for adapting a document designed to embody 17th and 18th century ideas of the relations of men and government, to the exigencies of a rapidly growing industrial society; for umpiring the federal system; and for educating the whole American people—including Presidents and the Congressmen—to the meaning and uses of the Constitution. It is as astonishing as it is gratifying that they have performed their tasks so well; indeed to the role of the Supreme Court we can apply the felicitous phrase of Winston Churchill: Never before in the history of law has so much been owed by so many to so few.

Landmark decisions since the fifties in three areas perhaps best illustrate the effect of the Court on urban areas.

In _Brown_ v. _the Board of Education_ (1954) the Court held that "separate" school facilities for Negro children, even if "equal," were in and of themselves unequal and that state-sanctioned segregation in public schools was unconstitutional. This decision lent a powerful impetus to the civil rights movement. Finally, the 1964 Civil Rights Act and the 1965 Voting Rights Act provided legislation which now had popular support in part through the visibility afforded by the decision in _Brown_.

For the cities one effect was to accelerate whites moving out of areas with increasingly black school populations. Another was the development of a more cohesive feeling of community among core city blacks. But at least segregated education no longer had legal sanction. Divisive racial tensions in the cities and elsewhere have not been resolved as a result, nor are schools desegregated in northern cities where neighborhood patterns result in _de facto_ segregation nor by any means in all southern communities either. But there has been a beginning and progress, and in many places minority groups are beginning to have more control over what goes on in the schools.

Another area in which Supreme Court decisions had a notable impact on cities was in apportionment of governmental bodies. In _Baker_ v. _Carr_ (1962) the Court held that federal courts did indeed have jurisdiction in cases involving apportionment of state legislatures and that inequitable apportionment violated the "equal protection of the laws" provision in the Fourteenth Amendment to the Constitution. In _Reynolds_ v. _Sims_ (1964) the Court ruled that state legislative districts must be apportioned substantially on population for both houses of bicameral legislatures, and, in _Lucas_ v. _Colorado_ (1964), that even a majority vote of the people could not impose on the minority an apportionment not based substantially on population.

These decisions and many others increased the city's share of representatives in state legislatures and protected minorities from being deliberately split in districting patterns to keep them from electing representatives of their own choice. In state legislatures particularly, implementing the Court decisions increased the political power of cities and especially of suburbs, providing better leverage to get some attention paid to their problems.

While the effects have not revolutionized legislatures' attitudes toward city problems, there are signs of change. By 1971, nearly all states had departments of community affairs or their equivalent, some of them, however, in the office of the governor. While they differ in function and performance among states, some have integrated several agencies into one department with broad powers in housing, redevelopment, social services, and municipal affairs. They sometimes provide research and planning aid to cities and regions, financial assistance, demonstration projects, or stimulate better use of federal, state, local, and private resources to meet urban problems.

Other signs of change include provisions to permit more flexibility among local units of government (such as city-county consolidation, regional arrangements, annexation). Such changes often provide a broader tax base, cooperative or consolidated services, sharing of resources, and involvement of suburban areas in helping to solve central city problems.

A third area in which Supreme Court decisions have had impact on cities is in fair access to housing. Decisions beginning in 1948 held that restrictive racial covenants were unenforceable in the courts and that money awards or damages in civil suits against violators of such covenants were denied. In 1968, in *Jones* v. *Mayer Co.*, the Court held that a hundred-year-old law which forbade all racial discrimination in the sale or rental of housing was constitutional and enforceable. The Court said:

At the very least, the freedom that Congress is empowered to secure under the Thirteenth Amendment includes the freedom to buy, the right to live wherever a white man can live. If Congress cannot say that being a free man means at least this much, then the Thirteenth Amendment made a promise the Nation cannot keep.

In spite of this decision and the Civil Rights Act of 1968, discrimination in housing still persists; since it is hard to prove, court action is costly and slow, and federal enforcement efforts are not noteworthy. However, more housing avenues have opened to minorities who wish to escape the slums. There is now hope, at least an outside chance, to live elsewhere.

While the Court decisions have not led all people to accept desegregated schools, integrated neighborhoods, or apportionment based substantially on population, they have provided legal remedies for injustice. They have also left the burden of achieving integration on the minorities themselves. It is not at all surprising that large numbers of blacks do not move out of slum neighborhoods, even when they can. It is not easy for people to go where prejudices exist against them. It is more surprising that, in order to acquire better education, so many do face the open and subtle antagonisms they so often endure in integrated schools. And it is not surprising that many minorities see "integration" as dispersion of their newly perceived political power.

### FEDERAL POLICY IN THE FUTURE

Effectiveness of current grant programs suffer from their multiplicity and overlapping, the "matching funds" requirements, and from having grown, like Topsy, often without consistent, clearly defined goals. Are we trying to save the big cities? to encourage development and growth of cities and communities of smaller size? to stem the influx into the city of the poor? Whatever the goals, do we patch up or do we try to prevent future deterioration?

President Nixon seems to interpret his overwhelming victory in the 1972 elections as a directive to implement his "New Federalism," the return of policy and decision-making in domestic affairs to the "people," to state and local governments. The five-year State and Local Fiscal Assistance Act of 1972 (PL 92-512) was a pre-election victory, despite strong opposition in Congress in the beginning but aided by vigorous support from mayors and governors. This act creates a trust fund to be administered by the Treasury Department, with a 5-year allocation of $30.2 billion, by-passing Senate and House appropriations committees. Two checks were sent in December 1972 and January 1973 to each of 38,000 state and local governments as payments for the calendar year 1972, for a total of $5.3 billion.

Two thirds of the money went directly to local governments (counties, cities, towns) to be used in any one or all of nine priority areas: public safety, environmental protection, public transportation (including mass transit), recreation, health, libraries, social services for the poor and the aged, financial administration, capital expenditures. The one third that went to state governments could be used for any legal purpose, including financing of school operations.

Cities, of course, benefit. These are revenues that do not require matching funds and can be spent, within the confines of the priority areas, without federal guidelines except that reports on the use of the money must be made to the public and Treasury, funds cannot be used for matching other federal grants (but can be used for matching state grants), and racial, sex, ethnic, and religious discrimination is not allowed in use of the money.

Another of Nixon's goals, consolidation of functions in restructuring of the executive branch plus special revenue-sharing broad grants to state and local governments, was outlined in the Budget Message for fiscal 1974. Nixon proposed four programs of broad-purpose grants, providing state and local governments with $6.9 billion to use in education, law enforcement and criminal justice, manpower training, and urban community development. These grants would replace about seventy categorical grant programs and would in many cases eliminate matching requirements. He also proposed a rigid ceiling, limiting total 1974 federal outlays to $268.7 billion, suggesting many program reductions and terminations of programs totaling $17 billion. Commitments already made under a variety of housing assistance programs will be honored but further commitments have already been halted by executive order, pending program deficiency review. No funds are requested for the Office of Economic Opportunity, and Community Action Agencies can only be continued by local communities using their own funds.

For example, in the areas of education, the budget proposed education revenue-sharing funds of $1,692.7 million. But it would allocate $1,331 million less for elementary and secondary education than was spent in 1972, and $422.8 million less in seven other programs. Including also a cut from 1972 spending of $519.5 million in impacted school aid (aid for schools with enrollments of children of federally employed personnel and long generally regarded as a "bad" subsidy), total federal funds for purposes to be included in the broad grant would be $580.6 million less than in 1972. Title I of the Elementary and Secondary Education Act has directives for use of the money in schools with large numbers of poor children, guidelines that would apparently not be part of education revenue sharing.

Special revenue sharing, if enacted by Congress, would supposedly alleviate problems of red tape, variations in grantsmanship skills, overlapping and numbers of grants, and certain inflexibilities. However, there are serious questions about broad purpose grants. What happens to citizen-participation requirements (lacking in the general revenue-sharing act)? civil rights guarantees (weak in the general revenue-sharing act)? fair labor practices built into federal performance standards? Would cities get their share of special revenue sharing if the legislation gives control of allocations to state agencies? Would money go to the people who need it most with more lenient or no controls?

Together with the 1974 budget proposals, the President has impounded (not spent) funds authorized by Congress for certain purposes. In order to avoid last-minute spending to use up appropriated funds, Congress has written legislation to allow for not spending in a fiscal year. However, the President has used this power to cut the budget and to establish priorities. Critics, and especially congressmen, say that such impoundment allows the President to usurp the powers of Congress, whose responsibility it is to vote on appropriations.

For example, Congress passed, over the President's veto, the Federal Water Pollution Control Act Amendments of 1972. A little more than $5 billion in 1973 and $6 billion in 1974 was to be spent for waste treatment plants in cities and research. The President impounded $6 billion of this $11 billion, leaving $5 billion that may be obligated in the first two years.

President Nixon's stated aims—to hold down federal spending and to return power to the "people"—mean the curtailing and dismembering of the "Great Society" programs begun in the sixties. However inadequate or beset by problems they may be, they were built around the concept that states and localities had neglected human needs, that citizens who were to be helped should have a say about what their needs and wants were, that many problems were national in scope and beyond the capabilities of state and local governments to solve, and that injections of federal money, incentives, and guidelines for its use were in the national interest. In spite of frequent references to returning decision-making to the people, involving citizens, except as volunteers or through their ability to vote officials out of office, has not yet been given much emphasis by President Nixon.

The general revenue-sharing funds, so widely acclaimed by state and local officials and so widely believed to be in addition to grant programs, are not being spent or committed in many places, being left to be used to support programs that have been cut through impoundment or curtailment.

The President, through impoundment, the shape of the budget proposal, and the shifting of programs from one agency or department to another, may accomplish congressional reform. Decisions in Congress for spending have been piecemeal, the result of independent appropriations subcommittees in each house, with little over-all examination of priorities or effect of spending in one area on another. The struggle in the Ninety-third Congress will be over executive v. congressional powers. There may result some improvement in how Congress goes about its business, some co-ordination of effort to establish priorities and a spending ceiling.

It may be that in the long run cities will benefit. In the meantime, the massive pollution problems, especially crucial in the cities, will probably be exacerbated. It may be that states, many of them in better financial shape than they were ten years ago, can pick up some of the slack, although most of them will need to design new arrangements for equitable funding of schools, should the Supreme Court decision in the Rodriguez case (regarding the constitutionality of the local property tax) arising in Texas require it. It seems unlikely that, without federal land-use policies and federal spending to help cities, the problems of megalopolis will be much alleviated.

Until the power struggle in Congress is resolved, there will be confusion and uncertainty. Cities will suffer. While almost no one defends how all of the Great Society programs work, no one can deny they pointed up neglected needs and problems, surfaced deep-seated, ugly national problems, and turned the spotlight of public attention on the growing deterioration of the cities. It seems drastic to perform massive surgery without more careful examination.

## FOR FURTHER READING

Cleaveland, Frederic N., et al. *Congress and Urban Problems.* Washington, D.C.: The Brookings Institution, 1969.

Friedman, Lawrence M. *Government and Slum Housing: A Century of Frustration.* Chicago: Rand, McNally, 1968.

Hamilton, Edith. *The Greek Way.* New York: The Modern Library, 1930.

Joint Center for Political Studies. *The Black Community and Revenue Sharing.* (January 1973)

League of Women Voters Education Fund. *Revenue Sharing: Stretch or Shrink?* Washington, D.C.: League of Women Voters, 1971.

Levine, Robert A. *The Poor Ye Need Not Have With You: Lessons from the War on Poverty.* Cambridge, Massachusetts: Massachusetts Institute of Technology, 1970.

Lindsay, John V. *The City.* New York: W. W. Norton, 1970.

Pechman, Joseph A. *The Rich, the Poor, and the Taxes They Pay.* Washington, D.C.: The Brookings Institution, 1969.

Schutze, Charles L., et al. *Setting National Priorities The 1974 Budget.* Washington, D.C.: The Brookings Institution, 1973.

Urban Coalition. *City,* Vol. 4, No. 2 (August/September 1970).

National Commission Reports:

National Advisory Commission on Civil Disorders. *Report . . . on Civil Disorders* and *Supplemental Studies.* Washington, D.C.: United States Government Printing Office, 1968.

National Advisory Commission on Intergovernmental Relations. *Urban America and the Federal System.* Washington, D.C.: United States Government Printing Office, 1969.

National Commission on the Causes and Prevention of Violence. *To Establish Justice, To Insure Domestic Tranquility.* Washington, D.C.: United States Government Printing Office, 1969.

National Commission on Urban Problems. *Building the American City.* Washington, D.C.: United States Government Printing Office, 1968.

President's Commission on Campus Unrest. *Campus Unrest.* Washington, D.C.: United States Government Printing Office, 1970.
President's Commission on Urban Housing. *A Decent Home.* Washington, D.C.: United States Government Printing Office, 1968.

# INDEX